Computer Science and Multimedia Technologies

Computer Science and Multimedia Technologies

Kunwar Singh Vaisla

ARCLER
PRESS

www.arclerpress.com

Computer Science and Multimedia Technologies

Kunwar Singh Vaisla

Arcler Press
224 Shoreacres Road
Burlington, ON L7L 2H2
Canada
www.arclerpress.com
Email: orders@arclereducation.com

ISBN: 978-1-77407-745-0 (Hardcover)

ABOUT THE AUTHOR

Dr. Kunwar Singh Vaisla is Ph. D. in Computer Science from Kumaun University, Nainital, MCA from University of Rajasthan, Jaipur, India and B. Sc. from Raj Rishi College, Alwar, Rajasthan, India. He is currently working as Professor at Department of Computer Science and Engineering at BT Kumaon Institute of Technology, India. He is editorial board member of many reputed international journals such as IJGCA, ITIST, IJIFR, CAIJ, ICACCE, IJWSC.

TABLE OF CONTENTS

LIST OF FIGURES

utilized for the addition of emotion and interest to the presentation, and other audio that is not speech utilized as section of the general interface

LIST OF ABBREVIATIONS

ACM	Association for Computing Machines
APS	Atlantic Packet Satellite
ARPA	Advanced Researches Programs Agency
BHO	browser helper objects
CD-I	compact disc interactive
COM	component object modeling
DAB	digital audio broadcasting
DDoS	distributed denial of service
DLP	data loss prevention
DRM	digital radio mondiale
DTV	digital television
DVB	digital video broadcaster
DVI	digital video interactive
EMF	enhanced metafile
EMI	electromagnetic interference
FCC	Federal Communications Commissions
FDDI	fiber distributed data interface
FLF	fluent laser fonts
FM	frequency modulation
GIS	geographical information systems
GM	general motors
HD	high-definition
IBOC	in-band on-channel
ICT	information and computer technology
IE	internet explorer
INW	international network working
IP	internet protocol

IPS	intrusion prevention systems
IPTO	Info Processing Techniques Office
ISDN	Integrated Services Digital Network
ISO	International Organization for Standards
ISPs	internet service providers
LANs	local area networks
MDCT	modified discrete cosine transform
MIT	Massachusetts Institutes of Technology
MOSFET	MOS transistor system
MPEG	Moving Picture Expert Groups
MS	Microsoft
NPL	National Physical Lab
NYC	New York City
OEM	original equipment maker
OOH	outdoor or out of home media
OS	operating system
PARC	Palo Alto Researching Center
PBS	Public Broadcast System
PNG	portable network graphics
PSTN	Public Switched Telephone Networks
RFI	radio frequency interference
SFN	solo-frequency network
SOA	service-based architectures
TCP	transmission control protocol
UCL	University College London
USADR	U.S. digital radio
UTP	unshielded twisted pair
VCE	video capsule endoscope
VoIP	voiceover internet protocol
WAN	wide area network
WMF	Windows metafile

PREFACE

Computer science is a discipline that's been growing in leaps over the recent few years. Nowadays, the technology applies to nearly every aspect of human life including media and communications. In fact, it has improved multimedia systems and made it accessible to nearly everyone. Computer Multimedia is defined as digital technologies that present information in multiple media formats, for instance, online TV platforms like Hulu and Netflix provide audio and video content to viewers while Amazon Kindle Books has text, pictures, and graphs for their audience.

Generally, information displayed through digital multimedia is of superior quality and capability compared to traditional media. Apart from being easier to understand, users can interact with the content according to their needs instead of just mere reading or watching. Case in point, virtual television allows you to choose the programs you want to watch from the list available. Unlike traditional TV where the programs have already been selected by the channel, and you have no say on what's displayed on the screen.

Nowadays, electronic networks have allowed otherwise traditional media channels to also have digital footprints, which has significantly increased their follower base. For instance, it's possible to subscribe to newspaper or magazine issues online instead of buying the paper format which is rather bulky and inconvenient.

Additionally, computers have inspired the invention of new multimedia technologies that were unheard of in the past, such as Twitter, Facebook, LinkedIn, and YouTube which are currently some of the most popular social media platforms. These networks are highly interactive and allow users to connect with others instantly from anywhere around the world, so long as you have internet it's possible to communicate with anyone from whichever country in the globe.

Furthermore, with devices such as smartphones and tablets, multimedia technologies have become more portable and accessible to everyone. It's now practical to access your favorite multimedia content digitally from the comfort of your device, it's not a must to be next to a stationary PC or computer in order to enjoy digital multimedia.

Computers have also simplified business procedures and made it easier for investors to manage their day-to-day operations more efficiently. For instance, through videoconferencing technology, companies can host live audiovisual meetings with their staff or clients from whichever location without worrying about logistics. This saves on operation costs apart from making the business more accessible to stakeholders.

Additionally, through email technology, you can send messages instantly without having to worry about buying papers, printing, and dispatching them manually to receivers like the past. For the health sector, multimedia technology is allowing physicians to attend to clients remotely without them having to physically visit the clinic for treatment. In some developed countries, doctors are even performing surgery using computer-assisted programs that run on multimedia system, which are proving to be more efficient and risk-free than manual operations. With rapid advancements in computer science and multimedia, the future looks even brighter for this field.

The volume is divided into 10 chapters that discuss different aspects of computer science and multimedia. Chapter 1 talks about introduction to multimedia, Chapter 2 explores into genesis of multimedia, Chapter 3 multimedia skill and training, Chapter four text in multimedia, Chapter 5 multimedia networks, Chapter 6 applications of multimedia, Chapter 7 multimedia software tools, Chapter 8 multimedia learning, Chapter 9 multimedia management, and Chapter 10 emerging trends in multimedia.

These 10 chapters were extensively prepared with more emphasis on the easiness of the content in order to make the volume clear and understandable to all readers.

It is my hope and trust that this volume will make a valuable contribution towards nurturing many to ride the wave of collaboration in different concepts discussed.

CHAPTER

1

Introduction to Multimedia

CONTENTS

1.1. INTRODUCTION

Multimedia involves utilizing a mix of different forms of content such as animations, texts, images, audios, interactive contents, and videos. This form of media is different from media that only uses computer displays that are rudimentary such as those that only have texts or materials that are produced by hand or printed.

Multimedia can be displayed, interacted with, recorded, and played, or accessed with devices that process information content, such as electronic or computerized devices. They can also be displayed as a performance that is live.

Devices that are used to for the storage and displaying of multimedia content are called multimedia devices. They are electronic. Multimedia can be presented and viewed by people on the stage, transmitted, played locally, or projected using the multimedia devices. A multimedia presentation that is either live or recorded is referred to as a broadcast. These can either be digital or analog electronic media technology. It is possible to download or stream digital online multimedia. This media may be live or high in demand.

Figure 1.1. Multimedia is an important part of our world today. There are so many applications that it provides. It has helped in making very many things easier for us.

Source: *http://www.lisbdnet.com/multimedia-its-components-and-applications/.*

There are also multimedia simulations and games which can be utilized in an environment that has special effects, with more than one user in a network that is online, or in a local environment with a computer that is offline, a simulator, or a game system.

Many different types of digital or technological multimedia are created so as to ensure the enhancement of experiences by the users, for example, making it much easier and efficient to pass information to a crowd, or even while displaying art or entertainment so as to engage a crowd.

Being able to combine different types of media content helps in enhancing the levels of interaction. Multimedia that is found online is developing to become oriented on objects and driven by data at a high rate, thus making it possible for one to personalize different forms of media as well as applications that promote innovation over time. For example, a variety of content on sites such as photo galleries that have both pictures and text, and also simulations that allow for modifications of videos, animations, etc. allowing for alteration of multimedia experiences, all without having to program the simulator again.

There is a form of technology that allows for virtual objects to be touched and felt in addition to hearing and seeing. This is referred to as haptic technology. There is also some technology that is emerging which will involve being able to taste and smell, and therefore helping in enhancing the experience brought about by multimedia.

1.2. TYPES OF MULTIMEDIA

In simpler terms, multimedia is a combination of different forms of media. For example, a webpage that has an animation in it. Video games, an information shop at the terminal of a subway, or even CD ROMs that help in teaching foreign languages are interactive forms of media and this is a form of multimedia as well. Hypermedia and Rich media are some of the other terms that are used to describe multimedia.

There are many different types of data that can be classified as multimedia data types. These are generally the contents that form multimedia environments and tools that can be used to integrate multimedia. The main types of multimedia include audio, texts, graphics, graphic objects, animation, and video (Mitra, 2004). Below are a few descriptions:

Text – there are many different ways in which a text can be stored. In addition to files that are based on the American Standard Code for Information Interchange, texts are normally stored in databases, spreadsheets, processor files, and annotations on multimedia objects that are more general. Due to how available and also the proliferative rate of Graphical User Interfaces, storage of texts is becoming much more complex and also providing additional effects such as shades, highlighting, and even coloring of texts.

Graphics – still images such as gifs and jpgs can be stored in many different ways due to a high variety of quality and size. Images that are digitalized are a pattern of pixels that help in representing a section in the graphical display of the user.

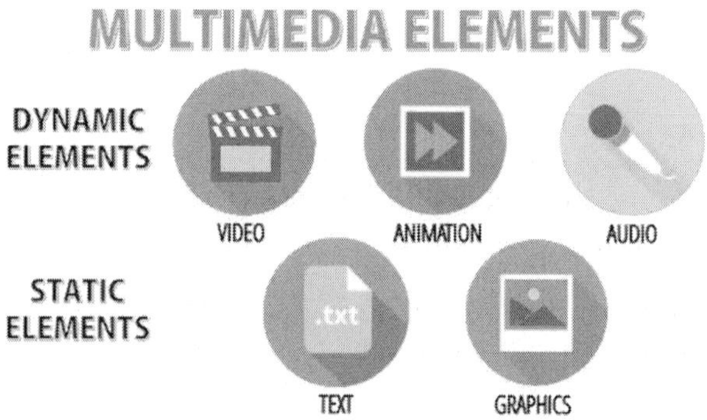

Figure 1.2. Above are the elements of multimedia. Texts are very common and they use words to express information. It is referred to as the most basic multimedia element.

Source: *https://storymaps.arcgis.com/stories/5df73b57c11a4630a5d0312a7166f74d.*

Audio – this data tape is well-known and is becoming very popular. It is the form of multimedia that is integrated in almost all applications. It takes up quite a lot of space. An audio file that is one-minute-long can take up to three megabytes of space. There are many different ways that one can compress an audio file to a format that is suitable.

Animation – these are created by displaying images that are still, one after the other, so as to give an appearance of motion. Most of the town, this type of multimedia is used for providing entertainment. They are also sometimes used to display a form of art, in addition to being used for entertainment. There are many film festivals all over the world that display and celebrates animations. They can also be used in schools for the purpose of education.

Video – Digitalized videos are the most space occupying multimedia datatypes. They are normally stored as frames in a sequence. One single frame can occupy up to one megabyte depending on its size and resolution. A continuous transfer rate is required so as to transmit, compress, and decompress digitalized videos in order to have a video playback that is realistic.

Graphic objects – these help in defining 2-D and 3-D shapes due to the special data structures they have, through which allows us to make definition of multimedia objects. Some examples of this include the different formats that are utilized by video and image editing apps.

1.3. ADVANTAGES AND DISADVANTAGES OF MULTIMEDIA

There are many different advantages and disadvantages of multimedia. These can help in allowing one to choose the type of media they want to use. Firstly, here are some of the advantages:

- They are much more affordable for the consumer in comparison to buying an illustrated book that is full-color. Multimedia forms are generally a quarter to a third of the price of a similar book in hard copy.
- They are also affordable to the producers seeing as they are created in print on-demand or small runs and they are red much easier to update or modify at an affordable cost.
- They are not heavy to transport. A paperback may weigh 600 grams per every 300 pages in comparison to fewer grams for a version in the multimedia form. This makes it easier for the transportation of content especially for wholesale distributors.
- Multimedia forms also help in saving the environment. Books that are in hard copy are made from cutting down of trees. Multimedia forms can reduce this and save the environment.
- They make it very convenient for searching texts instantaneously. It is possible to find a word or a phrase almost instantly within a multimedia publication especially when using it as a reference material.
- They have a higher advantage when it comes to storage space. Multimedia materials are normally much smaller than hard copy books, therefore saving space on a book shelf or in any other space.
- They are easy to carry around because they are found in electronic devices such as a laptop which is very portable. Multimedia content can also be carried on mobile phones and tablets. There are some wrist watches that can also allow one to access multimedia content on them. These are referred to as media-enabled wristwatches.

Figure 1.3. Multimedia has proven to be more appealing in comparison to the older methods that were used to teach. Students find it interesting, however, teachers are asked to make sure that the students do not get distracted by the over-stimulative form of media.

Source: *https://www.parentcircle.com/article/advantages-of-multimedia-courses/.*

- Texts can be enhanced on multimedia by adding sounds, video clips, videos, etc. which cannot be done on media that is printed.
- Multimedia types are much more entertaining than printed media. They can grasp the users attention and keep then engaged. This makes it very suitable for use in schools.
- Multimedia content is good for people who are more captivated by computers thus allowing them to stay interested. Considering the fact that multimedia can be loaded on CD ROMs, they can also be used by people who are not computer literate or are scared of computer functionality because they are very easy to use.
- They are franchised in an easier manner because they do not require much equipment for manufacturing and distribution.
- They help in gaining and holding the attention of people who are more interested in audiovisual media, due to the ability to combine video, graphics, texts, and audio. Studies on communication have shown that using this aids helps in offering a higher level of understanding, retaining information and are much more interesting to use.

- Multimedia helps in engaging all senses. It helps in engaging many different modalities of learning which appeals to different learners due to the various learning styles. They help in achieving learning by doing instead if learning by reading which has proven to be much more effective. Multimedia also helps in developing presentations that are much more engaging and persuasive. Multimedia immerses the users into the experience and this helps in making learning much more authentic.
- They can be done in different languages therefore allowing for many different people to access the data despite of their native language.
- They are also durable. CD ROMs are water proof and they can be dried, cleaned, and used times and times again. Hard copy material tears, and it can also get wet and water-logged.
- Multimedia publications cannot be affected by pests such as ants, moths, and mildew which always negatively affect hard copy materials.

Multimedia normally utilizes the natural abilities of processing information that we as humans already possess. Our brain together with our ears and eyes create a system that is formidable that helps in the transformation of sense data that is meaningless into understandable information. Especially when it comes to moving images, because the human eye adapts to detect and interpret movement (Mitra, 2004).

- Some of the disadvantages of multimedia include:
- Multimedia may have many problems when it comes to accessibility, because they need electricity to work, which may not be available due to blackouts and power shortages or even lack of electricity in rural areas.
- When used in the classroom or for a meeting presentation, it is possible for the students or members of the meeting to lose focus due to the formats that are used. These formats can grab the attention of the end users.
- Some forms of multimedia can be expensive to produce because they include more than one type of media. Producing multimedia also needs one to have an electronic device, and these might be quite expensive. The fact that multimedia also needs one to have electricity to use leads to additional costs, because one needs to pay for the electricity.

- Multimedia is also time consuming as it takes a lot of time to create.
- Creating multimedia also requires one to be consistent and practice time and time again so as to master the skill. Thus requires a lot of time and energy from the person creating the multimedia.

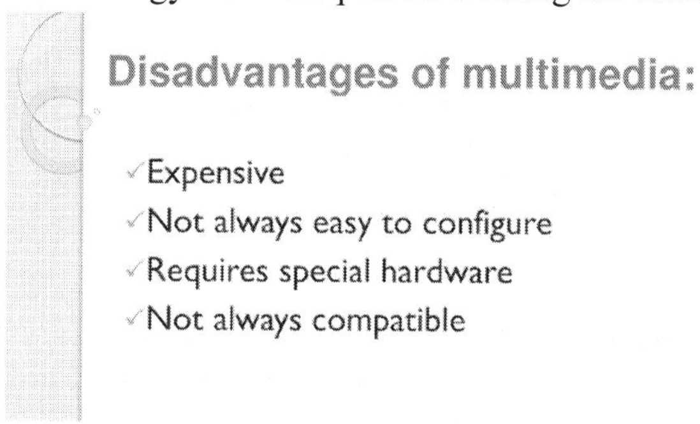

Figure 1.4. Above are some of the disadvantages of multimedia. When programs are designed poorly, some of these issues may occur.

Source: *https://www.slideserve.com/stasia/multimedia-powerpoint-ppt-presentation.*

- Some multimedia forms are not compatible on some gadgets.
- The electronic devices that are used to create and display multimedia need to be handled with a lot of care because they are fragile. Exposing them to humid environments and other harsh conditions can cause damage that is irreparable to the devices. This may require one to buy another device which is still expensive.

Multimedia normally needs computer systems that are high-end. Images, sounds, animations, and videos normally require a high amount of storage and this may lead to slowing down of computers that are low-end. Some of them might not even be able to fit in the low-end computer. In comparison to simple text files that are made using the Word Processor, creating multimedia content needs one to have a computer that is of high quality. One of the greatest disadvantages of multimedia content is that people without machines that are multimedia-capable might not be able to access large portions of the content. This requires the multimedia developers to be aware of the multimedia elements they are incorporating into apps and make sure to only use those that are important and significant (Rao, Bojkovic, and Milovanovic, 2006).

1.4. IMPORTANCE OF MULTIMEDIA

Multimedia includes video, audio, animation, text, graphics, interactive computing, etc. in a computer-based synchronized system. It is an important form of communication in the modern time. It has helped in enriching Medicare, education, business, entertainment, etc. by enhancing the utility of computers. Some of the uses and importance of multimedia include:

Education – multimedia has helped in revolutionizing the education field. It has ensured that the education system is much more effective and attractive in comparison to the older traditional ways of teaching. Creating a presentation using multimedia has helped in improving the level of retention and interest in the classroom. It helps in presenting information in a clear and attractive manner. There are many multimedia softwares available today, that allow students to even gain a large amount of knowledge from their homes on their personal computers. Students who prefer audiovisual learning learn much better with multimedia presentations. Teachers have also been able to use YouTube to post videos that the students can use to study in their free time. Multimedia is used in many schools for the production of computer-based training courses and even for books that are used for referencing, such as encyclopedias (Rao, Bojkovic, and Milovanovic, 2006).

Figure 1.5. When teachers equip their presentations with different types of media such as video and audio, they have high chances of retaining the students' attention.

Source: *https://www.kullabs.com/classes/subjects/units/lessons/notes/note-detail/1036.*

Entertainment – Multimedia has proven to be very important in the entertainment field. Most if the entertainment media such as television, radio, VCR, etc. use multimedia to provide the experience. In addition to this, being able to play games on a personal computer or using a game console also uses multimedia. Multimedia is also used to create special effects in animations and movies.

Marketing – companies have been able to develop CD-ROM software's that have data on uses, prices, outlets, etc. of the products and services they provide to their potential customers, so as to increase their profits. This allows the buyers to know the prices of what they want before they head there to purchase through the Compact Disk even at their houses or homes.

Communicating – due to development in technology, we are now able to communicate with people from different ends of the world due to audio conferences and video conferences. This form of communication is based on electronics and computers and has helped in making politics, economics, social, business, and international activities dynamic.

Medicare – medical services have become much more effective and efficient due to the use of multimedia. People are able to have consultations with their doctors from their homes due to multimedia-based electronic communication. Multimedia is also being used to diagnose and prescribe medication. Doctors are also able to have meeting with other doctors from different parts of the world, thus promoting networking and sharing if information for better diagnoses.

Helping in research – so as to conduct research and development works, researchers need various kinds of information. The internet has proven to be very helpful in this situation. It allows them to obtain any necessary information they may need to conduct their research. They get to collect all the information they need to carry out a research that is successful.

Virtual reality – this is a form of technology that gives a user the opportunity to interact with an environment that is computer simulated. It is possible for the simulated environment to be very similar to the real world. For example, pilots go through many flight simulations before they are able to fly a real plane. It is also possible for the simulated environment to be very different from the real world. For example, in virtual reality games which is based on multimedia bounder tech.

E-shopping – technology has developed to the point of allowing us to shop online. In E-commerce, people get an opportunity to see the object they are interested in before purchasing it.

Digital library – people no longer need to go all the way to the library physically so as to have access to reading material. It is possible to access books from the internet. This is due to digitization.

Multimedia has many more uses and has shown to be very important in our world today. It is great invention of modern technology. There are also some advancements that are still being researched on, so as to further develop this technology to the next level.

Figure 1.6. In addition to the digital library, we now have Kindles that users can use to purchase novels and other reading materials to read. It is portable and very convenient.

Source: *https://www.cnet.com/google-amp/reviews/amazon-kindle-paper-white-2018-preview/.*

1.5. LINEAR VS. NON-LINEAR MULTIMEDIA

Multimedia projects are referred to as linear when:

- They are not interactive; and
- The user is not able to alter the content that they are viewing.

An example of a linear multimedia is a movie.

Multimedia projects are referred to as non-linear when:

- They are interactive;
- The users have control over what they are viewing; and
- The end user has navigation control.

An example of a non-linear multimedia is a video game.

It is also possible for Multimedia to be either recorded or live. A presentation that has been recorded allows for the user to achieve interactivity using a system for navigation. A multimedia presentation that is live may also allow for interactivity, however, with the person presenting the work, or the person performing it (Mitra, 2004).

1.6. HYPERTEXT VS. HYPERMEDIA

Hypertext is a tool that is used for cross referencing and it is meant for access that is driven by the user for a whole lot of information that is interconnected, either dynamic or static. It is all in the electronic format. In other words, it is a simple text that has links that allow one to gain access to many more texts that are either a different or same document. It helps in providing information to end users in a well-organized and easy to access manner. It is used for representing information that is textual and linked all together so as to ensure the provision of much more control as well as flexibility. All this provides users with the opportunity of moving from one location to another with the help of hyperlinks. The links help in connecting nodes to different documents which can then undergo activation once they are clicked on by a pointing device.

Hypermedia, on the other hand, is an extension of hypertext that uses different forms of media including audio, videos, graphics, etc. It has a similar structure to the hypertext, however, it is not based on texts only. It can make extensions of the hypertext systems capabilities by the creation of links that are clickable within webpage's so as to ensure the creation of a network of nonlinear information that is interconnected, which the users are able to gain access to and also have interactions with it for a multimedia experience that is much better than usual. One of the main types of hypermedia includes a link of an image which is linked to different webpage's. Hypermedia is used for many different functions including sophisticated learning, qualitative research, problem-solving, etc. (Mitra, 2004).

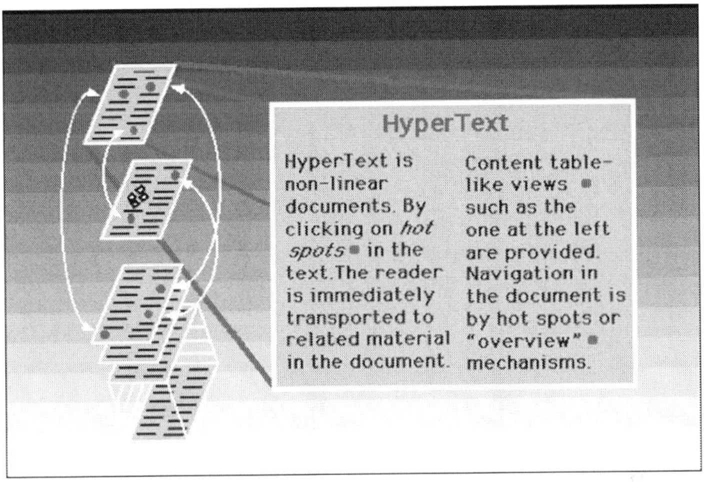

Figure 1.7. Above is the basic concept of how a hypertext works. One piece of hypertext can send you to many others including sounds and images.

Source: *https://users.cs.cf.ac.uk/Dave.Marshall/Multimedia/node11.html.*

1.6.1. Differences between Hypermedia and Hypertext

In terms of their definition: Hypertexts are texts that have links to a different set of texts that the user can access by clicking on the link with a mouse. These documents are linked into one using hyperlinks allowing users to move from one to the other whether the webpage is the same or not. Hypermedia is used in a similar manner, however, it does not only use texts. It has different elements of media such as video, images, audio, etc.

In terms of their representation: Hypertexts refer to a network of documents together with other media that have been interconnected and they have links between them that reference them. It contains electronic data in either dynamic or static forms. The content that is static cannot be modified during delivery to the end user, while dynamic content can be altered based on the input the user applies. Hypermedia is referred to as the peak of the multimedia experience, allowing the hypertext to also have many different firms of media such as audio and video.

In terms of technology: The hypertext technology has been there for a long period of time, despite the fact that it is associated with the Work Wide Web. Hypertexts are mainly based on the interaction between the computer and a human by hyperlinks. It allows for the user to effectively utilize links and texts as well as their implementation on the World Wide Web. The technology used by hypermedia is based on a media form that is non-linear, including not only texts but also different forms of media for enhancement if the experience. This has really been helpful in the education field.

In terms of their application: There is more than just being able to click and access links from different locations on the internet when it comes to hypertexts. This model can be used for many different purposes, and its ability to link dynamically is not only possible on the internet. It can also be used in qualitative research, literary exploration, and electronic studying. Hypermedia has many different documents that are interconnected and linked together by hypertexts. For example, the World Wide Web.

Both hypermedia and hypertexts have similar structures, however, hypermedia includes many types of media. The major difference is in how they undergo implementation. Hypertext is used for the representation of multimedia content in a text format that is electronic, while hypermedia involves both multimedia and hypertext for the provision of access to a lot of information in a sequence that is non-linear. Hypermedia is mainly used for the extension of how multimedia elements function, making the information relayed much more interesting and accessible (Li, Drew, and Liu, 2014).

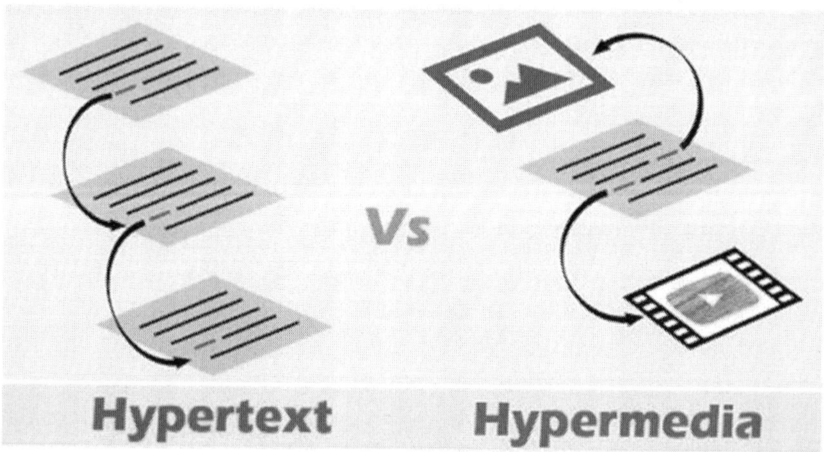

Figure 1.8. The main difference between hypertext and hypermedia. Hypermedia incorporates different forms of media such as videos and audios.

Source: *https://techdifferences.com/difference-between-hypertext-and-hypermedia.html.*

1.7. DELIVERY TECHNOLOGY USED AND ITS DIGITAL APPLICATION

Multimedia technology has been developing more and more each year. They have been very many advancements that are significant in relation to the different components of multimedia technology: processing if images, computer processing, digital audio, technologies for display, scanning, telecommunications, optical storage technologies such as CD-ROM, digitized video technologies, consumer electronics, etc. all which have helped in providing major contributions to developing multimedia apps.

There are so many different types of media in the optical technology area, such as:

- CD-ROM – Photo CD;
- Compact Disc-Interactive;
- CD-ROM extended Architecture;
- Digital Video Interactive; and
- CD-TV.

Despite the fact that they have some similarities including durability, portability, large storage capacity, quick random access, etc. they have some differences in the manner in which they function. They can be used as tools that offer reliable solutions to problems that are related to information when they undergo integration with information systems that are computerized. Below are some of the explanations.

1.7.1. CD-ROM

Figure 1.9. These were very popular for distributing software and data for computers. It was also used for video game consoles in the fourth generation.

Source: *https://en.wikipedia.org/wiki/CD-ROM.*

In this area, the number of CD-ROM products as well as the number of installed drives has been growing at a fast rate. As of now, the number of CD-ROMs with a base that is installed have gone up to two million drives from around 170,000 drives back in 1988. There were certain issues when it came to CD-ROMs being accepted by the public such as their performance, price, etc. and these have been changed. It is also possible for one to publish a CD-ROM on a desk-top now due to existent software's and peripherals that are affordable, together with lower costs of reproduction for producing a master disc that is 600-MB with 10 copies.

1.7.2. CD-ROM Jukebox

These help in providing access to full image databases that are networked. These are considered as a major aspect of an information system that is well integrated. This technology takes up very little space, however, it can hold 240 discs each with a storage capacity of 600-MB. They can store a total of 1.45 million full-page images. This technology can also be daisy-chained together, so as to allow for its connection to a network system that can help in delivering full-image and full-text documents to users of the system in a short period of time.

1.7.3. Compact Disc Interactive (CD-I)

This technology was introduced in 1986 and it is a consumer multimedia product that is new. It is able to store video, audio, and graphic materials in a simultaneous manner on the CD format. Its system is able to handle a large amount of data that is interrelated in real-time. This leads to an integration of synchronized text information, video, and audio. The different types of video and audio data that are interrelated normally share the disc capacity of the CD-I. They make a wide variety of video images and interactive effects available, such as scrolling, full screen video, full motion, etc. They also make it possible for one to store a maximum of 16 languages for audios in one disc. This however, is not done often due to its impracticality.

1.7.4. Digital Video Interactive (DVI)

This technology provides a combination of high quality graphics and interactivity while presenting motion digital videos that are in full-color, audios, and stills. This is all possible in a personal computer that is IBM compatible. Application developers have been able to create applications that are interactive with multiple track audio, full-motion videos, dynamic graphics, and still video games, due to the introduction of the Application Development Platform in the 1980s. This has therefore provided multimedia applications in many different markets especially in industries.

1.7.5. Photo CD

An example of this is the Kodak Photo CD system that works by transferring photos that have been taken on a 35mm film, that is exposed and processed, onto a CD that is writable. An audio/photo CD player that is dual purpose can read the data and thereafter display the image onto an appliance that is user-friendly, such as a television set. There are many different possibilities after the processing of a roll of film that is exposed or a certain number of photos. Because the images are stored digitally, the finishers get the chance to retouch and crop the digital prints in a much easier manner. This technology also allows for one to create certain products in an easier manner, such as business cards and postcards using the desktop personal computer.

1.7.6. CD-WORM

Besides being able to use the CD-ROM for publishing in the electronic publishing area, we are not only able to have ROM products in CDs, but also be able to write on Compact discs once with the CD-WORM disc by utilizing its technology. This was able to provide u with the opportunity of writing 600 megabytes of data on a Compact Disk.

1.8. MULTIMEDIA SYSTEM

A multimedia system refers to a system that is able to process multimedia applications and data. It is mainly characterized by its ability to process, store, generate, manipulate, and render multimedia information (Mitra, 2004).

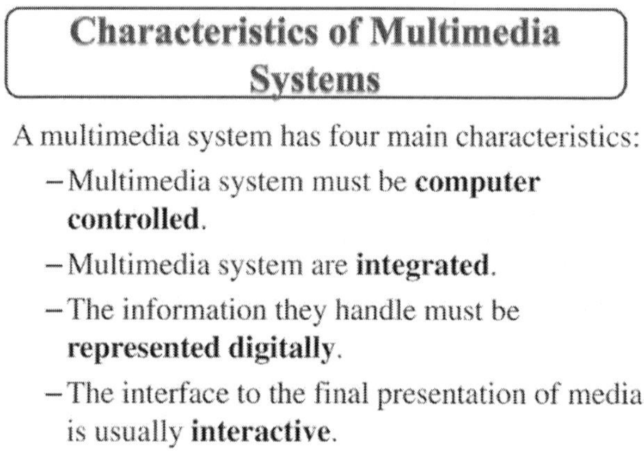

Figure 1.10. Above are some of the characteristics of an efficient multimedia system. All multimedia systems need to represent their information digitally.

Source: *https://slideplayer.com/amp/12810303/.*

There are four main characteristics of any multimedia system. These include:

- The system has to be controlled by a computer.
- All systems have to be integrated.
- Any data that is handled by the system has to be digitally represented.
- The interface for the last presentation of the media needs to be interactive.

Below are some features that make the Multimedia system more effective and efficient:

Extremely high processing power – This is required so as to allow the system to process large amounts of data and ensure delivery of media in real-time. Some if the media normally has a high capacity, such as videos, depending on their definition.

A file system that is Multimedia capable – this is required so as to be able to provide media in real-time including streaming audios and videos. RAID technology is a hardware that can be used to achieve this. Representation of data and file formats that can support multimedia – the representation of data and file formats need to be easy to manage and at the same time give one permission for one to compress and decompress in real-time.

High and efficient input and output – the input and output to the subsystem of the file are supposed to be fast and efficient. They also need to allow for one to record and playback data in real-time, for example, direct to disk recording systems.

Special operating system – this helps in allowing for accessibility to the file system and also for the processing of data in a fast and efficient manner. They also are required to be able to promote the supporting of scheduling in real-time, input, and output streaming, direct transfers to disk, interrupt processing that is fast, etc.

Memory and Storage – they should be equipped with large storage units with more than 50GB, and also large memory of more than 50MB. They should also have large caches and they should either be level 2 or 3 hierarchy so as to manage the system efficient.

Network Support – they should well-distributed systems.

Software tools – they should have tools that are user friendly so as to handle media, deliver media, develop, and design applications.

1.8.1. Components of a Multimedia System

There are a couple of different software and hardware systems that are needed to run a multimedia system. These include:

Capture devices – These include keyboards, mice, video cameras, graphic tablets, audio microphone, Virtual Reality devices, tactile sensors, 3D input devices, etc.

Storage devices – DVDs, CD-ROMs, Hard disks, Zip drives, etc.

Computer systems – workstations, DSP Hardware, VIDEO hardware, etc.

Communication Networks – Intranets, Ethernet, ATM, Internet, FDDI, Token Ring, etc.

Display Devices – Color printers, HDTV, CD-quality speaker, Hi-resolution monitors, etc.

Figure 1.11. For audio Multimedia to be expressed efficiently, there is a need for quality speakers. This will help in expanding the multimedia experience. It is important for the input and output of any multimedia system but of good quality.

Source: https://www.theverge.com/platform/amp/circuitbreaker/2018/7/9/17534710/shinola-speakers-studio-quality.

1.8.2. Challenges for Multimedia Systems

A multimedia system can have the task of rendering more than one form of media at the same time, and this is very different from other applications. Many forms of media playing at the same time have a temporal relationship. Two problems may arise from this:

- The inability to play the frames in the correct time frame or order in a video and therefore a lack of sequencing within the media.
- Lack of synchronization, for example, the lip movement and the audio in a movie. These two need to be in synchrony for the user to enjoy.

Some of the main issues that multimedia systems need to deal with include:

- The correct manner in which they can represent and store information that is temporal.

- How to ensure that the temporal relationships on playback as well as retrieval are strictly maintained.

1.9. DELIVERY OF MULTIMEDIA

There are two ways in which multimedia can be delivered: via traditional methods such as CDs and through the internet. We will discuss these two below.

1.9.1. Traditional Methods of Multimedia Delivery

Figure 1.12. Above is a DVD player. These are used to play DVDs so as to relay either audio or video information. They were very popular for storing movies.

Source: https://shop.etcnet.fi/shop/datortillbehor-en/usb-mini-dvd-burner/?lang=en.

DVDs provide full motion videos that are of high quality and in a standard format, and these can be played using a television or a standard player. Multimedia DVDs and CDs can be viewed using most personal computers, and they can be used to play any form of media including videos. Any content that can be delivered online can also be delivered on a CD or a DVD. These traditional methods are very portable and they can be viewed at the users' convenience at any place and time, however, they are not quite interactive. When being delivered across different places, they can take a while to arrive, around a few weeks or days. When they are distributed in this manner, they can get outdated and it is not easy to update them in a timely manner. This method of delivery is only efficient for delivering lower volumes. Compact Disks can store up to 650 megabytes, Digital Versatile Discs can store up to 4.7 Gigabytes, and Bluray Discs can store up to 27 Gigabytes (Savage and Vogel, 2009).

1.9.2. Internet Multimedia

These days, most of the multimedia content is delivered using the internet in so many different ways, such as blogs, social media sites, public web sites, chat rooms and public web sites, amongst others. One can access content online using a desktop personal computer when the content being viewed is on-demand, and it can also be downloaded for one to view later.

One can access multimedia content at any place and time, based on the constraints of the internet service provider or Local Area Network that the viewer is using, as well as the person who owns the content. It is also possible to add control so as to give permission to users who are authorized to access the content that is deemed appropriate from a specific location. Internet technology can provide a whole lot of interactivity. It is also easier to update content in real-time, allowing for the content to always be fresh; however, it thus can be intensive for the bandwidth for the Local Area Network of the viewer. The consumption of bandwidth is relative to the quality of the video as well as the number of people who are using the same network at the same time. One can control the overall bandwidth consumption by using open solution cache devices, by temporary storage of content locally (Savage and Vogel, 2009).

Some of the main differences between the traditional method of delivery and the internet method are:

- The web-based method has a limitation when it comes to the size of the picture and videos that have low resolution, while CDs and DVDs are able to store multimedia elements that are high end.

Figure 1.13. The World Wide Web has all the information one would need. It has information in all forma of media: video, audio, text, etc. Internet content can however, be false, because there are many people who have access to the content and can change and add false statements.

Source: https://depositphotos.com/135808950/stock-illustration-download-or-upload-internet-contents.html.

- The content on the internet can be changed, destroyed or deleted by people who are not responsible, while that on a CD or DVD can be stored permanently, and it can also not be altered. If the disc is placed in harsh conditions, it is possible for it to get spoilt and one would not be able to obtain the content from it anymore.
- On the internet, it is easier and cheaper to update information, while on the CDs and DVDs, the information on them can get outdated very fast and cannot be changed.

1.9.3. Audio Multimedia

Audio is referred to as the sound that can be heard by humans, which means that it is within our acoustic range. We are able to produce acoustic sounds due to audio frequency which is an electrical current that is constantly alternating within 20–20,000-hertz range.

When it comes to computing terms, audio is referred to as the sound system that either is bought together with the computer, or even that which can be added to the computer. The computer has an audio card, that has a special processor which has been built in, as well as the memory, so as to be able to process audio files and later on send them to the speakers in the computer. An audio file is the term used to refer to captured sound that has been recorded and this sound can also be played back. The audio card is equipped with a microchip that is referred to as an analog to digital converter which helps in converting sound, which is a sequence of analog signal that are natural, into digital signals. When the computer plays sound, the digital signals are then transferred to the speaker where they undergo conversion back into signals that are analog and then produce sounds that vary.

Figure 1.14. Audio can be utilized for the enhancement multimedia applications in many different ways, such as in the delivery of lectures over the internet, music is utilized for the addition of emotion and interest to the presentation, and other audio that is not speech utilized as section of the general interface.

Source: https://www.sleepytimegorillamuseum.com/multimedia-audio/.

For storage and faster transmission, audio files are normally compressed. It is possible for audio files to be sent in standalone segments that are short, such as in the wave file format. It is important for sound to be delivered as streaming sound, so as to enable the end-user to receive this sound in real-time when they are listening to music, for a multimedia effect, or even so that they are able to take part in a video or audio conference. There are audio cards that are more advanced and these are able to support tables of sound that are pre-captured. The most commonly used format for audio files today is the MP3.

1.9.4. Audio Coding

The format that is used for audio coding, and also sometimes referred to as audio compression, is a format that is able to represent content so as to allow for the transmission or storage of audio that is digital such as digital radio and television, or even in video and audio files.

Some of the commonly used audio coding formats include MP3, Opus, FLAC, AAC, and Vorbis. There is a software or hardware that is specific for implementing compression and decompression of audios either to or from an audio coding format that is specific, and this is referred to as an audio codec. LAME is an example of an audio codec, and it is one of the various codecs that are available which helps in the implementation of audio encoding and decoding in the MP3 format for coding audio in software (Mitra, 2004).

Figure 1.15. This format allows for coding digital audio. It was upgraded from the MPEG-1 3rd part, allowing it to support many more audio channels.

Source: *https://www.freepik.com/free-icon/mp3-audio-file_740342.htm.*

Some of the formats that are used for coding audio files undergo documentation by a technical specification document that is detailed, and it is referred to as an audio recording specification. Standardization organizations normally write and approve some of the specifications as technical standards, and these are normally referred to as audio coding standards. "Standards" can be used to refer to both de facto and formal standards.

Audio content that has gone through encoding in a specific audio coding format normally undergoes encapsulation in a container format. This means that they use that does not have a aw Advanced Audio Coding file, however, they have a M4A audio file which is stored in the MPEG-4 format in a container that has Advanced Audio Coding encoded audio. The container is also equipped with metadata, including the title of the audio as well as other tags, in addition to an index that is used for seeking the audio faster.

One of the main exceptions are the MP3 files, which have been audio coded in a raw manner and do not have the container format. The De facto standards that are used to add metadata tags including artists and titles in MP3 files are ways that work by ensuring the tags to the MP3 are appended, and thereafter being able to rely on the MP3 player to establish the malformed audio coding and in this situation, be able to skip it. In the video files that have audio in them, the audio content that has been encoded is put together with the video, in a format for coding videos, within a multimedia container format.

Not all the algorithms that are used by the codec that is ensuring implementation of the format, are dictated by the audio coding format. Lossy audio compression works in a very important way, by ensuring that data is removed in a manner that the human ear cannot hear, in accordance with the psychoacoustic model. According to this model, the encoder implementer is able to choose the data which should be removed.

Audio coding formats (Lossless, lossy, and uncompressed): The lossless audio coding format lowers the total data that is required for the representation of sound, however, it can still undergo decoding to its original form which was uncompressed. The lossy audio coding format works by adding the reduction of the bit resolution, of the sound that is at the top of a compression, which leads to a reduction in the data at the cost of lost information that cannot be retrieved (Mitra, 2004).

Figure 1.16. FLAC is a format for coding audio files for lossless compression of audio that are digital, and it is also the term that is used to refer to the software project that is free and produces the tools for FLAC, the software package that is used as a reference and is inclusive of a codec implementation.

Source: *https://blog.teufelaudio.com/flac-lossless-audio-codec/.*

Lossy audio codecs are mostly used for the compression of consumer audios, because the size that is smaller allows for convenience during distribution. MP3 and Advanced Audio Coding are the commonly used audio coding formats, and both of them are lossy formats that are based on perceptual coding algorithms and also modified discrete cosine transform (MDCT).

FLAC and Apple Lossless are lossless audio coding formats, and these can also be used but at a coat similar to that of larger files. Pulse-code modulation is an uncompressed audio format are used but rarely. The Pulse-code modulation was the main format that was used for Compact Disc Digital Audio, before there was the use of lossy compression which became the main format after MP3 was introduced.

1.9.5. Image and Video Multimedia

There are some properties that light has that allow it to appear to have particles and also at other times it appears to behave like a wave. Light is energy that is electromagnetic and it is emitted from an energy source in wave forms. Light that is visible is in the range of 400 to 700 nanometers on the electromagnetic spectrum.

Candela or a candle power is a unit that is used for the measurement of the radiation strength from a source if light. Radiance is the term used to refer to the total energy from the source of light, inclusive of all electromagnetic radiation and heat. This measurement is expressed in watts. The strength of light that the human eye is able to perceive is referred to as luminance. Radiance and luminance can be compared in that; radiance measures the whole output from the source of light and luminance refers to only the part that is perceived (Rao, Bojkovic, and Milovanovic, 2006).

The brightness is a measure of perceived intensity that is psychological. It is a subjective measure. It is practically impossible to measure brightness in an objective manner because it is relative. An example of this can be seen with a candle in a dark room, which may seem bright to the person using it; however, it is not bright in a room full of sunshine or light. The strength of light decreases with increase in distance of the light source, as it is inversely proportional to the square of the distance from the light source. This gives a reason to why there is a requirement of projectors that have a high intensity so as to show a multimedia presentation to an audience, on a screen.

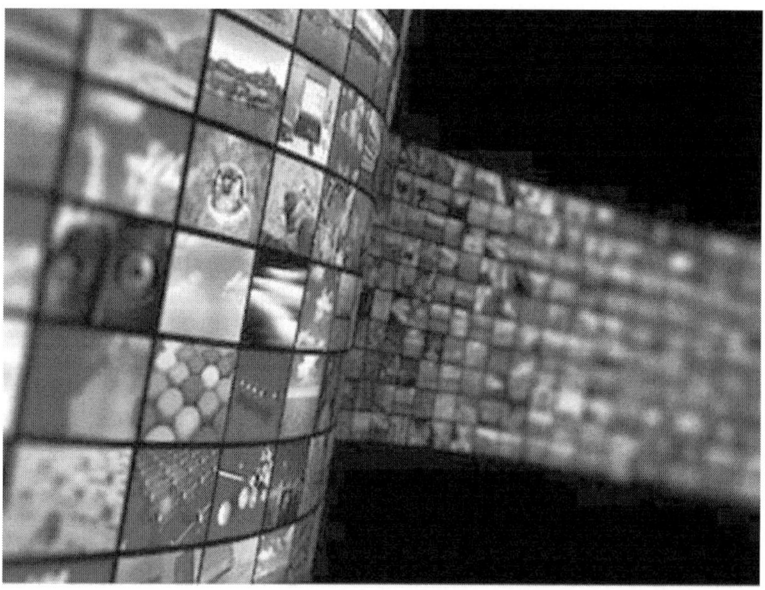

Figure 1.17. Images have a higher chance of influencing around 30% of people to click through from social media to a website whereas videos are only able to do so by 1/3rd, at 15%. Videos are still considered very important in the different types of content, however, images have shown more success at driving clicks.

Source:https://www.google.com/url?sa=i&source=web&cd=&ved=2ahUKE

wiml4nq0LjnAhUV5uAKHXgkC8gQjhx6BAgBEAI&url=https%3A%2F%2Fwww.shutterstock.com%2Fsearch%2Fmultimedia&psig=AOvVaw0KBXqrjXk5pstF28h1uYHW&ust=1580930921904131.

What are the basics of color?: Color is referred to as the sensation that one registers when light in various wavelengths undergoes perception by the brain. It is seen in objects that emit or reflect various light wavelengths. When appropriate amounts of the three primary colors are mixed, it is possible to create the sensation of any color. These colors are red, blue, and green.

Colors are created on the monitors of computer by emitting three light wavelengths in combinations that are appropriate. Hue helps in distinguishing amongst colors like yellow, green, and red. The level at which a color is far from a gray that has a similar intensity is referred to as saturation. Lightness helps in the embodiment of the notion that is achromatic, of perceived intensity of an object that is reflecting. We use the term brightness instead of lightness for an object that is self-luminous such as a cathode-ray tube.

Image data Formats: Firstly, there are the standard system independent formats. These include:

- The Graphics Interchange Format which was initially created to transmit images over phone lines. It was created by Compuserve and UNISYS, and it has a limitation of 8-bit color images.
- The JPEG bitmap which is the standard for compressing still image files. It is able to achieve high rates of compressions due to its ability to take advantage of the limitation of the human vision system. It also uses the Lossy compression which provides users with the opportunity to set level of quality that is desired. It was created by the Joint Photographic Expert group.
- The Tagged Image File Format is a lossless format that is able to ensure the storage of various types of images. It is not considered better than the JPEG, seeing as it is not user controllable. Thus was standardized by the Aldus Corporation.
- The Encapsulated PostScript is a typesetting language. It is inclusive of structured graphics, as well as images that have been bit-mapped. It is utilized by many popular graphics programs such as Adobe. It does not allow for the images to be compresses, and it only provides large files.

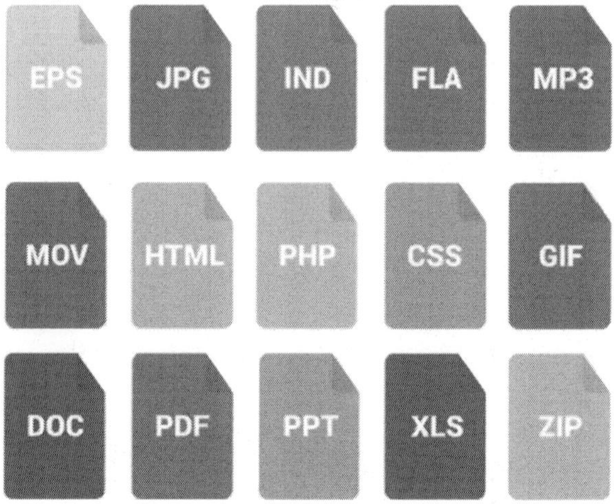

Figure 1.18. Above are some of the most commonly used file formats. There are normally 5 main formats that are used for storing images. These include: JPEG, TIFF, GIF, PNG, and Raw image files.

Source*: https://www.analyticsvidhya.com/blog/2017/03/read-commonly-used-formats-using-python/.*

Secondly, there are system dependent formats. These include:

- The bitmap image file format is one that supports 24-bit bitmap images for Microsoft Windows.
- The X BitMap is able to support any 24-bit bitmap images for the X Windows System.

Video coding format: This is also referred to as the video compression format which is a format that helps in representing video content such as in bitstream or in a data file, with the purpose of it being stored and transmitted. It normally uses a video compression algorithm which has been standardized, and is mostly based on discrete cosine transform coding and motion compensation. Some of the formats that are commonly used include HEVC (H.265), H.262 (MPEG-2 Part 2), Theora, VP9, MPEG-4 Part 2, and AV1. The video codec is the software or hardware implementation that is able to compress and/or decompress to or from a certain video coding format. Xvid is an example of a video codec, and this is one of the many that helps in implementing encoding and decoding of video files using the

MPEG-4 Part 2 format if coding that is found in the software (Li, Drew, and Liu, 2014).

Some of the video coding formats undergo documentation by a technical specification document that is detailed, referred to as a video coding specification. They are sometimes referred to as video coding standards due to the fact that they are written and approved as technical standards by organizations that have been standardized.

When a particular video coding format is used for the encoding of video content, it is normally encoded with the help of an audio coding format inside a specific multimedia container, for example, MP4, AVI, FLV, Matroska, and also RealMedia. Due to this format, the user has no access to a H.264 file, however, they will have access to the MP4 video file containing an MP4 container with a H.264-encoded video, always next to an Advanced Audio Coding encoded video.

These multimedia container formats are able to have any one of the various formats that are used to code videos, for example, there can either be an MPEG-2 Part 2 or H.264 video coding format in an MP4 container format. We can see this as well in the first specification that was given for the WebM file type, which specifically needed to use Matroska, and also gave the specific audio and video compression formats they needed to use with Matroska container (Vorbis and VP8 respectively), despite the fact that the container format for the Mateoska itself was able to contain other different video coding formats such as Opus for audio amd VP9 for video support, which was actually later added to the specifications for WebM (Li, Drew, and Liu, 2014).

Video coding formats (Lossless, Lossy, and Uncompressed): Lossy video codecs are mostly used for the compression of consumer videos, because they provide significantly smaller files in comparison to lossless compression. Despite the fact that there are video coding formats that are made specially for wither lossless compression or lossy compression, there are some video coding formats that are able to support both, such as H.264 and Dirac.

Video formats that have not been compressed such as Clean HDMI, are considered a form of lossless videos, and these are rarely used, but can be used in a few circumstances such as being able to send video to a display through connecting a HDMI.

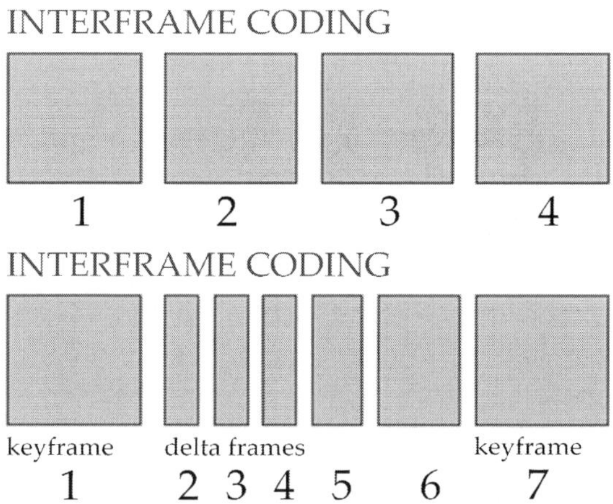

Figure 1.19. Above shows one of the main differences between the intra-frame coding and Inter-fame coding. The intra-frame coding, unlike the inter-frame coding, allows each frame to use an equal amount of data as seen above.

Source: *https://www.yourdictionary.com/interframe-coding.*

Intra-frame video coding formats: Inter-frame makes being able to edit a video sequence that is encoded complicated. The Intra-frame video format is a subclass of the various formats that make it relatively easy to code videos. An example of this is the DV, which is able to independently compress each frame of the video stream without having to refer to the other frames in the same stream. In addition to this, it does not attempt to take advantage of how successive pictures correlate over a period of time, for them to be compressed in a better manner.

An example of this is the Motion JPEG, which is generally a succession of JPEG images that have been compressed individually. This method is faster and simpler; however, the video that has been encoded is much larger than the format that is able to support inter-frame coding.

Due to the fact that Inter-frame compression is able to copy information from one frame to another, if the frame that was originally there gets lost in transmission or cut out, the frames that follow it cannot undergo reconstruction in an effective manner. Being able to make a cut in a video that has been compressed using intra-frame while editing a video is quite easy and almost as easy as the ability to edit a video that has not been compressed. It is done by finding the start and end of each frame, and thereafter copying bit-for-but of each frame that one is interested in keeping, and then discarding of the frames that are unwanted. Another dissimilarity between the inter-frame and the intra-frame compression is that, each frame in an Intra-frame system uses the same amount of data. In the Inter-frame system, some of the frames such as the I-frame in MPEG-2 is not able to copy data from the other frames, and therefore need much more data than the other frames that are close by (Savage and Vogel, 2009).

One is able to build a video editor that is based in a computer that is able to spot issues that occur when I-frames are edited out, despite the fact that other frames need them. This has promoted the use of other newer formats, such as HDV, for editing. This process however, needs much more computing power in comparison to editing a video that has been compressed with the Intra-frame format with a similar quality of the picture. This compression is however, not fully effective for its use with audio format.

1.9.6. MPEG Coding Standards

The Moving Picture Expert Groups (MPEG) standards are a set if standards that are always evolving for the compression of both audio and video, as well as for the delivery if multimedia which was developed by the Moving Picture Expert Group.

MPEG-1 was created to code videos that are progressive at a 1.5 million bits per second transmission rate. It was mainly created to use with CD-I media and Video-CD. Another evolution from the early MPEG work is the MOEG-1 audio layer-3 which is normally referred to as the MP3.

MPEG-2 was created so as to code images that are interlaced at four million bits per second transmission rates. It is utilized mainly for broadcasting on digital TV and also for DVDs. The MPEG-2 player is also able to deal with MPEG-1 data.

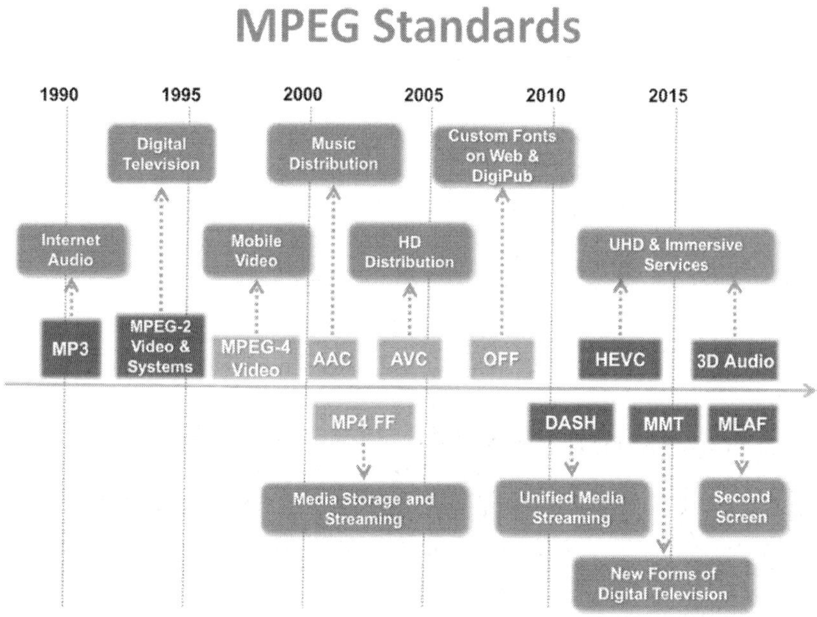

Figure 1.20. *Above are the MPEG standards that have been used since 1990 to 2015. Most of these are still used up to today.*

Source: *https://records. sigmm. org/2017/05/09/standards-column-jpeg-and-mpeg/.*

The two MPEG designs make definitions of methods they use to compress videos that are digital using factors that vary up to 50:1 from 25:1. They are able to achieve this compression through 5 main methods:

- Using the Discrete Cosine Transform which is a transform that is based on frequency;
- The use of quantization which is a method that helps in losing selective information, which is also referred to as lossy compression, and this can be lost acceptably from information that is visual;
- Another technique is the Huffman coding, which is a lossless compression that utilizes code tables on the basis of statistics in the data that has been encoded;
- Another technique is the Motion Compensated Predictive Coding, where the dissimilarities in the changes that have occurred between a certain image and the one that precedes it, are counted

and only these dissimilarities undergo encoding; and

- There is also the Bi-directional prediction which helps in making predictions of some images from the pictures that precede immediately and thus being able to follow the image.

The first 3 methods are normally used for the JPEG File compression as well. There was the merging of a proposed MPEG-3 standard, which was initially created to be used with High Definition Television, with the MPEG-2 standard. This however, did not last because the MPEG-2 standards were able to meet the requirements of the HDTV.

The MPEG-4 is considered a standard that is very ambitious and is able to address video and speech synthesis, computer visualization, fractal geometry, as well as artificial intelligence as the main approaches to reconstruct images. It is also able to address a standardized way for the creation and definition of media objects by the authors in a multimedia presentation, the ability of them to be synchronized and in relation to each other while they are being transmitted, as well as how the end-users should have the ability to have interactions with the media objects (Gries and Gries, 2005).

MPEG-21 is able to provide a framework that is larger and architectural, so as to create and deliver multimedia. There are 7 main elements that are defined by this:

- Representation of content;
- Reporting of events;
- Declaration of digital items;
- Handling and using content;
- Networks and terminals;
- Management and protection of intellectual property; and
- Identification and declaration of digital items.

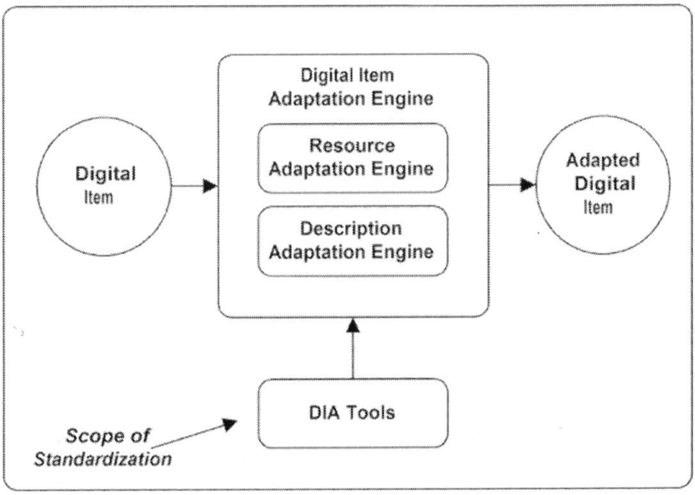

Figure 1.21. The MPEG-21 standard was created so as to define a framework that is open for multimedia applications. It is from the moving picture experts group.

Source: https://www.researchgate.net/figure/Overview-and-scope-of-the-MPEG-21-DIA-standard_fig7_220205129.

1.9.7. Advanced Video Coding

This is also referred to as MPEG-4 Part 10 or H.264. It the mostly used format when it comes to being able to record, compress, and distribute video content, utilized by 90% of the multimedia industry. It helps in supporting resolutions that are up to and also including 8K UHD.

This project was created so as to use it for the creation of a standard that is able to provide videos that are of good quality at lower bit rates in comparison to the earlier standards, without having to the complex level of the design to an extent that would make it less practical or too expensive to do. They were able to achieve this with certain features such as the integer DCT, multi-picture inter-picture prediction, and variable block-size segmentation (Mitra, 2004).

One of the added goals was in the provision of adequate flexibility so as to give permission to the standard to be applied in many different applications on many different systems and networks, including bit rates that are both low and high, broadcasts, videos that are of high and low resolution, RTP/IP packet networks, DVD storage, and ITY-T multimedia telephony systems.

It is also possible to view the H.264 standard as a family of standards that are made of many different profiles, however, the highest profile it has is the format that is most commonly used. They have a specific decoder that is able to decode a minimum of one, but not exactly all at the same time. The standard is able to describe the format of the data that has been encoded as well as how the manner in which the data is decoded. It however does not give specifications on the algorithms that are used to encode the video. That is normally as it is so as to allow the encoder designers to choose for themselves, and due to this, there are very many encoding schemes that have been developed (Mitra, 2004).

H.264 is normally utilized for lossy compression, despite the fact that one is still able to create lossless coded regions inside pictures that have been lossy-coded or also in the support of cases that are of rare use, where in this situation, the whole encoding is lossless.

The advanced video coding was standardized by the ITU-T Video Coding Experts Group in collaboration with the Moving Picture Experts Groups. This ended up in the Joint Video Team. They are all maintained in a joint manner so as to use technical content that is identical. In May 2003, there was completion of the final drafting work on the original version of the standard. Many different extensions of its capabilities have been included into the other editions. The same organizations are the ones that developed the High Efficiency Video Coding, which is also referred to as the MPEG-H Part 2. It succeeds the MPEG-4 AVC. The standards that cane earlier are the ones that are mainly used as of today.

The H.264 is the most commonly used format for encoding videos on Blu-ray Discs. Streaming Internet Sources also use this format often, including Hulu, Netflix, Vimeo, Prime Video, YouTube, and even the iTunes Store. Other Web softwares including Microsoft (MS) Silverlight and Adobe Flash Player are able to broadcast over terrestrial satellites and cables, as well as systems. The H.264 normally gets protection by patents that are provided by different parties. There is a patent pool administration by the MPEG LA that administers a license that covers most of the patents (Mitra, 2004).

Figure 1.22. This format has many different applications that are able to cover a variety of forms of video that have been digitally compressed, from an internet streaming application that is low bit-rate to digital cinema applications that nearly have lossless coding.

Source*:* *https://www.dreamstime.com/multimedia-video-streaming-web-banner-background-multimedia-video-streaming-web-banner-background-television-wall-broadcasting-image126169509.*

Payments have to be made to certain royalties to MPEG LA as well as other owners if the patent, for the commercial use of H.264 technologies that have been patented. Free use of the H.264 technologies has been permitted by the MPEG LA so as to be able to stream internet videos that are free to the end-users. The Cisco System then makes the payment to MPEG LA on their behalf so as to have an open source.

1.9.8. Video Production

This is the process of creating video content. It is almost similar to making films; however, with images that have been digitally recorded instead of using film stock. There are three steps to producing a video: pre-production, principle production and post-production. The planning aspects that are done in production of the video before filming, are what are referred to as pre-production. This involves writing the script, logistics, scheduling, and other duties that are administrative.

The principle production stage in the production of videos is the point at which the content of the video is captured, including moving images and videography, and it also deals with the time to taken to film the subjects that are going to be in the video. The post production stage involves combining the video clips in a selective manner through editing of the videos into a final product that is able to narrate a story or communicate certain information either during live production or even after a certain event has already happened.

As of now, most of the video content circulating has been captured using media that is electronic, such as a solid state storage or SD card for cameras that are consumer grade, as well as flash storage for cameras that are professional grade. Video content that undergoes distribution in a digital manner normally appears in formats that are quite common such as QuickTime, Windows Media Video, Moving Picture Experts Group Format, and DivX (Gries and Gries, 2005).

Types of Videos: There are many different types of video production. Some of the ones that are used more commonly are TV production and film, web commercials, television commercials, marketing videos, wedding videos, product videos, corporate videos, and event videos. For content creation to be referred to as video production, it has to have gone through all the stages of production. It also has to have been created while having a certain audience in mind. A video that is recorded by someone who is creating the content with either a video camera or a smartphone so as to record a video for the purpose of creating a memory is not referred to as video production, but home video.

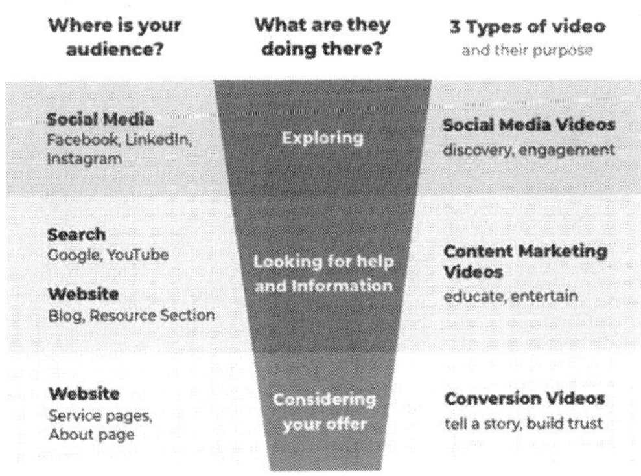

Figure 1.23. Above shows three types of video and what they are used for in different applications. It is important to consider your audience wham you are using videos to enhance a multimedia presentation.

Source: https://www.orbitmedia.com/blog/types-of-marketing-videos/.

1.9.9. Multimedia Protection

The ability to provide services that are legitimate to user is the only way we are able to use the distribution of digital media on a large scale. This needs for us to allow the use of digital media in a convenient manner, while still being able to compensate all members in the chain of information distribution in a manner that is equitable, inclusive of consumers, creators, and providers. There is a huge need for multimedia security.

Our world right now is full of pervasive mobile digital media that can be acquitted, distributed, and consumed. The fact that it is distributed digitally means that it is permitted to introduce business models that are cost effective and flexible and they are greatly beneficial for multimedia commerce transaction. In addition, having the information in a digital manner also makes is much easier for people to duplicate, access or manipulate the media information to a higher degree than that which is permitted in the terms and conditions that had initially been agreed upon in the specific transaction. Due to this, the protection content as well as the rights management has become a problem that is highly influential in the networks of delivering content.

Figure 1.24. Information security refers to is a group of actions that are carried out so as to ensure that data is kept secure from access that is not authorized or from being altered, either when it is undergoing storage, or transmission from one place to another.

Source: *https://www.csoonline.com/article/3513899/what-is-information-security-definition-principles-and-jobs.amp. html.*

Multimedia Security: This is a form of protection that is based on content. When it comes to creation of information, being able to process it, transmit it, and store it, there is a high level of representation and the data semantics are also available.

This generally means that it is possible for multimedia content to be compromised in many different forms, including videos, images, audio, texts, and even graphics inclusive of the many different formats that are digital. Due to this, there can be a high level of variations that occur in the characteristics of the information. For example, the needed maximum acceptable error, bit rate, display requirements, and decompression complexity may be deviated in a significant way which ends up in the creation of many issues when it comes to the protection of content (Mitra, 2004).

The forms of computer and network security that were traditionally used are not able to address the necessity of protecting content, due to the fact that information is normally processed at the bit level, which does not provide an allowance for considering the semantics of the information in an appropriate manner. This needs to be considered if we should be able to design mechanisms that can properly secure and have the ability to process information that is of high bandwidth, such as a video that may go through format conversion, at the same time allowing for the possibility to retain a certain level of control over the intellectual property after transmission. An example of this includes the ability to encrypt and authenticate functions which have to be accommodated by data formats that vary, as well as lossy compression. In addition, the issue of piracy cannot only be managed by network and computer security.

Multimedia security can deal with these issues using certain attributes, including:

- Tying protection to content that is of a higher level, in opposition to the actual bits, for the provision of security that is effective and efficient. This security can be created in a manner that makes in more robust so as to enable conversion and recovery to be formatted from an error in communication. For example, signatures that are digital can be based on features of information that are of a higher level, instead of using bit representation for it to be authenticated even when using lossy compression.
- Processing of security, for digital watermarking or encryption, undergoes integration with other tasks for processing signals such as decompression and compression, so as to have the ability to deal with any occurring fluctuations in but rate. Combination of digital watermarking and encryption with processing of the

signals does not only provide an opportunity for one to reuse blocks that are used for processing for a greater level of efficiency, but also can have the provision of a method that is well structured for the attachment of security processing to various forms of content and bandwidth.

- Metadata, which is semantic Information, have an association with the security mechanisms of the content so as to make sure that the content is utilized in the manner that was initially negotiated in the situation of an Information commerce.

Digital rights Management is a major motivation and application for developing and using multimedia security, in addition to network and computer security.

Management of digital rights: This is the manner in which user rights to content are managed digitally. It deals with the ability to link specific user privileges to media so as to be able to control what the users view, duplicate, access, and distribute, in addition to many other operations. The digital rights management system aims at balancing the protection if information, its usability, and its prices for the provision of an environment that is beneficial to all users in the information commerce transaction; all this is inclusive of cost effectiveness, new marketing opportunities, and expanded functionality.

Figure 1.25. Digital Rights Management refers to the various processes by that the publisher or author of a certain piece of work used to make sure that they have control on the actions that the buyer of his or her work is allowed to do.

Source: *https://www.locklizard.com/digital-rights-management/.*

All in all, we are able to achieve management by ensuring that business models interact effectively, technological, and legal policy.

The rapidly changing environments as well as the characteristics that are always conflicting in each of these aspects that make Digital Rights Management an issue that is both interesting and challenging at the same time.

As of now, there is research that is being done on ensuring that digital fingerprinting, media encryption, digital watermarking, tamper-assessment technologies and media authentication for Digital Rights Management applications.

1.9.10. Online Distribution

This is also referred to as digital distribution or electronic software distribution. It is the distribution or delivery of media content that is digital including video, audio, video games, e-books, and different software's.

It is generally used to refer to content that is distributed over a delivery medium that is online, for example, then internet, therefore being able to bypass distribution methods that are physical, including optical discs, paper, and even video cassettes (Savage and Vogel, 2009).

Online distribution refers to products that are freestanding; add-ons that are downloadable for other products are mostly referred to as downloadable content.

With the capabilities of network bandwidth being constantly advanced, distribution if content online has become very important in the 21st Century, with platforms that are well known including Netflix, Amazon Video, etc.

Multimedia content that undergoes distribution online has the ability to be downloaded or streamed, and it mostly includes films and television programs, music, books, video games, and software.

Being able to stream means having the ability to download and use the content on-demand, instead of giving permission to the user to have it stored permanently. In contrast, downloading this content fully to a storage media such as a hard drive, may allow for one to access the content offline in the future.

Figure 1.26. The distribution of content refers to the ability to distribute content to audiences that are found online, in many different media formats through many different channels. There are three groups of categorizations of these channels: Those that are owned, those that are earned, and those that are paid.

Source: *https://www.mailmunch.com/blog/content-distribution-strategies/.*

Content delivery networks are specialist networks and these help in distributing content on the internet by making sure that the have high performance as well as high availability. There are also alternative technologies that are used for delivering content. These include peer to peer file sharing technologies. In contrast, platforms that deliver content are able to ensure the creation and syndication of content in a remote manner, acting like management systems that have hosted content. Without any relation to the information above, digital distribution is used to refer to content distribution through digital media that is physical, instead if using analog media such as the magnetic tape. This is used in this manner in film distribution (Savage and Vogel, 2009).

CHAPTER

2

Genesis of Multimedia

CONTENTS

2.1. INTRODUCTION

Multimedia refers to content which applies a blend of varying content forms like text, sound, images, video, animations, and communicating content. Multimedia differs with media which uses just basic computer displays like text-only or conventional types of hand-produced or printed content. Newspaper was probably the original mass communication channel to use Multimedia – it was applied mostly for text, images, and graphics. Later in 1895, Marconi Gugliemo sent their original wireless radio broadcast at Pontecchio, Italy. Some few years later, the same inventor noticed that radio waves could beam over the Atlantic in 1901.

Originally designed for telegraph, later the radio became a key channel for audio broadcasting. TV also grew to become the new source of media during the 20th century, further bringing video to the front and changing the realm of mass communications.

2.2. BIRTH OF PRINT MEDIA

The Guardian

Alliance woe helps Labour poll surge

Thatcher in new confrontation

Figure 2.1. Newspapers were the earliest multimedia forms than combined pictures with words.

Source: *https://www.theguardian.com/gnm-archive/2002/jun/11/1.*

Historically, the Chinese became the first people to devise printing. They created wooden blocks for printing letters. It began during the era of Tang Dynasty back in 600 AD. Currently, the oldest preserved printed artwork in a wooden block is the Buddhist spiritual text of 684 AD.

It's presently displayed in the Tokyo calligraphy museum in Japan. The original printed book issued in China was a Buddhist script called the "Diamond Sutra," written by the scholar Wang Chick during the year 868 AD. A few copies of the Buddhist texts printed in 1377 have been stored in Chinese museums.

However, many scholars believe "The Peking Gazette," printed in China was the earliest newspaper. It was launched in 618. During the initial phases, this paper was hand-written and circulated to readers. But later it got printed and officially circulated. Henceforth, The Peking Gazette persisted its publication up to the start of the 20th century.

In more recent times, the newspaper was originated when publishers living in Protestant territories started to create printed editions of the hand-written journals which had delivered information for Europe's elites. Newspapers experienced lot of variations in their structure and content afterwards.

For instance, in England a newspaper called "The Weekly News" got launched in 1622. While the first newspaper bearing the modern print concept was printed in Oxford during the year 1655. This paper was called the "Oxford Gazette."

Today, the biggest newspaper in circulation is "Yomi Yuri Shimbun" that's published in Japan. This piece has an average circulation of about 14,323,781 copies a day. Similarly, the 2nd and 3rd largest dailies in distribution around the globe come from Japan.

Generally, the modern-day newspaper is considered a European invention. Among the oldest known ancestors of print media however, were handwritten newspaper sheets, which circulated extensively in Venice during the year 1566.

The weekly news sheets became filled with information concerning politics in Europe. Soon, the initial printed newspapers were officially published as weekly papers in Germany starting from 1609. Normally, they were highly censored by the state and featured only foreign news, or information deemed favorable to the government.

However, after the UK government eased censorship in 1695, the newspapers thrived in London and different other cities such as Philadelphia and Boston. Come the 1830s, high speed presses were capable of printing 1000s of papers affordably, allowing for reduced daily costs of production.

2.3. THE LONDON GAZETTE

While not considered a public newspaper in its traditional sense, The London Gazette is rather an official journal of UK's government. In the first years, it was mostly sent through post to subscribers, instead of being available for purchase at the newspaper stand. It has led to many other newspapers saying that they got to publishing first in the UK-key among them is The Stamford Mercury which started publishing to the public in 1712.

The London Gazette emerged during an especially turbulent period for Britain. The UK Civil War that had ceased in 1651 was lingering in people's memories, having led to the death of 4% of the country's population. There was also a lot of propaganda between the opposing sides, with each one employing inventions in print media to promote their causes and criticize their opponents (Costello, 2016).

Meanwhile, during these times the English press hadn't develop professionally, and truthful news was hard to come by. Equally, it's reasonable to say that at the period Britain had quite a pervasive fake news problem where propaganda was rife. Despite these setbacks, there have been tremendous improvements in the UK's print media industry over the years, from where numerous modern day newspapers like The Observer, Daily Mirror and Morning Star have emerged.

The term newspaper became widespread during the 17th century. Nevertheless, in Germany, journals that may today be regarded as newspaper publications, began showing during the sixteenth century. They were noticeably newspapers for these following explanations: they were published, dated, appeared at fixed and regular publication intervals. Similarly, then, while the printing press for the physical, technical sense was developed, 'the press' within the broad sense of the term also came into its most historical phase."

The first professional English-language newspaper was called the Corrant, officially published out of Germany and Italy during the year 1620. Approximately 1yr later, Corante, which is a weekly publication was made available in Germany, Hungary, Italy, Poland, France, Bohemia, and Low Countries. The newspaper was officially published in England through an "N. B" label, basically thought to mean Nicholas Bourne or Nicholas Bourne.

During the year 1814, The Times bought a printing press that was capable of producing 1,100 impressions every hour. It was later adapted to print format on either sides of the page at once. The invention made newspapers affordable and thus accessible to a greater portion of the populace. In

1830, the original penny press newspaper entered the market. Furthermore, newspaper editors swapped copies and effortlessly reprinted material.

Come the late 1840s, the telegraph networks connected major and minor towns and allowed overnight news broadcasting. The discovery of wood-pulp papermaking during the 1840s considerably reduced the rate of newsprint, having formerly been developed from rags. Improved literacy during the nineteenth century further enhanced the scope of newspapers' audiences (Costello, 2016).

2.4. COMING OF MODERN TECHNOLOGY

Have you ever questioned how the newspaper pages are printed? Right from the times of wooden block print, the era of newspapers has passed through a sea of changes. Technical revolution has upgraded the print media. Starting from way back, they were formed through hand composing. Later on, these were swapped through monotype and linotype. For this process, an appliance run by the key board was employed to compose letters. While this has also gotten obsolete now, computer typesetting, offset printing as well as laser production have taken over. Desktop publishing has also become quite common now than in the past.

Today internet cafes have become as regular as STD /ISD cubicles. If you haven't visited a web café before, then please go and check what's happening there. The Web is a computer-based global interlink system. It has no nation barriers. Hence an individual found in India can easily access the web in U.S over the computer system. This has made radical alterations in communication throughout the world. Lately, nearly all newspapers have web editions. For instance, the Hindustan Times from India is readable over the web over their net editions. Every paper has a dotcom term for their website, such as www. hindustantimes.com. Though you must pay to purchase a newspaper, the web version of that paper is completely free and, accessible in case you own a PC and internet connection.

2.4.1. Invention of the Television

The TV is a network for transmission of visual pictures and sound which are replicated on screens, primarily used for broadcasting products for entertainment, IT, and education. The TV set has grown to become an ordinary appliance in several households, companies, and institutions. It's a key driver for advertising. Only a few innovations have had as greater effect on modern U.S. society as TV.

A certain media observer, recalled that "TV is the pervasive US pass time that cuts across geographic, ethnic background and cultural diversity, it's the single binding fiber of the modern world, having a major impact on experiences that affect young and old, the rich and poor, educated, and illiterate." For instance, in 1948 just 1% of U.S's households owned a TV set; besides by 1953 well over 50% possessed one; and from the early 60's, well over 90% of all households have a TV set. From mechanical TV to electronic, there remains to be a swing in how TVs are seen today.

Brief history of TV: During the year 1880, the invention of the TV was put forth. Moreover, the cathode-ray tube, which is a forerunner of the television picture tube, merged aspects of electricity and camera. TV images couldn't float over the air, thus technicians established a technique of encoding pictures at a TV channel and decoding them for the TV set.

Generally, Paul Nipkow, is considered the father of TV, and is said to be the inventor of the original rotating disk. The device would allow the pictures to be transferred over conductors during the 1830's. Similarly, John Baird, who is from Europe, became known for creating the first image in motion. Shortly later, he participated in engineering the first colored tube. Vladimir Zworykin, who is yet another Russian inventor, coming from America in 1919, presented the iconoscope that was an automated camera tube applied in TV. Zworykin landed some work at Westinghouse then later started to work for RCA.

In America, another inventor called Philo Farnsworth matured as a teen in the farm setting. Farnsworth invention permitted for a way of transmitting photos over 60 horizontal lines, known as lines of resolution. These are outlines of lighted dots which constitute a TV picture image. The dots are known as pixels. Moreover, they're the slightest dot found on the display unit that creates a TV photo image. Both Zworykin and Farnsworth contributed towards the invention of what is called the modern-day television.

Zworykin still worked at the broadcasting innovation leader RCA, while Farnsworth got challenged for his patents courtesy of RCA. Similarly, the business sensed that the technology which Zworykin applied was derived from Westinghouse and RCA. Farnsworth returned back to his secondary school instructor and they were capable to finding the inventive drawings coming from 1922. Thus in 1930, the inventor was capable of ultimately gaining the user patent for the original television.

Following Farnsworth and RCA's legal settlement, the RCA; president, David Sarnoff, eventually was capable of working out a contract alongside

Farnsworth to officially license his patents for RCA and AT&T, which are to be used in the creation of TV on a profitable level. By the conclusion of the creation process of TV, Farnsworth was capable of demonstrating for the initial time the widespread use of television. It happened at Franklin's Institute in Philadelphia during the year 1934, 5yrs before RCA's official demonstration of the TV in 1939's World Fair. Following these demonstrations, rich individuals could afford to buy these TV sets. The original sets were sold for around $55–$125 apiece.

The Colored TV: During the year 1953, the federal communications commissions or (FCC), the state agency responsible for regulating satellite, wire, cable, and TV, permitted CBS to perform scientific tests on the colored TV systems. The existing black and white television consoles couldn't handle its transmission, since it was mismatched. At that time, majority of Americans had only recently began getting used to black and television white sets. But not dispirited by the discordancy, RCA constantly press forward so that by 1954, this business was able to develop the colored TV standard, which allowed for color signal which could operate with the typical black and white version. Come 1966, NBC was capable of broadcasting their TV programs in a colored layout. Since that period, the Big 3 Networks (CBS, NBC, and ABC) started to transmit their network's programs for color which was put in the evening schedule. This then prompted the rise of color TV sets being sold to the general public.

Broadcasting: Following the emergence of color broadcasting channels on prime-time TV, the nation became increasingly captivated with television. Nevertheless, they were only limited to what showed on the 3 major networks namely: NBC, ABC, and CBS which were the leading broadcasters back then.

These three networks bought time to showcase their programs from associates in every major town in the U.S. The programs were developed to access a mass audience. The CBS channel presented basic comedies like The Beverly Hillbillies, further starting the program of situational comedies like 'All within the Family' that was launched in 1971. Most programs were typically around 30 minutes to an hour in length, dealing with family and a set of co-workers, dramas or cowboys. Furthermore, daytime TV included soap operas as well as quiz displays. The three main networks were constantly in a race to gain ratings and marketing dollars.

By 1967, the Carnegie Commission study recommended the formation of a 4th, noncommercial, public TV network constructed around the learning nonprofit stations that were already in place. Also, the Public Broadcast

System also known as (PBS) was formed and created programs which are displayed through the network, plus are spread throughout the country. Among the most prominent programs delivered through PBS channel was for preschoolers, known as Sesame Street.

The PBS received funding through state appropriations, witness donations, and business underwriters. State funds may also lead to state interference as well as the requirement for viewer donations which prompted on–air fundraising. Furthermore, broadcasting stirred the rise of multiple new channels, though was soon met with rising competition coming from cable TV networks.

Cable TV: Cable TV, also known as Community Antenna TV or CATV became the first cable network that was engineered. It was invented in states such as Pennsylvania, New York and Oregon since the mountains as well as skyscrapers prevented the signals from connecting to TV sets. When cable got introduced, the cable firms were able to dispatch the signal using a coaxial cable, comprising of a dual conductor cable which is concealed to prevent electronics interference.

This developed more channels, including a clearer image compared to that of an over-the-air system. Afterwards, the CATV was capable of producing a lot more channels for audiences than previously. This stirred major competition for broadcasting. But the only setback from cable TV was that the co-axial cable needed to be solidly connected to the TV set in order to start receiving signals.

Nevertheless, broadcasting through the antenna only needed connection to the local antenna. Same as radio, which needed no wires, cabling technology could only work with some form of connection. During the 50's and 60's cable only was able to transfer up to 5 channels. With the progression of cable TV, in the early 90's, cable TV had hit well over 100 standard channels. Once the technology started to swiftly increase, the cable companies started to offer Pay-Per-View service. The concept permitted clients to buy program shows and movies which were to be viewed instantly. This charge was further added onto their cable bill each month. By this crucial moment in the business, owning cable TV was quite popular, because of the additional networks and the extra features. Furthermore, cable providers needed to improve protection of the cabling system, through scrambling the network they were capable of preventing cable theft.

Clients would then have to configure the signal in order to check content. As innovation advanced, the usage of descramblers soon became obsolete. The hackers started to gain awareness of the new innovation and developed their unique edition of the descramblers. Due to this obstruction, cable providers developed a more technical virtual box which was needed for each TV set which was to get cable.

2.4.2. Birth of the Internet

The internet's history derives its foundation in the endeavors to interlink computer systems which emerged from science and innovation in the U.S. and entailed global collaboration, especially with scientists in the UK and France. Computing grew to become a popular field during the late 50s, where people began to develop interest in time-sharing among users and, much later, the probability of attaining this over vast area networks. Individually, Paul Baran suggested a dispersed network depending on data kept in message blocks during the early 60s, whereas Donald Davies came up with packet switching within the year 1965 for (NPL) or National Physics Laboratory in UK, becoming a basis for research for nearly two decades (Mitra, 2004).

The American Department of Defense bestowed contracts in 1969 towards the growth of the ARPANET program, managed by Robert Taylor as well as Lawrence Roberts. This project executed the packet-switching invention suggested by Baran and Davies, supported by mathematical programs during the early 70s by Leonard Kleinrock. This network was established by Beranek, Bolt, and Newman.

Early packet switching systems like the NPL network, Merit Network, Telnet, CYCLADES, Merit Network and ARPANET were also developed during the 70s undergoing thorough research and providing data networking. Furthermore, the ARPANET system and global working groups prompted the creation of conventions for internetworking, whereby multiple separate networks might be combined into a system of networks, which delivered various standards (Mitra, 2004).

Additionally, scholars from the Stanford University came up with the Internet Protocol (IP) and Transmission Control Protocol (TCP) during the year 1973, including two inventive protocols of the Web protocol suite. The project consisted of models from the popular French CYCLADES program managed by Louis Pouzin.

Furthermore, ARPANET changed to TCP/IP as well as other networks which connected to it, plus each other, through those protocols via time, establishing the Web of today. During the start of the 80s, NSF financed nationwide supercomputing centers at different universities in U.S. and delivered interconnectivity during the year 1986 in the NSFNET program, therefore creating network admission to these supercomputer websites for research and educational institutions in the U.S. and globally.

Additionally, business Internet Service Providers (ISPs), started to materialize during the late 80s. The ARPANET however, was decommissioned by1990. Few private connections to sections of the Internet through officially commercial programs arose in different U.S. cities by the late 1989 up to 1990.

NSFNET was officially decommissioned during the year 1995, eliminating the last limitations on the usage of the Web to carry exchange traffic. Studies at the CERN institute in Switzerland by UK computer expert Tim Berners-Lee during the year 1989 up to 90 occasioned the Internet, combining hypertext files into a data system, available from any point on the network (Mitra, 2004).

Ever since the mid-90s, the Web has had a radical effect on society, culture, business, and innovation, plus the development of almost-instant networking through instant message, electronic mail and Voiceover Internet Protocol (VoIP) phone calls, dual-way collaborative video calls, plus the Internet with its chat forums, social networking, blogs, and virtual shopping websites. Greater amounts of information are transmitted at advanced and higher speeds through fiber optic systems running at 1 Gbit/s, even up to10 Gbit/s.

The Web's takeover of the international communication landscape was quick in historical context: only communicating 1% of the data passing through dual-way telecommunications systems during the year 1993, rising to 51% by 2000, including well over 97% of the telecommunicated data by 2007. Currently, the Web continues to grow, propelled by an ever growing rate of virtual information, business, social networking and entertainment. Nevertheless, the prospects of the universal network might be shaped through local differences.

Historical Context: The notion of data communication – transferring information between two unique spots via an electromagnetic channel like radio and electric wire – it pre-dates the launch of the original computers. These communication structures were usually limited to only point-to-point networking between dual end devices (Mitra, 2004).

Furthermore, semaphore lines, telegraph structures and telex equipment be regarded as initial precursors of this type of communication. Plus, the telegraph during the late nineteenth century became the original fully virtual communication system. Early processors possessed a central processing component and remote terminals. But as the invention evolved, fresh systems were developed to foster communication over extended distances (for terminals) plus with increased speed which helps with interconnection of local devices, which were required for the mainframe workstation model.

These innovations allowed for exchange of data (like files) between distant computers. Nevertheless, the point-to-point networking model was limited, since it didn't permit for instant networking between any dual arbitrary structures; the physical connection was necessary. The innovation was also regarded unsafe for planning and military use, since there were no substitute routes for the networking when enemies launched attacks (Mitra, 2004).

Multimedia systems: Basic theoretical work in information transmission as well as information theory was established by Ralph Hartley, Claude Shannon and Harry Nyquist during the early twentieth century.

Moreover, information theory, as pronounced by Shannon during the year 1948, offered a solid theoretical underpinning for understanding the trade offs existing between network-to-noise ratio, error-free transmission and bandwidth within the presence of noise, especially for telecommunications systems.

The invention of transistor innovation was essential to a fresh era of electronic devices which later impacted nearly every element of human experience. The long-searched understanding of the field-effect transmission, as a form of MOS transistor system (MOSFET), by Bell Labs institute in 1959 encouraged the creation of fresh prospects for miniaturization and largescale generation for a vast range of uses (Mitra, 2004).

This became the fundamental building block for the data revolution including the information age, plus established the basis for power electronic innovation which later allowed the creation of wireless Web technology. Furthermore, Network bandwidth has steadily been expanding after every 18 month period since the 70s, something that found manifestation in Edholm's law, same to the scaling mentioned by Moore's theory for semiconductors.

About 15yrs later, the original computers became functional, scientists started to understand that an interconnected system of computers might provide solutions that surpass the capacities of a single structure. By this time, processors were becoming more powerful, besides a considerable number of researchers were starting to consider applications which went far past basic numerical calculations.

Probably, the most convincing and earliest definitions of these prospects was shown by Licklider in 1960, he mentioned that, in the next few years, PCs would become adequately powerful to collaborate with people in solving research and technical issues. Licklider was a psychologist working for the Massachusetts Institutes of Technology (MIT), he began noticing his vision upon becoming the manager of the Info Processing Techniques Office (IPTO) based at the Advanced Researches Programs Agency (ARPA) during the year 1962. He remained working for ARPA up to 1964, later convincing his successors, Robert Taylor and Ivan Sutherland, of the significance of finding solutions to complex, long-term problems.

Moreover, Taylor, after becoming IPTO's executive leader in 1966, became concerned with the replication of costly computing resources at different venues with ARPA contracts. The expert proposed a networking system, whereby users at one venue accessed computers at a different site. A project he worked on together with Licklider. Due to these efforts, ARPA grew to become a major supporter of programs in networking at this period.

Different from NSF, which granted awards to personal researchers, on the other contrary ARPA gave research contracts. For instance, the IPTO project managers, normally hired from academia for about 2yr tours, with substantial latitude in describing projects and detecting academic and business groups for executing them.

For many cases, these scholars worked together with researchers that they sponsored, delivering intellectual leadership and financial support. Besides, one major strength of ARPA format is that it doesn't just produce artifacts which promote its missions but further develops and coaches upcoming researchers.

Furthermore, the internet researchers gathered together the graduate learners participating in projects. This invention assisted in developing the community which would trigger the growth of the field as well as the Internet during the 80s. By the 60s, there was a significant number of scientists who had already started investigating technologies which would develop the foundation for computer networking.

A good part of this preliminary networking research focused on packet switching, which is a method of subdividing a conversation into several smaller, independent units, with every part carrying the ultimate address of its terminus and is routed via the network autonomously (Mitra, 2004).

Special workstations at the branching units in the network may affect the route followed by packets, from a moment-by-moment basis in reaction to network jamming or link failure. Among the earliest innovators of packet switching technology was Paul Baran from RAND Corporation, he was interested in techniques of arranging networks to endure nuclear attack.

Furthermore, Baran suggested a richly interrelated set of network terminals, having no central control system—both aspects of the modern day Internet. This same project was ongoing in the UK, whereby Roger Scantlebury and Donald Davies from National Physical Lab (NPL) devised the word "packet."

Indeed, the U.S. already had a broad communications network, with systems like public switched telephone networks (PSTN), whereby virtual switches and broadcasting lines were utilized during the year 1962. Despite this, the telephone network didn't feature highly in early PC networking. Computer researchers working to connect their networks spoke a unique language from that of engineers and researchers working in conventional voice telecommunications.

They read diverse journals, attended unique conferences, plus used unique terminology. Furthermore, data traffic was considerably unique from voice traffic. For the PSTN, a recurrent connection, or circuit, can be established at the start of a call, while maintaining it for a period. Computers, alternatively, connect in bursts, plus unless a certain amount of "calls" are combined on one transmission path, then the line and switching range is wasted (Mitra, 2004).

Originally, telecommunications specialists were mostly focused on improving the voice network, besides they were skeptical about alternative technologies. Therefore, although phone lines were applied to offer point-to-point communication for the ARPANET, still the switching module of the PSTN wasn't used. During the original Association for Computing Machines (ACM) Symposium touching on Operating System (OS) Principles in 1967, an IPTO program director managed to present an early blueprint for the packet-switch network, which was to grow and form into the ARPANET.

Additionally, Roger Scantlebury managed to present the NPL project referencing Baran's previous RAND report. The response was positive, besides Roberts presented a request towards helping with quotation (RFQ), with regards to the formation of a 4-node network.

Progress from Arpanet Network to Internet: Even though the ARPANET became ARPA's biggest networking project, by no stretch was it the only system. They also promoted research on land packet radio as well as packet satellite networks. By 1973, researchers such as Vinton Cerf and Robert

Kahn had started considering new ways of interrelating these networks, which consisted of a rather different bandwidth, interruption, and error features than did telephone lines connected to the ARPANET. Ultimately, this resulted in the formation of TCP/IP, originally mentioned in a 1973 at the International Network Working (INW) Conesus meeting in England.

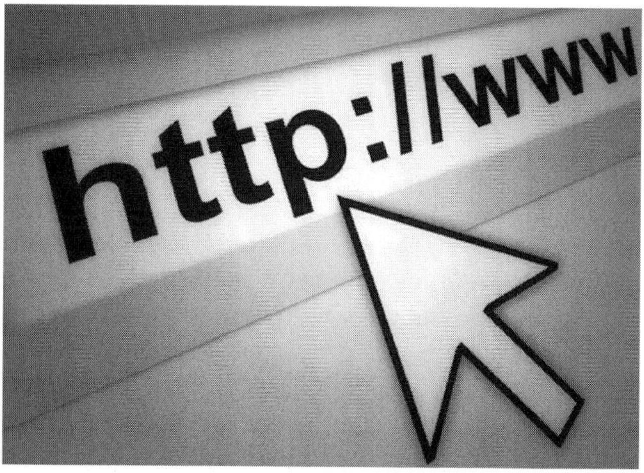

Figure 2.2. The Internet inspired new multimedia platforms like digital TV.

Source: *https://www.newznew.com/the-rise-of-the-internet-entrepreneur/.*

Different NCP, which allowed the hosts of one network to connect, TCP/IP was developed to interconnect different networks to create an Internet. The protocol suite described the packet format, including the flow-control as well as error-recovery system to permit the hosts to advance gracefully from network faults.

It further highlighted an addressing mechanism which could sustain an Internet consisting of almost four billion hosts. Additionally, the work needed to convert TCP/IP from a theory into a useful structure was carried out under ARPA agreement by teams from BBN, Stanford University, and (UCL) University College London.

Even though TCP/IP has advanced over the years, it's still widely used today being the Web's basic packet transport system. In 1975, the ARPANET had advanced from its initial four nodes to almost 100 nodes. Within this period, two factors—the creation of localized area networks (LANs) as well as incorporation of networking into (OS) operating systems—contributed towards a sharp increase in the overall size of the system (Mitra, 2004).

Local Area Networks: Even though ARPANET scientists were experimenting using dedicated phone cables for packet transmission, scientists from the Hawaii University, supported by Norman Abramson, began trying diverse approaches, such as with ARPA funding.

Same as ARPANET team, they sought to offer remote access for their primary computer system, however, rather than a network of phone-lines, they applied a shared radio system. The program was shared in a sense that every station employed the same channel towards reaching the main station. The approach had a probable drawback: in case two stations sought to transmit during the same period, then their transmissions shall interfere with one another, and neither transmission shall be received.

However, such interruptions were improbable since the information got typed on keyboards, sending very short waves to the computer, and leaving significant time between the pulses by which time the channel became clear for receiving keystrokes from another user (Barz and Bassett, 2016).

Furthermore, Abramson's system, commonly referred to as Aloha, produced significant interest in applying mutual transmission mediums, besides various projects were started to establish on the idea. Among the two best-known programs were the Ethernet and Atlantic Packet Satellite (APS) Experiment. In particular, the packet satellite network showed that the protocols created in Aloha for

Managing contention between coinciding users, together with more conventional reservation schemes, occasioned the efficient usage of the accessible bandwidth. Nevertheless, the long latency natural in satellite communications restricted the practicality of this approach.

Additionally, Ethernet, established by a team controlled by Robert Metcalfe from Xerox Group's Palo Alto Researching Center (PARC), is among the few instances of a networking innovation that wasn't directly sponsored by the state. The experiment revealed that utilizing coaxial cable in form of a shared medium caused an efficient network. Different from the Aloha system, whereby transmitters couldn't get any signals, Ethernet channel could notice that collisions had happened, stop transmitting instantly, and repeat a short while later (and randomly).

The approach enhanced the proficiency of the Aloha method and made it feasible for actual use. Furthermore, shared-media LANs turned to become a dominant type of computer-to-computer networking inside a building or surrounding area, even though differences from (Token Ring) IBM, plus others also captured a portion of this rising market. Besides, Ethernet was originally used for connecting networks of around 100 of PARC's Alto-processors, applying the center's time-sharing structure as an entryway to ARPANET (Barz and Bassett, 2016).

Originally, many assumed that the lesser size and reduced performance of computers would impede their application as network hosts, though, with DARPA funding, a team from the MIT, having received multiple Altos from PARC, was able to create an effective TCP operation for the program plus, later, for IBM PC. Moreover, the increase of PCs linked by LANs during the 80s drastically improved the Internet's scope.

Internet Television: The rise of internet technology also sparked the invention of online TV. Usually, with our busy lifestyles, we don't have a lot of opportunities for sitting right in front of TX. If you fail to get the opportunity for sitting down to watch, then you'll most definitely be using a smartphone device, PC or laptop. Emerging technologies are also making viewership of TV exceedingly expedient for the audience. Figures show that conventional TV is the media system losing the most followers in courtesy of the Internet. According to internet scholars, a digital TV has two key roles: one of content producers while the other for content distributors (typically a license is required from other channels or produced by expert or beginner users) (Savage and Vogel, 2009).

Furthermore, the web has opened up fresh ways of watching content, plus even the means of storing media has dramatically changed. There are critics who aren't really fans of watching TV on the computer monitor, but it has its advantages. TV on the web broadcast by request plus the audience response is quick. There are various alternatives to your standard TV channels through options like Video on-demand, that's a device with the capacity to access fresh film and cinemas at whichever time.

In addition, companies such as Netflix (a provider that allows users to stream television shows and movies digitally through electronics devices), Amazon Video and Hulu make access to modern-day shows and movies much easier, having less than $20 dollars per month you can easily stream and view all you preferred movies and TV shows. Besides, it has become more affordable than having satellite or cable TV.

In America, the biggest streaming service is called Hulu. Their subscriptions typically have time shifts, whereby viewers determine when they prefer watching a given program. Presently, there's a tiny niche of individuals who may sit and view a 2hr movie on their workstation. Now when watching media from these web-based sources, you can connect your

PC or laptop to your Plasma Television for viewing. Apart from that option, TV users are able to access the Web via their smart television. Much newer plasmas moreover have twice the picture resolution and pixels found in a typical definition (Savage and Vogel, 2009).

The rate of the merger is advancing at an extremely high rate, with the smartphone devices becoming even smaller and more sophisticated. Individuals are still going to continue using these systems to watch TV. With a slight shift in how the material is conveyed to the audience, something that will eventually affect the large networks and make them to alter the way that they do their broadcasting. As TV continues integrating with the web, there would be a change in normal TV usage, which shall decline over the next few years as people continue to favor online viewership.

2.4.3. Web Browser Applications

Nexus browser: The Nexus browser was invented by Tim Berners-Lee but was initially known as the Worldwide Web browser. In its original form as a browser-editor, the system could be applied to develop new pages and browse them as well. Furthermore, it allowed for user-centric and text-centric browsing. Just like modern day browsers, Nexus also required certain tools in order to operate smoothly. You needed to have Adobe 10.1 Flash Player or higher to utilize the Record Audio function, while also ensuring that your browser contains Cookies and JavaScript functions that are enabled (Savage and Vogel, 2009).

Originally, released in 1991, Worldwide Web was somewhat buggy. The second version, from 1994, got retitled the Nexus Browser from where it became clear that the retrieval system and the utility space were separate. The Worldwide Web and Nexus jointly are known as "hypermedia browsing-editors, an activity in universal information accessibility" (TBL was extremely busy for spell-check however). The key point here is that the two browsers may be applied to develop and edit pages, or to find and extract them.

Remarkably, in the Worldwide Web system Edit was just on top of Find in the user menu, while they have exchanged positions for the Nexus browser. This probably shows that in 1991 forming pages was the main purpose, though by 1994 an extra passive web had now begun to arise and finding and showing pages was the main requirement.

This early browser was updated in 1994 to form Nexus which Tim Berners-Lee had named The Project, the program was launched within its original browser and the main thing to remember is that the index page sits distinctly from the main browser. Furthermore, the webpage isn't enclosed by any browser but instead floats in its unique window inside it. The second aspect to remember is that URL isn't shown anywhere on Nexus. But can only be discovered by applying the Inspect feature within the File sub-menu (Savage and Vogel, 2009).

Once a hyperlink inside the page has been clicked, a fresh page opens, also in its own unique window. With more pages being opened, ultimately the screen may become quite crowded. Nevertheless, by pushing Function+M, selected pages got minimized and packed up at the base of the screen. Then a list of available windows may also be witnessed in the Windows system sub-menu. Remarkably, there's a second means of navigating the website using the steering panel within the Navigation sub-menu.

Nexus' navigation panel consist of 5 buttons which are– Home, Preceding, Backup, Next, and Support – all common terms. Nevertheless, these buttons don't behave like people may come to expect. For instance, Previous, and Next don't draw you backwards or forwards through your user journey, but instead opens links successively as they show on the preceding page.

By Clicking Next, a link is opened following the one which has recently been clicked, thereby saving users the problem of heading back to the former page. It means that the website can be browsed in two unique ways. The first one is user-centric, involving opening of links following any order that you prefer, or a file-centric method, which involves opening the links exactly how the author put them out within the page. This function may have been hidden to history, since the original browser has since been vanished to history (Savage and Vogel, 2009).

Looking back to the origins of the web as well as seeing the first web page inside the first browser, shows us everything that we should know concerning Tim Berners-Lee's dream. The first browser to be launched as highlighted was a browsing-editor. The Internet wasn't intended to be some passive browsing experience, rather the internet was supposed to become a multi-author setting from the start. Successive browsers extracted that editing capacity, disrupting the original vision. Furthermore, a distinction was established, between the inventors of websites as well as the users of websites. Even though the social web cuts away at this delimitation, the world is still a way off the wholly collaborative space like it was initially planned by its designers.

Microsoft, Internet Explorer (1996): Internet Explorer (IE), previously called MS IE or simply Windows IE became the first browsing multimedia tool to be released following Nexus. The program is a set of graphical internet browsers established by Microsoft (MS) and incorporated in the MS Windows group of OSs, beginning in 1995. This program was first launched as an aspect of the extra package, including Windows 95 for that particular year.

Future versions were accessible as free download options, or even in-service packs, including the original equipment maker (OEM) service launches of Windows 95, plus preceding editions of Windows. Before its discontinuity, IE was among the most popular web browser, achieving a peak of roughly 95% user share by the year 2003 (Savage and Vogel, 2009).

Coming after MS first used bundling as a means of winning its browser contest against Netscape that was the most dominant browser during the 90s. However, its user share has henceforth declined following the release of Firefox in 2004 and later Google Chrome in 2008, including the rising popularity of OSs like Android and iOS which don't support IE.

Estimations for IE's overall market share is roughly 1.7% across different platforms, ranking it 8th worldwide. For desktop processors, the only setting on which it's ever had considerable share (discounting mobile and Xbox) it's ranked fifth at 3.67%, with MS Edge, which is its successor coming fourth with a 4.57% market share.

IE reveals a group of Component Object Modeling (COM) interfaces which allows for add-ons to modify the use of the browser. Generally, extensibility is subdivided into two forms: content extensibility and browser extensibility. The latter involves including context menu entries, menu items, toolbars, and Browser Helper Objects or (BHO) (Leopold and Garcia, 2003).

BHOs are widely used to expand the function arrangement of the browser, while the other extensibility choices are applied to reveal that feature as displayed in the user-interface.

Furthermore, content extensibility provides support for non-native material formats, allowing IE to manage new file setups and fresh protocols, for instance, WebM or SPDY. Additionally, web pages can incorporate widgets called ActiveX controls that run on Windows exclusively but have immense potentials to expand the content functions; MS Silver light and Adobe Flash Player are good examples.

Furthermore, add-ons can easily be installed locally, or straight through a web site. Considering that malicious add-ons may compromise the system's security, IE applies various safeguards. For instance, IE VI with Service Pack II and later consist of Add-on Managers for facilitating or disabling personal add-ons, supplemented by the "No Add-Ons" module. Beginning with Vista,IE as well as its BHOs operated with limited privileges and are detached from the remaining of the system (Leopold and Garcia, 2003).

IE 9 later introduced a fresh component – Extension Performance Advisor. This Add-on Performance Guide displays a notification once one or several of attached add-ons surpass a pre-set activity threshold. The notification shows in the Notification Space once the user activates the browser.

Moreover, both Windows 8 and RT have introduced a Metro-format edition of IE which is fully sandboxed and doesn't operate using add-ons completely. Additionally,

Windows RT can't download or connect ActiveX controls totally; even though existing ones grouped with Windows RT are still operating in the conventional edition of IE.

The browser itself, nevertheless, is able to be hosted alongside other applications through a group of COM platforms. This may be used to entrench the browser functionality within a computer system, or creating IE shells (Leopold and Garcia, 2003).

2.4.4. Digital Radio

Digital radio refers to the application of digital innovation to convey or receive audiovisual information across the radio waves. Digital transmission through radio waves covers digital broadcasting, particularly digital audio-radio solutions.

For virtual broadcasting systems, normally the analog auditory signal is digitized, and compacted using an auditory coding format like AAC+ or MP2, plus transmitted through a virtual modulation scheme.

The ultimate goal is to improve the quantity of radio programs available within a particular spectrum, enhancing the audio quality, removing fading issues in mobile settings, and allowing extra data casting services, plus limiting the transmission influence or the overall number of transmitters needed to cover a particular region.

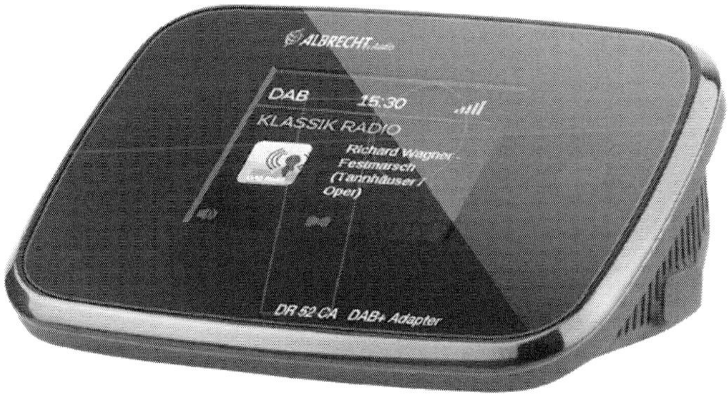

Figure 2.3. Digital radio allows for streaming of online or satellite music from any location.

Source: *https://m.reichelt.com/de/en/digital-radio-adapter-for-stereo-systems-albrecht-dr52ca-p213809.html.*

Nevertheless, analog radio consisting of AM and FM are still the most popular options and hearing radio stations over the IP, is an activity that's rising in popularity. During the year 2012, a total of four online wireless radio programs are identified by the Global Telecommunication Union: a pair of European style Digital Audio Broadcasting (DAB), as well as Digital Radio Mondiale (DRM), Japanese ISDB-T or the in-band per-channel technique applied in the U.S. and Arab countries and branded in form of HD Radio.

A much older definition that's still applied in communication mechanical literature, is virtual digital transmission innovations, such as, microwave, and radio channel communication principles whereby analog information signals and virtual data are transported by an online signal, through a digital modulation technique (Al-Khatib and Alam, 2007).

This definition covers broadcasting systems like online TV and online radio broadcasting, including also dual-way virtual radio standards like the second era (2G) cellular-phones and thereafter, short-range communication like online cordless phones, virtual computer networks, and online micro-wave radio connections.

A not so common description is that of radio receivers and transmitter systems that are reliant on virtual signal processing, though may transmit or acquire analog radio transmission modules, for instance FM radio. Something that may lessen noise and jamming brought about by the electronics. This also permits for software radio applications, whereby the transmission innovation is changed simply by choosing another set of software. For the most part, this would nevertheless improve the energy usage of the receiver apparatus. Also, one-way (broadcasting) structures have for years been recommended by researchers as an emerging form of multimedia.

Broadcast standards: Digital audio radio program standards might offer terrestrial or cable radio services. Digital radio channel systems are normally designed for portable mobile devices, such as mobile-TV units and unlike other virtual TV systems that normally need a stationary directional antenna. There are some virtual radio systems that offer in-band on-channel services (IBOC), which may co-exist together with or relay with either analog FM/AM transmissions, whereas others are developed for select radio frequency waves (Al-Khatib and Alam, 2007).

The latter permits one wideband radio wave to transmit a multitude of different radio-channels of varying bitrates, including data solutions and other types of media. There are also virtual broadcasting systems which allow for solo-frequency network (SFN), whereby all land transmitters within a region sending a single multiband of radio programs might use one frequency channel without experiencing any self-interference issues, further enhancing the structural spectral efficiency.

Even though digital broadcasting provides many potential advantages, its introduction has probably been obstructed by the lack of universal licensing standards and various other setbacks. The DAB-Eureka 147 principle for online radio is harmonized by the Global DMB Forum. This concept of virtual radio technology was described during the late 80s, plus is currently being applied in some European nations.

Commercial DAB receivers started to be sold during the year 1999 plus, by 2006, around 500 million individuals were in the covering aspect of DAB broadcasts, even though by this period sales had just spiked in the UK as well as Denmark. By 2006, there were roughly 1,000 DAB points in operation. Meanwhile, there have been some contrary voices in the multimedia industry of the Eureka-147 standard, such that a fresh 'DAB+' system has been introduced.

Furthermore, the DRM module has been applied for multiple years to transmit digitally on frequencies under 30 MHz (short, medium, and longwave). Besides, there's now the protracted standard DRM+ that's developed for VHF bands. Additionally, DRM+ Tests have been done in countries like Germany, France, Brazil, UK, and India. The DRM+ program is furthermore considered a more transparent but less expensive standard as compared to DAB+, therefore a better choice when it comes to local radio, business-oriented or community broadcasting Al-Khatib and Alam, 2007).

Even though DAB+ has officially been launched in Australia, the state nevertheless determined in 2011 that any preference for DRM+ or DRM higher than HD Radio may be applied to supplement DAB+ solutions in (various) local and regional zones.

Status in the united states: The U.S. has implemented the patented HD Radio technology, which is a form of in-band on-frequency (IBOC) technology. For iBiquity, they believe that "HD Radio" is more of a trademark name for its patented virtual radio system, however, the name doesn't imply either high-definition (HD) or "hybrid digital" like it's sometimes incorrectly referenced.

Broadcasts use orthogonal frequency-separation multiplexing, a method that's also applied for European land virtual Television Programming (DVB-T). The HD Radio system was created and is licensed courtesy of iBiquity Digital Company. It's generally believed that a key goal for HD radio innovation is providing some limited virtual radio services, whereas conserving the relative "stick principles" of the stations covered, and ensuring that fresh programming services can be managed by registered licensees.

Furthermore, the FM virtual schemes in America offer audio solutions at rates of between 96 to 128 kilobits a second (kbit/s), plus with supporting "subcarrier" broadcasts of around 64 kbits. In addition, the AM online schemes handle data rates of around 48 kbits, alongside auxiliary services which are offered at a reduced data rate.

In addition, both AM and FM systems utilize cutting-edge compression methods to derive the most benefit from limited bandwidth. During the year 1999, U.S. Digital Radio (USADR), Digital Radio Express and Lucent Digital Radio began conducting tests of their different schemes for online broadcast, with a goal of reporting their final outcomes to the country's Radio Systems Committee by December 1999.

While the outcome of these tests still remain uncertain, something that generally describes the condition of the land-based virtual radio broadcasting endeavor in North America. Moreover, some terrestrial and analog broadcasting stations remain apprehensive concerning the impact that digital satellite radio has on their firms, whereas others intend to adapt to online broadcasting when it's economically and technically viable.

Though traditional land-based radio broadcasters are attempting to "go online," many major U.S. vehicle manufacturers are supporting digital satellite radio, where you can listen to favorite radio stations from across the globe and even see your presenters live in the studio. Similarly, HD Radio innovation has been adopted into the vehicle manufacturing sector with default options available in brands like BMW, Volvo, Mercedes, Ford, and Jaguar.

Likewise, satellite radio is defined by its liberation from FCC censorship present in the U.S., its comparative lack of advertising, plus its capacity to allow individuals on their travel to tune to similar stations at any region in the country. But listeners must still pay a yearly or monthly subscriber fee so as to gain access to the service, plus must connect a different security card for every radio or receiver system that they tune to.

Manufacturers such as Daimler AG and Ford have partnered with Sirius Satellite Station, formerly known as CD Radio, from (NYC) New York City, while General Motors (GM) as well as Honda are associating with XM Cable Radio from Washington, D.C. to develop and support broadcast DAB radio structures for North America, every one of them providing "CD quality" audio plus around 100 channels.

Sirius Satellite Radio, which is among the most renowned globally, instituted a group of 3 Sirius satellites in the year 2000. These satellites were developed by Space Systems/Loral, besides they were propelled by Russian Proton boosters into the atmosphere. Same with XM Cable Radio, Sirius executed a series of land-based ground repeaters, whereby satellite signal would normally be blocked by massive structures such as multilevel buildings and natural structures. In total, XM Satellite Radio covers a constellation of 3 satellites, 2 of which were propelled into space in the spring of 2001, then another following later during the year 2005. These satellites go by the name of Boeing 702 comsats, having been launched into circuit by powerful Sea Launch boosters.

Additionally, back-up surface transmitters (repeaters) shall be developed in cities whereby satellite signals might be jammed by tall buildings. In 2007, XM Satellite Radio joined forces with Sirius Satellite Radio, eventually developing Sirius XM Radio. Also, the FCC has managed to auction bandwidth allotments for satellite transmission in the S bandwidth range, which is around 2.3 GHz.

Terrestrial broadcasting has benefits in being no-cost and local. But satellite radio is none of these things; nevertheless, during the early twenty first century it grew by offering uncensored material (most remarkably, the border of Howard-Stern from land-based to satellite radio) plus commercial-free, all-online music networks that provide same radio formats to native stations.

Even so, the "HD Radio" frequency of FM transmission station in America has a restricted listening distance compared to the broadcasting tower station. FCC regulations presently restrict the influence of the online aspect of the station's broadcasting to 10% of the present analog power allowed by the station.

Up to this power level, existence of the virtual signal just near the station's analog transmission can make older radios to pick up noise because of trouble declining the nearby digital signal. Still, there are some fears that HD Radio when streamed on FM shall heighten interference between diverse stations, but HD Radio even at the 10% power ratio fits inside the FCC spectrum mask.

"HD Radio" allows every existing transmission station to add extra "channels" in America by transferring an online signal on either section of its frequency, just beyond their present analog Frequency Modulation (FM) signal. Moreover, the HD Radio frequency covers the 0.1 MHz which starts 0.1 MHz both above and beneath the carrier broadband station.

Case in point, if a station's physical signal's carrier broadband is 93.3 MHz, then the online signal shall fill 93.1MHz to 93.2 MHz, and 93.4 MHz to 93.5 MHz inside the FM Transmission Band. Different online audio streams, or "sub-channels," may be transmitted within this one digital information stream, with the amount of audial of sub-channels and bandwidth provisions at the selection of the station.

As shown on the radio selector, these will show as "93.3–2" and "93.3–3." The bandwidths that are applied don't change as more frequencies are included to the primary radio station. Rather, a fixed overall quantity of bandwidth is basically re-allocated across the acoustic streams, so that each program now gets less bandwidth, and thus reduced audio quality, compared to previously.

DAB adopters: Statistics show that roughly 20 countries around the globe use DAB/DMBDigital Audial Broadcasting (DAB), commonly referred to as Eureka-147, it has widely been implemented by different nations around the globe. It's centered on the (MPEG-1) Audial Layer II acoustic programming format, besides this has been synchronized by the WorldDMB. The later pronounced in 2006 that DAB shall be implementing the HE-AACv2 auditory coding format, better referred to as eAAC+. Equally being embraced at a high-rate is the MPEG Frame format, including stronger error correction programming known as Reed-Solomon coding.

The improved version has been called DAB+. Receivers who support the fresh DAB standard commenced with its release in 2007, launching hardware updates accessible for a few older receivers. While DAB and DAB+ can't be applied for smartphone TV since they don't comprise any video codecs, DAB-related principles (DMB) Digital Multimedia Broadcasting, as well as DAB-IP are appropriate for smartphone radio and television both since they contain WMV9 and MPEG four AVC respectively in form of video programming formats. Nevertheless, a DMB film sub-channel might easily be included to any DAB frequency – since DMB was developed from the start to be supported on a DAB sub-channel. DMB transmissions in Korea transmit traditional MPEG-1 Layer II DAB auditory solutions together with their DMB audiovisual services.

CHAPTER

3

Multimedia Skill and Training

CONTENTS

3.1. INTRODUCTION

Multimedia deals with the production of film, video, and animation. It is a broad field and is an area of the allotment being picked up by several individuals with various jobs emerging from multimedia. It involves the use of technological tools such as computers to come up with the products. This is more so applicable for animation which will rely on computer tools to produce them. To succeed in the field of multimedia, one is required to have skills. These skills will keep them at the top when it comes to production. For multimedia, most employers in this field opt to have their employees working in teams so that they can share their ideas and come up with content that will be interesting for the consumers of the production. For the individuals to make the team then they have the necessary skill and experience in the field of multimedia.

Not only the skills but also the required training that is required. The training held them to apply the skills they have acquired. They can learn how the skills should be applied in the various roles that they may be appointed to work in the team. It is also a form in which they gain experience in the field of multimedia. For this reason, various institutions offer training on multimedia. This is due to the much emphasis on the skills and training generally required in multimedia.

3.2. SKILLS AND BACKGROUND

Here we get to further discuss the skills that are required and the responsibilities of each of the software team. There are a variety of skills required in the development of good multimedia. They include:

3.2.1. Creativity

Creativity is the process where an individual comes up with a new idea that was not discovered before. Creativity is an important tool because it enables individuals to think out of the box and come up with a new invention in creativity an individual has the opportunity to carry out research and develop new things that are interesting and amazing progress.

Creativity plays a key role in multimedia. Many of the individuals who work in the field of multimedia have to embrace creativity. The skill of creativity is what the team to come up with new content that has never been thought of or produced before. Every individual has a different level of creativity. In the field of multimedia, the more the creativity the better.

However, the skill of creativity is not taught in learning institutions. It is a skill that an individual has to develop on their own. The learning institution will only assist the individual to embrace creativity as they progress in the work-life (Costello, 2016).

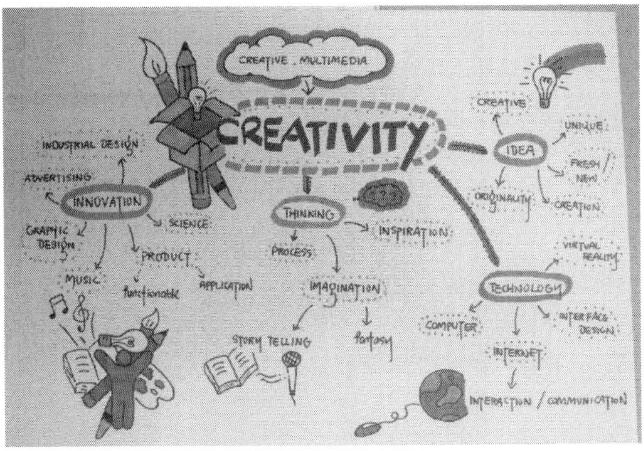

Figure 3.1. Creativity brings about creative mindset.

Source: *http://vicky-creativestudies.blogspot.com/2010/08/week-9-creative-multimedia-mind-map.html.*

In creativity, one has to come up with strategies that were not discovered by anyone else. They have to think widely and in case they suspect that the idea was discovered by another person they should come up with new and better alternatives. The advantage of creativity is that it enables competition to be a leading factor and a fair one for that matter such that the more creative one is the more competitive he is as compared to the rest. It is also a fun process to deal with.

3.2.2. Creative Mindset

The creative mindset is where an individual has it more emphasis on creativity such that his or her mind is more on creativity. They always look for good multimedia content in their interactions as well as their day to day life undertaking. For such individuals, the creative mindset helps them to develop an eye that is out for creativity. For instance, an individual who produce short comedy films. Most of them get content from day to day life scenarios or natural human behavior. They observe they come up with ways of presenting the content to the audience in a way that will be fun for them as well as educative.

3.2.3. Communication Skills

Communication involves the passing of information from one individual to another. No organization may exist without communication being a leading factor or else the organization will fail to function. This is because communication determines how the workflows and instructions are given out through the process of communication. Communication may be applied in the multimedia team, for example, when the work output is being delivered to the source population it is mainly passed through the use of communication and the use of words. Communication is, therefore, a factor that cannot be escaped in any organization at any time or occasion.

Communication is very essential in the production of multimedia. The fact that the individuals will be working in groups means that they will need to be able to have good communication skills. Multimedia involves conveying of messages through tools such as ad the television. This means that there is the presence of media personalities. These media personalities need to have hood communication skills. They need to convey messages with much clarity to the audience. Good communication skills involve audibility, clarity of the message, good speed and being able to convey messages without repetition. The message will be heard worldwide so they need to have communication skills as it adds up to the name of the media group.

Also, the narrators used in the making of advertisements need to have hood communication skills. They also focus on the voice as it is a tool used in the marketing process.

They choose the voice that will attract a larger audience. The communication skills are also applied within the multimedia team. With good communication skills, they will be able to communicate better therefore the outcome will be good quality media products.

Communication can be face to face or through media. When communication is being applied in any organization it must involve the elimination of factors that hinder communication. These factors include noise such that when it is noise in a place then communication may be impossible and it may fail. Another factor that may hinder communication is biases such that an individual is biased to what the other party is saying to them and this is a major hindrance to communication since it makes people not be open to ideas from other parties and they may receive incorrectly and misinterpreted information (Costello, 2016).

3.2.4. Problem-Solving Skills

Problem-solving is the ability of an individual to discover a solution to any problem that may arise along their way. There is no time that a problem may fail to arise in the work and life of any individual at any one time. An individual with problem-solving skills, therefore, do not waste a lot of time dealing with problems that may arise in their life but they can easily find suitable solutions for their problems and move forward with their lives normally as if the problem never occurred from the start. It is, therefore, necessary for every individual to have problem-solving skills.

Every individual in the multimedia team needs to have problem-solving abilities. In the course of production, they face a variety of challenges which they need to know how to solve. T

hey need to be able to come up with solutions within a short period. For instance, if one of the multimedia tools which they expected to use during production is not available, they can think of solutions like improvising and use of a different media to be able to complete the allocated work.

The problem-solving skills also apply in solving issues among the team members.

For instance, any arguments between the employees. Depending on the issue, they can come up with the appropriate solution to the issue. The problem-solving skills are essential to individuals who come up with without the software used in multimedia.

They need to identify the problems in the existing software so that they can come up with much better software that will enable the smooth running of the multimedia production. Problem-solving skills are an important point of choosy ng individuals to work in production (Costello, 2016).

3.2.5. Critical Thinking Skills

Critical thinking is the ability of an individual to think very deeply and find a deeper meaning of an idea rather than judging it from its upper idea. Many individuals often judge so quickly without digging further to find the root cause of a problem or to know more about an idea.

Critical thinking is mainly used to solve a problem at hand and it enables individuals to solve problems in the right and diligent way rather than making guesses that may not be right and that may affect others.

3.2.6. Management Skills

Management skills affect a broad field in the line of multimedia production. Management runs from the top most to the least person in the firm. The management of the individuals in production. This means the allocation of resources as well as their job description and the different roles they will play in the multimedia team. T

hey also manage individuals and identify whether there is a need for more individuals to be added to the team. For the very team members, they need to have management as they will be having a variety of things to work on be it data among other things.

Management skills are the ability of individuals to take a role and part in the leadership of a specific project. It is not a skill that is familiar to many as many of them may fail to be transparent enough and they may also succumb to vices like corruption and they may end up leading to the failure of the company or the organization. Management skills can, therefore, be gained through training that the individuals can be taught what is expected from them and what they should not do. They can also have mentors who may enable them to reach their target.

3.2.7. Time Management

The keeping of time is an important factor when it comes to good multimedia and any other organization. When individuals are good time managers they can do things in the appropriate time that was set for that thing to be done without fail. The advantage of being and maintaining good time management in multimedia is that they avoid having to disappoint the public that is watching and they do their things in the appropriate and designated time that is normally allocated for them to be done.

Every member of the multimedia team must, therefore, be in a position to keep time and do things at the right time that they were meant to be done and avoid having to procrastinate for it makes individuals have a lot of work to do later and they may end up doing this work in a rush that will make them not do the work correctly as required.

It also leads to them having to slow down the progress of the other workers since they hinder them from performing their duty in the case where the stage of the specific lazy worker is a key stage in the production process and cannot be skipped at any one cost (Costello, 2016).

3.2.8. Active Listening

Active listening is the ability of an individual to take part in the listening progress and listen attentively to what is being said without making conclusions first without getting the main idea. It is a key skill in the multimedia faculty because they need to listen attentively to what is being said first and know what is going on before they can make their conclusions that may not exist. Active listening avoids and makes people avoid jumping in conclusions that may be circumstantial and consequential in such a way that it may end up hurting the feelings of others or it may end up leading to results that were not desired or planned for. It also enables people to know a deeper meaning and gain a deeper understanding of what is being said so that the individuals might know what is being talked or communicated about. Active listening involves listening attentively without disrupting the speaker and also it involves asking random questions that may have a connection to what is being talked about in such a way that the individuals can gain a better understanding and a deeper meaning of what is being communicated about (Costello, 2016).

3.3. MULTIMEDIA SKILLS ARE ACQUIRED IN THE FOLLOWING WAYS

3.3.1. Self-Learning Multimedia Tools

An individual can acquire multimedia skills by learning and teaching themselves without having to involve a third party. Self-learning is the use of the computer, the internet and other books to gain knowledge that could be offered by a teacher in a classroom. Self-learning can be done at the comfort of one's home without having to pay school fees to be taught and one does not have to attend skill daily to receive these skills but they can teach themselves some skills at the comfort of their homes.

The internet also has multimedia tools that can help the multimedia self-learners add up to their skills as they source information from the internet. These multimedia tools include the software like Photoshop that the students can spend their time editing random photos and coming up with new designs that will enable them to practice how to edit photos and they can use this knowledge for the future. It also enables them to acquire important skills that may not be acquired before and they can use these skills in the multimedia career which will be of great benefit to them (Hin and Leo, 2009).

3.3.2. Watching Movies, Videos, and Tutorials

By watching movies, videos, and tutorials that are available on the internet students can increase their skills in the sector of multimedia. A good example is when a person wants to edit a photo and they do not have any clue of what is done they can use the internet and watch YouTube tutorial on how to edit a photo. The tutorial will give the student and individual steps that they need to follow to edit this picture and when the individuals and students follow these steps they end up with an edited picture.

3.3.3. Keeping Up with Multimedia Trends

Just like fashion and other sectors, multimedia trends keep on changing from time to time. The new trend keeps coming up that are different from the original existing trends and they are more improved than the previous trends. For instance, the Photoshop keeps on changing with time and it keeps on improving into better versions when the software is updated and these improvements enable editing to be simpler, faster, and more fun than before. When the individual studying multimedia keeps up with the changing trends, their lives become more interesting and fun and their work is minimized by a great percentage.

3.4. RESPONSIBILITIES OF MEMBERS OF THE SOFTWARE TEAM

The software team consists of several individuals whose main aim is to ensure that they perform work as it is required. Working as a team is an important factor as it leads to better performance than the performance of a single individual working alone. Each individual has to perform depending on the type of skills every individual has and with these skills each individual is given responsibilities in the team. Individuals in a software team include:

- Project Manager;
- Multimedia Designer;
- Interface Designer;
- Writers;
- Video Specialist;
- Audio Specialist;
- Multimedia Programmer; and
- Multimedia Producer for the Web.

Their roles are most at times linked with things to do with the internet. The internet involves things such as websites. Their functions involve coming up and producing websites. The website content depends on the client's needs and requirements. For the website, the producer has the task of coming up with the pages for the websites. Usually, the minimum number of pages for a website is six pages so depending on the content they come up with more than six pages. They are also tasked with the duty of making changes and updates or upgrades to the website.

The following are the responsibilities of each:

3.4.1. Project Manager

A project manager is an individual who works under the field of project management. A project manager has to plan and procure a project and then execute it. When an organization wants to come up with a project it is the work of the project manager to design the project.

The management of a project and how it should run is the work and duty of a project manager. The work of the project manager mainly involves the beginning of the project and they may not take part in the end but they take a major role in the intermediary processes that leads to the end. The project manager has the following major responsibilities:

Giving out or coming up with workable projects and that can show results. A project manager must design projects that can be attained and to give these projects so they can be worked on.

Stating and explaining what the project requires so that it can come into accomplishment. A project manager must explain what the project needs and the materials that are required for the project to be complete. They state what kind of workforce is required and the basic structure of the whole project.

Lastly, they have to come up with ways to avoid any constraints that may come up. The project manager manages any constraints that may arise that may range between the amount of time it takes, how much money it will consume and the quality of the outcome. A project manager is, therefore, a major part of what takes part in the project as he is the designer of the project itself and they also have a lot of duties to perform.

The project manager is in charge of the overall projects in multimedia. They make the mist of the important decisions dealing with the project. They are in charge of the development of the project from the start of the project to its progressive stages. They are also in charge of the implementation of various decisions. They do so by monitoring the day to day operations involved in the project. Project management involves designing the project as well as managing the project. The project managers come together and choose the design that will be more suitable and they actualize it (Hin and Leo, 2009).They are tasked to choose the software that will be used during the project. They are therefore required to know the best software available. They make this decision based on the strengths and weaknesses of the software. They choose the individuals that will be involved in actualizing the projects. The individuals are chosen based on the skills that the individuals have. They also relay information from the client to the software team this way they produce the software according to the client's desires. The project managers should, therefore, have organizational skills (Hin and Leo, 2009).

3.4.2. Multimedia Designer

The work of a multimedia designer is designing presentations that involve images and data for multimedia which are the televisions, the web, video games and movies. Multimedia designers design these presentations by the use of the present advanced technology such that they came up with an artistic work that they present it to the individuals. They, therefore, should be individuals who have a taste of art so that they can come up with something artistic.Some traditional methods are also used by the multimedia designers which include drawing or photography skills that they use in their designing process. They are used to develop the image and can also be used in the coming up of the 3D designs. A multimedia designer has to, therefore, know these skills so that they can apply them in their work.

Figure 3.2. A multimedia designer.

Source: *https://unsplash.com/s/photos/republic.*

To come up with multimedia designs, Multimedia developers and designers have to know some tools which are very crucial in their work process. The tools that they should be familiar with include the Adobe Photoshop which is important for the process of editing and presentation of the pictures that are used in the multimedia field. These photos are required to be of high standards and maintain the high standards all along and therefore there is a need for editing them to meet the desired quality. Editing can be done by adding brightness and contrast and balancing effects and multimedia designers have to perform this task. For multimedia designers, they have to be very thorough and good at their job due to the high competition levels and therefore they have to undergo a lot of practice and training to improve their skills. They, therefore, take most of their time doing a lot of practice to improve their skills more and more and they have to ensure that their work is perfectly done to the required standards (Costello, 2016).

These individuals have the crucial role of coming up with the content. This applies to the websites. They work with the multimedia producer by coming up with the content that will be added to the website. The deal with the scripting of animation plays. They control the voice-overs as well as the actor narrators. This more so for the making of cartoons. They control the synchronization of the actor's narrators and the animations were made. They write proposals within multimedia and carry out test screens for the produced projects ensuring that they are okay before being sold.

In the creation of animations, they create the characters in the animation. They coordinate the motion of the characters as well as make them do various actions such as jumping, laughing or even walking (Costello, 2016).

3.4.3. Interface Designers

The work of an interface designer is to ensure that they create web elements that assist users of the web to have an easier experience when they are designing it. The following are the duties that these interface designers have:

The design storyboards that bring out the concept of the design. It is the role of the Interface designer to come up with a storyboard that shows what the design is about and bring out the concept about it to those who are not familiar with it. They conceptualize the design in other terms.

The interface designers come up with the timeline and the deliverables and this is a major role. There are many advantages of determining the timeline for a project such that it enables individuals to remain on the same page and therefore the interface designers are endowed with this duty and role.

The interface designers also test the applications that are formed and the software to ensure that they are working in the right way. The carryout tests on the websites and they give out clear feedback on them.

They are endowed with the duty to work with other engineers to assist them in case their help might be required.

3.4.4. Writers

Writing is a major important part of the software team and it is also an interesting part. Their role includes putting down information and data in the form of words into the computer software. They include the article writers who write articles that are found and useful when individuals are carrying out their research in specific fields. Writers have to be very keen and specific when they are carrying out their roles and their work has to be detailed and up to date. It should also be accurate and timely as desired.

3.4.5. Video Specialists

A video specialist is an individual who works on videos editing and coming up with videos that can be viewed by the people. Videos are recordings that are displayed in the form of moving images and often are accompanied with a voice or tone especially viewed in the televisions or other technological devices. Videos are a major key to entertainment in today's world and many people spend most of their alone time watching videos to pass time while they still enjoy themselves. It is, therefore, a major sector in the software and the multimedia team and organization.

The roles that a video specialist has to play include: Capturing photographs in the studio that are of good quality and meet the desired quality. Video specialists are specialized in the field of photography such that they are equipped with the skills to capture very good pictures that are of high standards and that can meet the requirements of the society. Aside from taking good photographs, they are taken very quality videos that they use in broadcasting and carrying out their jobs. Video specialists as the name states are therefore individuals who are specialized in the field of video and photography at large (Costello, 2016).

Another responsibility of video specialists is to work both on-site and off-site. When a video specialist is hired it does not necessarily mean that they have to carry out their duties from the workplace but they can also carry out fieldwork and go off-site to perform their duties. The video specialist must, therefore, be willing to adjust to any condition and work from any sector and it is their responsibility to ensure that they are specialized at this. This is advantageous because it eliminated monotony in the work and their profession.

The other responsibility of a video specialist is to produce and edit videos and other content and have a collection of these videos and content. A video specialist has to produce content regularly and keep editing them such that he has a lot of content in his store and collection that he can hire to other companies and they can showcase their work at any one time. The advantage of having a collection of their work is that they are always ready to showcase their work and they can readily hire it to companies. This role is beneficial since it keeps the video specialists always ready for anything that may be becoming.

Another responsibility of the video specialists is they are the managers who are behind the process of recording a video such that they are the ones who manage and state how the video will be recorded and the theme, costume, and where it will be taken from. They also oversee how the videos are taken and from these, they can find and connect the parts where they find it inappropriate. The Video specialists are supposed to be behind and take the lead in the producing of the videos and they, therefore, play a key and major role (Costello, 2016).

The video specialists are involved in media dealing with the visual and audio aspect. They know which mode the videos should be delivered. For instance, those people relayed on video players then the videos were delivered in the form of DVD. There are other forms in which the videos are delivered such as CDs, DVDs or even the internet. They also need to know how to shoot videos with very high quality that will be more appealing for the audience. They are required to know how to transfer the video footages from the devices such as the camera to the computer. The mode of transfer that they choose should be efficient in that the whole video is transferred with none of the sections omitted. They should be able to properly use computers as their work involves them editing the video footage. They should be able to use both digital and non-linear editing systems. The final version of the exciting footage should be able to be displayed in digital formats.

3.4.6. Audio Specialists

They are like the video specialists the only difference being that they deal with the audio aspect of multimedia. The fact that the latest digital technology is used in multimedia, the audio specialists are required to store the recorded materials within the computer. They also use computers to digitalize and edit the recorded materials. They are also required to locate and select individuals with talent. The talent either in music or in narrators. They are then required to make schedules for the recordings. The identified individuals are then given time and date for the recording sessions.

3.4.7. Multimedia Programmer

They are also referred to as software engineers. They kind of do what software engineers do. They have to the role of incorporating the various multimedia elements into a project. They do so by using the most appropriate systems. They are required to know the right programming language to be used in incorporating multimedia element into the project. They also control and manage the timings in the progression of videos. They select the transitions that will be used in the project.

They are in charge of keeping records of the projects. Programming deals with the creation of codes. The multimedia programmers write the codes that are later on displayed. The codes are used in displaying the various elements in multimedia. For them to be able to make the codes, they need to know about controlling the peripheral devices such as computers. With such knowledge, he or she can be able to manipulate the devices for them to work to his advantage (Costello, 2016).

3.5. BACKGROUND/TRAINING AND SKILLS REQUIRED BY THE DIFFERENT MEMBERS OF THE SOFTWARE TEAM

According to the roles that the individuals play, the must have the necessary skills in line with their roles. The project managers should have good interpersonal and communication skills which will enable them to work well with the individuals they interact within their line of work. They should also have good organization skills as they will be required to create an outline of the priorities of the project. They essentially give a guideline on how the project is to be conducted. They should also have good decision-making skills this is because they are the ones to call the shots when it comes to making the important decisions concerning the projects (Kim et al, 2011).

For the multimedia producers, the skills that they are required to have are almost similar to that of the project manager. For a TV or film producer, they will be required to have leadership skills as their role will entail them being in charge of other individuals. They should also have communication skills as they will be involved in the various broadcasting channels. The training they are given involves them using different media tools and training them on using such facilities.

The multimedia writer needs to have skills in creativity. This will enable them to come up with content that has not been seen before. The use of their creative skills will enable them to develop objectivity. They will also need to have communication skills. For the multimedia writer, they will have to write scripts among other things. Writing is a form of communication and therefore they will have to use their communication skills in their writing making the skill to be of much importance.

They also make use of observation skills. Through observation, they can get ideas which they can incorporate into their writing. Apart from that, they will also need to have problem-solving skills. When writing content, they may be relaying a problem to the audience and they may be required to give out a solution to the problem. They are given training and need to have a background on writing which will enable them to be the best at what they do. They need to have a good background in good grammar (Kim et al, 2011).

For the video specialists, they need to have a good background on video and editing this will enable them to easily interact with the various tools provided for them. Among the skills they are required to have is problem-solving. As a video specialist, he or she may encounter various challenges which they will be required to solve. They also need to have management skills. The management will be in terms of aspects such as time which is very crucial for a video specialist. They need to manage their time so that they can strike a balance between shooting a video and editing of the video. They should also have good communication and interpersonal skills that will enable them to work efficiently with other individuals. They should have great observation skills which will help them improve the quality of images produced.

The audio specialist requires almost the same skills as video specialists. They need to have good time management skills. This is because they are involved in activities such as recording sessions scheduling as well as editing of the recorded material. They also need to have problem-solving skills that will be applied in case they face any challenging situation. They need to have a good background in editing equipment. They are given training on handling the technical equipment such as the microphones and the speakers ensuring that they are properly used and can run for long periods.

A multimedia programmer needs to have the training and a good background on programming. This ensures that they are knowledgeable on the various programming languages and they will be able to work will the one they have more knowledge on. With such knowledge, they need to have analytical skills.

This they will use when coming up with the various codes used in displaying multimedia elements. Communication skills are also essential as they will need them when interacting with other individuals. They will also need to have technical, team working and creativity skills. The training they are given involves equipping them with knowledge and experience in coming up with codes used in displaying multimedia elements (Kim et al, 2011).

For the multimedia designer, the skills and training they are required to have depended on the role they have. For instance, for the graphics designers need to have a background on computer graphics. They need to have skills such as creativity which they will be applied in coming up with new and fresh graphics design.

Generally, multimedia designers need to have communication skills. This will enable them to present their ideas and content. They do so employing technological and programming skills to be able to make the content to be more presentable for the audience making it easily understandable by the audience.

Creative skills are also employed in various fields such as graphics design. The creative skills will help the individuals to approach in the designing of the projects. They also need to have organizations skills that will be used in formulating the projects. They also need to have management skills.

These skills are discussed as per all the members of the multimedia team since different teams have different skills that are involved. It is, therefore, necessary for the individuals to take part in understanding the skills that are involved in each sector so that each individual in the software team can know what skill they are required to obtain in their work process and to enable them to know what skills they have to reveal in their work process. Although most of them share the same skills, the following are some skills that each individual has to reveal in their work (Kim et al, 2011).

3.5.1. Skills Required By Each Member of a Multimedia Team

Project manager: A project manager mainly takes up the leadership role and the skills he requires most include:

Communication: A project manager needs to have the ability to send information from one individual to another in a way that he can ensure the information being passed is the correct information. Communication is an important factor in any group and organization because it enables each individual to know what they are supposed to do and in case of a problem the individuals can know the point where they need to correct on early enough. A project manager is an individual who manages a project and also designs a project and they need to have the communication skills so that they can give out duties to every member of the project team that he is managing. They also require communication skills so that they can share the ideas they have generated from the project and when they are explaining it to the other members they should explain it in such a way that it will enable each member of the team to know what they are dealing with and they will get a clear image of what is involved.

- Leadership: Leadership is the ability of a person to lead a team to an attainable goal that is set. Leadership skills are not common to many people and many individuals fail to know what is expected of them as leaders. Project managers are the individuals behind the success of a project and they should have leadership skills so that they can lead their team to the end of the project where the goals they had set will be achieved and also they can ensure that their team works to produce the best results that were expected. Some leadership skills that project managers require include transparency where they need to be open and they should avoid corruption at any one time. Transparency enables individuals to gain trust from the people they are leading as they are assured that the money invested in the project will not be squandered or used for the benefit of one individual but it will be used for the advantage of the project. Project managers should, therefore, be very transparent and they should also be fair in a way that they will give out duties to their team in a fair and just manner.

- Problem-solving skills: In every organization, some problems always arise that if they are not dealt with appropriately they can lead to the fall of a project. Project managers need to have the skill of solving problems diligently and they can handle any problem that comes their way appropriately and give out the solutions that are most applicable to this situation. Problem-solving skills mostly involve critical thinking where the individuals need to think deeply into the issue and find out causes that may have led to the problem so that they can find the most suitable solution for the problem.
- Listening skill: The project manager must always be ready to listen to what their team members have to say. They should not view their idea as the best idea but they should be willing to listen and by this, they can receive corrections in areas where they had overshadowed. Project managers are therefore individuals who are humble enough to welcome the ideas of others without any biasness. In case of a problem arising in the project, Project managers should listen attentively to know the cause of the problem first before judging and making conclusions.

Multimedia designer: A multimedia designer has to have skills that will enable them to design multimedia in the most desired way. The skills that multimedia designers should possess include:

- Creativity: Creativity is the ability of an individual to create a new thing that was not created before and to design multimedia, multimedia designers need to be very creative and to have a lot of creativity skills such that they can design a new thing that they can be proud of.
- Problem-solving skills: A lot of problems may arise in the process of inventing a new thing or creating a new multimedia and therefore, multimedia designers need to have the skills of solving problems that may arise and they should ensure that these problems are solved as early as possible before they lead to more harm and before they damage anything in the organization. The multimedia designers need to look deeply into the issue and discover the cause of the issue then they should find out the possible solutions and from this, they should derive the most suitable solution and apply it.

- Critical thinking: A project manager should think critically so that they can come up with new ideas and so that they can design new multimedia. Thinking critically is the ability to dig deep and thinking widely by being open to new ideas so that they can create new things that were not discovered by anyone before. If their idea was discovered before, the multimedia designers need to think critically on ways that they can improve this idea and come up with a more improved thing than the one that was present before and then apply it.

Organization: A multimedia designer should be very organized. The organization is the ability of an individual to carry out their duties in a way that is properly planned such that they can avoid any distraction due to being disorganized. The organization is a key factor in multimedia designing because every step of the process must be defined clearly and they must be followed as desired so that the result can be as required. If the multimedia designers fail to be organized and they do not follow the processes appropriately then they can end up having a big problem at the end. Also, the organization enables individuals and multimedia designers to have peace of mind and avoid a lot of stress and struggles since they are following the processes step by step and they cannot end up getting mushed up and confused that could lead to a lot of stress and struggles. Lastly, by being organized it enables individuals to gain respect since when an individual is organized and smart physically then they are seen to know what they are doing and therefore they gain respect from the other members of their team and they also become confident.

Writers: Writers are individuals who require a lot of skills for the success of their work.

Communication skills: Every content writer must have communication skills so that they can deliver their message in the most appropriate way and that which is desired.

Strong research skills: A written need to do a lot of research so that they can find out and acquire a lot of information that they require for writing. A written must, therefore, have the ability to conduct research and come up with a piece of organized information that they can translate and put it down in an appropriate manner. Strong research skills can be acquired by carrying out a lot of practice and visiting as many books as possible that they can use to get information from. Strong research skills are therefore very important skills in the process of writing.

Organizational skills: Just like any other skills organizational skills are also important in an organization because it enables the writers to have the ability to put down their knowledge in the most desired form. Just like in the multimedia designer, organizational skills by being organized it enables individuals to gain respect since when an individual is organized and smart physically then they are seen to know what they are doing and therefore they gain respect from the other members of their team and they also become confident and hence they do not have to be shy.

Video specialists: Video specialists should have the following skill.

- Time management: Video specialists should be good timekeepers such that they do things at the required time and submit before the deadline. Good time. Good time management enables things to be done at the required time without fail and by this, it enables everything in an organization to flow smoothly. In case an individual fail to keep the time it may delay the whole process and it may lead to failure of some processes hence the results may not be desirable and they may breed unwanted results. Video specialists should, therefore, be very careful to keep time as it is desired.
- Editing skills: Video specialists must know how to use various editing software because their work demands that they get the best of what they are doing so that they can conquer the competition that is in existence in the market. Video specialists, therefore, edit the pictures and videos making them more lively and increasing the pictures brightness, contrast, balancing the effects of the picture and making it more visually attractive. Video specialists are therefore trained on the editing of pictures and they can also train themselves and perform a lot of practice to improve their skills.

Audio specialists: For these individuals, they are referred to as specialists as they have expertise when it comes to using and handling of audio equipment. In the software development team, they tend to work mostly on thing related to broadcasting. Their work is to ensure that the broadcast produced is of good quality. They capture audio which will be transmitted during the broadcast. They also work on audio tracks as some of them are involved in the music industry. They use the computer software to come up with beats or even balance the sounds in a music track or video.

For one to qualify to be an audio specialist, they need to have knowledge of computer software making it easier for them to work with the given software on the production of audio. They can manipulate the software to suit their needs as audio specialists. They also need to know the audio equipment. This comes in handy when they experience challenges with the equipment. They will be able to identify the problem and sort it out. Their knowledge of computers will enable them to mix audio tapes enabling the production of a new variety of music.

Among the responsibilities of an audio specialist is the proper positioning of equipment. The positioning will be s major factor in determining the quality of sound produced. This is more so applicable in broadcasting. The audience needs to get a good quality of sound to understand the content. They are also in charge of booking the recording sessions. They identify an individual with musical talent and bring them to the studio to record. The recorded music may be used in advertisements or incorporated into animated films. They also control the actor narrators when producing animation films so that the sound of the actor is consistent with the action of the character (Hin and Leo, 2009).

Some of the skills that an audio specialist should have included good communication skills that will be used whilst interacting with other individuals. They also need to have time management skills as they will be required to make a schedule for the recording sessions. They need to have management skills that will assist them in handling a variety of tasks. Problem-solving skills are essential as they will be required to solve problems that may arise when handling the audio equipment.

Multimedia producer: As the name states, they are in charge of production. These individuals had a major role to play in the software development team. One of their roles involves them being in charge of creating and designing digital content. Some of the digital content include websites and digital films. They also have to interact with the clients to know their preference and their view on the products the team produces. They are then required to give feedback to the development team so that they can evaluate and strategize on what to do.

For one to qualify to be a multimedia producer, there are some qualifications needed to be surpassed. One of the qualifications being that they need to have knowledge and experience in using software programs. This knowledge is applied to the production of websites among other products. They also need to know the different fields of digital media. This allows them to take up other roles in the production process such as the illustrator and the web designer. They may need to know programming which may be useful in the creation of websites.

The multimedia producer also needs to have s variety of skills. As most of the time they will need to manage the project, they need to have project management skills. The skill will be useful as they will be overseeing projects from the initial stages until the final product. They will also need to have decision-making skills which will be useful ad they are among the members who make decisions concerning the project. They need to have leadership skill as they will play the role of team leader at times. Time management is essential. It will help them ensure that the project is completed within the allocated time. They need to have communication skills that will help them interact with clients as well as the members of the team (Hin and Leo, 2009).

Multimedia programmer: These are individuals who use technical and creative abilities to come up with digital products. Some of the products include mobile applications and animated films. They also play an important role in the software development team as shown by the number of responsibilities that they have. Among the responsibilities of multimedia, the programmer is to carry out a variety of tests on multimedia products. The tests help them identify any bugs that may be present. They also research the latest advancements in technology concerning the type of technology to be used or the latest programming languages.

It is also up to them to make any updates or changes to the applications that were initially made. The client's feedback is used in determining the type of change that should be made. As they know to code, they can solve any issue with codes by either changing them or making new codes. They are also required to work with the other members of the team and offer them any form of assistance in something related to programming.

The multimedia programmer needs to have a variety of skills one of them being programming skills. They need to have developed the skill of programming for them to be called programmers. They also need to have interface designing skills which are used in interface design. Communication skills to enable them to communicate with other individuals. Problem-solving skills. Their problem-solving skills should mostly be logical as they will be dealing with logical operations. The management skills will be useful in assisting them in handling a variety of tasks (Hin and Leo, 2009).

The multimedia programmers need to know computer software, a programming language such as java and markup language such as HTML.

Good multimedia: For us to understand what good multimedia is we need to know what multimedia is to classify multimedia as good or bad. Multimedia is a technology that facilitates storage of data in its form be it in text or photo or animation format and is giving users a way through which they can add or modify the data. Therefore, good multimedia is on that effectively allows the storage and the modification of data to suit the user's needs. For multimedia to be good, it must meet all the characteristics of a good multimedia system. A multimedia system is a system that can integrate a number of the different types of media such as graphics and audio.

The characteristics of a good media system include:

- The system is controlled by a computer: We live in a generation where technology is everything. The use of technology means that everything is automated. Therefore, if multimedia is computer-controlled, then it improves the quality of the multimedia. For instance, text. The computer is fitted with applications and programs that control how text is presented thereby increasing the quality of the text.
- All the multimedia systems are integrated: For the multimedia system to efficiently work then it has to be whole. Meaning that all of its important elements have to be in it. The different types of media also have to be incorporated into it. That is the text, video, audio, and graphics among others. If the multimedia system has been integrated, then the multimedia will have a variety of resources at its disposal.
- The information must be digital: This means that the information to be fed to the audience should be presented in a digital format. This is why the multimedia system should be computer-controlled. The use of computers in the presentation of information is resourceful as computers provide a variety of tool at the user's disposal. For instance, tools such MS Access allows the user to present information on bar or pie charts.

The interface of the multimedia should be made in such a way that it allows the presentation of the final product to be interactive. It should give room for feedback from the viewers of the content making it be an interactive session.

If the multimedia has all the above characteristics in its system them the multimedia can be termed as good. It can also be termed as good if its system can facilitate the shifting of the technologies to cater to the use of the latest technology. This will allow the addition of the tools that can be used to make the multimedia more interactive and productive.

CHAPTER
4

Text in Multimedia

CONTENTS

4.1. INTRODUCTION

In multimedia systems, texts refer to words, numbers, and special characters used to pass across thoughts, concepts, and facts in almost all aspects of life. Nowadays, multimedia products also rely on texting for many things like explaining how the program works, guiding users in steering through the application, plus delivering the data for which the program was designed.

Text is the simplest form of digital communication and the most effectual way to pass a message across. However, users must provide sufficient attention to the presentation as well as flow of text for the multimedia application, in order to prevent misrepresentation of facts and delivering the text's central message. Most individuals are accustomed to text even if they've never handled computers before. It forms the basis or foundation for word processing systems, besides being the central information channel used by most multimedia programs.

Figure 4.1. A smartphone operator using digital text to communicate.

Source: *https://www.plummerslade.com/2015/12/email-text-messages-documents/.*

As a matter of fact, most multimedia programs rely on the format of converting written text to computerized form. The conversion provides users with instant access to text, while allowing them to showcase pop-up windows, thereby giving meanings to certain words.

The Windows OS gives users a nearly infinite variety of expressing text. Being a multimedia programmer, it's easy to choose the kind of font for displaying your text in, including how large or small it must be, plus what color it must be presented in. Through displaying text in different formats, it means that the text a multimedia system is attempting to portray may become more comprehensible. One form of application where multimedia text applies is in Windows Help Engine. It's basically a text-based data viewer which makes accessing information pertaining to a given topic simple.

4.2. HYPERTEXT

Hypertext is text exhibited on a digital display or some form of electronic device, having references (hyperlinks) linking to other text that the reader may instantly access, or whereby text may be shown progressively at different angles of detail, commonly known as Stretch Text.

Usually, hypertext paragraphs are linked through hyperlinks, which are initiated through a simple mouse click, key press chain or simply touching the screen. In addition to text, hypertext is occasionally used to define tables, pictures, and other presentational material forms through hyperlinks. Hypertext forms the underlying principle that defines the makeup of the internet today, with pages mostly captured in HTML or Hypertext Markup Language. This allows for ease of usage and dynamic connection, including sharing of data over the Web (Figliola and Stevens, 2012).

Basically, hypertext works in the same manner as general text – it's possible to store, peruse, search, or edit at any given time – though with an exception: the hypertext refers to content with pointers connecting to other text. Usually, browsers allow you to handle pointers in a rather transparent manner—simply choose the pointer then you're directed to the text which is chosen.

Hypertext documents may either be stationary (readied and stored beforehand) or dynamic (constantly changing in reaction to user input, like dynamic web content). Static hypertext may be applied to cross-reference groups of data found in files, software applications and books on drivers (Figliola and Stevens, 2012).

4.3. HYPERMEDIA

Hypermedia can be defined as a mega-set of hypertext. Most hypermedia texts have links to not just other documents, but also different types of media – including sounds, pictures, and movies. Pictures themselves can be chosen to connect to sounds or files. It means that browsers may not demonstrate a text document, but instead show images, animations, and sound. Basically, hypermedia combines aspects of multimedia and hypertext.

The Internet or Worldwide Web is a great example of hypermedia, while a non-interactive cinematic presentation forms a classic example of regular multimedia because of the existence of hyperlinks.

Additionally, Hypermedia is sometimes applied as a medium or constraint in some application programming platforms. In fact, being the driver of Application State, Hypermedia can be a constraint to the REST system architecture, whereby clients connect with the server completely through hypermedia delivered dynamically through application servers (Figliola and Stevens, 2012).

It means that theoretically no API filing is needed, since the client doesn't require any prior knowledge concerning how to connect with any individual application or server outside the generic comprehension of hypermedia. For other service-based architectures (SOA), users, and servers communicate through a secure interface shared via documentation or even interface description communication. An example is when you're reading some text in the Japanese dialect. You choose a Japanese term, and then hear the word as expressed in the native language (Figliola and Stevens, 2012).

4.4. TEXT STRUCTURES

All texts comprise of two main structures which are linear and non-linear.

4.4.1. Linear

It's a single means of progressing through the text, commencing at the start and reading up to the finish. The linear active content advances often without any directional mechanism for the viewer like a cinema presentation. Basically, linear multimedia text is a form of a multimedia which is crafted to be availed in a sequential way. The writing has a clear beginning and end. Furthermore, it moves on a consistent flow from the beginning point to finish. It's usually projected for display reasons with not a lot of interaction or distraction coming from the audience.

Due to its nature whereby audience participation isn't required, Linear Multimedia text can also be called "Passive Multimedia." For this form of presentation, developers are in total control of the text multimedia. This form of text media is preferential in case interaction isn't essential in the presentation.

Key objectives include: entertainment, passing knowledge, and making individuals familiar on a particular subject without any kind of diversion.

A PowerPoint presentation is a good example. The advantage of linear text is that audiences must focus and deliberate on one particular topic. There's also organization since the presenter manages the presentation flow. This strategy is effective in cases where you need the audience to grasp the text information well. The disadvantage is reduced interactivity, or even none completely. The audience doesn't have much say on the subject they wish to dwell into (Pearson Education, 2004).

4.4.2. Non-Linear

In this text format, information is presented in a semantic way where different related parts of the document are linked to one another. The user might then search through parts of the text, going from a particular text unit to the next.

Moreover, non-linear multimedia text is a non-sequential form of digital communication, whereby the individual's participation is key. For this kind of media, one must connect with a computer system, thereby making him in charge of the experience. Through the existence of an interface, both the individual and computer are able to interact with one another.

Right from the starting point, an individual using a non-linear multimedia text is provided a variety of options which, based on their individual preferences, shall direct them to fresh information. An example of non-linear text is with a website content. An advantage of non-linear text is in how an individual controls and uses multimedia depending on their preferences and requirements. The only disadvantage of non-linear text is that it needs some form of computer literacy coming from the user (Pearson Education, 2004).

Font vs. Typefaces: All texts consist of elements which include alphabets, numerical, and special characters. The alphabets are A – Z, Numbers from 0 – 9 and Special Characters include punctuations, signs, and symbols. These symbols may comprise of unique icon or drawing signs, even Greek letters and mathematical symbols,

A 'font' is defined as a group of characters which are of a given size and style consisting of a specific typeface family. Fonts also largely vary based on type size and style. Mostly sizes are measured as points, it really doesn't offer any distinct height/width for the text. This comprises of the letter set, number set, and special characters or diacritical marks which you obtain by dialing the shift, option, and command/control buttons.

On the other hand, typeface is defined as the general design of lettering; this design may include variations like bold, standard, light, italic, shortened, and extended. Every one of these typeface variations basically is a font. Currently, there are 1000s of new typefaces in existence, though new ones are being established constantly (Pearson Education, 2004).

The technique of designing typefaces can be referred to as type design. Generally, the designers of typefaces can be referred to as type designers plus are typically hired by type foundries. For digital typography, the type designers are occasionally known as font designers or developers. Each typeface represents a group of glyphs, where every character represents a particular letter, number, symbol or punctuation mark. This same glyph can be applied for characters from diverse scripts, for example. Roman uppercase A resembles Cyrillic uppercase A as well as Greek uppercase alpha. Some typefaces are tailored for particular applications, like astrology, map-making, and arithmetic. The phrase typeface is commonly confused with the word font. However, before the arrival of digital typography as well as desktop publishing, these two phrases had more visibly understood meanings.

Among the major traps when discussing type, is combining fonts with letterings or handling them as synonymous. There are some typographic experts who may correct beginners for wrongly using the term font, when they should have instead said typeface. Plus, for those individuals who consider fonts only when picking one from Microsoft Word, it means the difference between the phrases may seem unclear, esoteric, or even arcane. Generally, a font is the text format you use, while typeface is the aspect you see (Pearson Education, 2004).

Does their use matter any longer: Even among type experts, there's an increasing acceptance that for a majority of people, the words font and typeface may be applied interchangeably. It's only the experts who really have to be concerned with this question.

For individuals in many situations, these terms can be swapped around without so much trouble. The difference may matter in type format, obviously, however, also contexts that involve engineering, such as web design or app development can be included. Many people, apart from type designers, simply say 'font." For graphic designers, however, it's more of a generational thing. Most of the older generation of still say 'typeface.'

4.4.3. Digital Type

Digital type rose to become a dominant version of text during the late 80s and early 90s. These digital fonts are designed to record the copy of every character in form of a bitmap that's in the bitmap font, or through mathematical depiction of lines and arcs in a sketch font, also known as vector font. Typically, the Bitmap fonts were utilized during the earlier phases of digital type, though are seldom used today. The bitmapped typefaces were originally created with help from Casady and Greene, Inc. where they were called Fluent Fonts. They became largely obsolete following the formation of downloadable Post Text fonts, plus these new fonts often are known as Fluent Laser Fontsor (FLF). Once an outline font has been used, the rasterizing routine (involving the OS, application software or printer) identifies the character outlines, deducing the vector guidelines to determine which pixels must be black and those ones that are white.

Moreover, rasterization is typically straightforward at great resolutions like those applied by laser printers, as well as in top-end publishing systems. In computer screens, each single pixel can denote the difference between sanctioned and illegible characters. But for digital fonts, there are some that use hinting algorithms for purposes of creating clear bitmaps at small sizes. Virtual fonts may also comprise of data demonstrating the metrics applied for composition, such as kerning pairs, module creation information for accented characters, and glyph substitution policies for Arabic typography, plus for joining script faces, or basic everyday ligatures such as fl.

Some common font formats comprise of PostScript Type 1, TrueType, and Open Type, whereas Metafont is still applied by TeX as well as its variants. Some applications that use these font types, including the rasterizers, show in Microsoft (MS) as well as Apple Computer OSs or OSs and Adobe Systems items and those of different other establishments. Oftentimes, digital fonts are formed with font editors like RoboFont, Glyphs, Font Forge, Font Lab Studio, Asia Font Studio, Fontographer, and Fontlab'sTypeTool.

4.4.4. Typeface Anatomy

Typographers have established an all-inclusive vocabulary for defining the different elements of typography and typefaces. There is vocabulary that apply just to a subgroup of all scripts. Case in point, Serifs are a wholly decorative aspect of typeface that's applied for European scripts, while the glyphs applied in East Asian or Arabic scripts feature characteristics (like stroke width) which may look similar in some ways but can't solidly be referred to as serifs, besides they may not be fully decorative.

Generally, typefaces can be subdivided into two key categories which are sans serif and serif. Serifs consist of the small structures at the finish of letter strokes. Stakeholders in the printing sector call typefaces without serifs to be sans serif (borrowing from the French word sans, which means without), or grotesque (which is grotesk in German). Immense variety exists among the serif as well as sans serif typefaces (Pearson Education, 2004).

The two groups comprise of faces that are developed for setting huge volumes of body text, while others are exclusively intended for decorative purposes. The absence or presence of serifs represents just one of several factors to contemplate when selecting a typeface. In many cases, typefaces with serifs usually are deemed simpler to read in lengthy passages compared to those without. Research on the subject is still ambiguous nonetheless, showing that majority of the effect arises because of increased understanding of serif typefaces. Generally speaking, printed works like books and newspapers nearly always apply serif typefaces, probably for the text structure only.

Websites don't need to specify any font, since they can merely refer to the user's browser settings. Though for websites which actually specify a font, many of them use contemporary sans serif fonts, since it's widely believed that, different from the scenario for printed material, most sans serif fonts tend to be simpler than serif fonts for reading on low-resolution PC screens.

In addition, text fonts can be divided into two groups which include proportional and monospace typefaces. A proportional typeface comprises of glyphs of different widths, whereas a monospaced (straight-width or non-proportional) typeface applies one standard width for different font glyphs (Pearson Education, 2004).

Dual-spaced fonts are same as monospaced fonts;however, characters may also be paired character widths rather than just one-character width. Most individuals typically find proportional typefaces to be better-looking and simpler to read, hence they appear more regularly in professionally published text content. For this similar reason, GUI PC applications (like web browsers and processors) normally use proportional fonts. Nevertheless, most proportional fonts comprise of fixed-width (tabular) statistics so that numerical columns may remain aligned.

The monospaced typefaces work better for some reasons since their glyphs align in neat, standard columns. There's no glyph which is added any extra weight than the other. Majority of manually run typewriters use mono-spaced fonts. Same as text-only PC displays and 3rrd or 4tth generation gaming console graphics computers, which handle the screen as one uniform network of character cells. Many computer programs with text-based interfaces (such as terminal emulators, for instance) use just mono-spaced fonts (or add extra spacing to comparative fonts to arrange them in single-spaced cells) within their configuration (Pearson Education, 2004).

Monospaced fonts are typically used by computing experts for showing and editing the source code, such that some characters (like parentheses applied to group arithmetic expressions) are simple to see. The monospaced fonts might also make it simpler to perform visual character recognition. In most cases the SCII art needs a mono-spaced font for correct watching, with the exemption of Shift JIS systems which make use of proportional characters present in MS PG othic fonts.

For web pages, HTML tags such as <code></code>, <tt></tt> and <pre></pre> may further be used as monospaced fonts. When it comes to LaTeX, it means the verbatim setting or Teletype font unit (example, {\ttfamily.} or \texttt{.}) apply monospaced fonts (for TeX, use {\tt.}). there's no two text lines that have the same amount of characters since every line forming the monospaced typeface must be shown as equivalent in width, whereas the same dual lines in the proportional typeface might have fundamentally different widths. It happens because in a normal proportional font, the glyph widths differ, so that wider glyphs (normally those for characters like, M, D, O, W, Q, Z U and H)

Utilize more space, as well as narrower glyphs (like those meant for 1, i, t, and l characters) use lesser space compared to the average font. For the publishing sector, it was initially the standard that editors read documents in monospaced fonts (usually Courier) for editing ease and word count estimations, besides it was considered unmannerly to submit a text in proportional fonts. This has become less widespread in recent times, such that writers must check first with editors concerning their preferences, however, monospaced fonts are largely the norm (Cranny-Francis, 2005).

Most texts have a common baseline concept: comprising of an imagined horizontal line where characters rest. For some scripts, there are sections of glyphs that fall below the baseline. This descent extends through the distance across the baseline up to the lowest downward glyph in the typeface, including the section of the glyph which slopes below the baseline that bears a name descender. Alternatively, the ascent extends through the space amid the baseline and highest point of the glyph which spreads at the farthest point from the baseline.

Both the ascension and descent may include or otherwise omit distance captured by diacritical marks and accents. For Greek, Latin, and Cyrillic texts, one may refer to the space going from the baseline up to the peak of standard lowercase glyphs or (mean line) as x-height, including the section of glyph that's rising past the x-height being the ascender.

Moreover, the stretch from the baseline up to the highest section of the ascent, or regular uppercase glyphs can be referred to as cap height. This ascender height may have a drastic impact on the readability as well as look of a font. The fraction between the x-height as well as ascension or cap height typically helps to characterize typefaces. All typefaces which can be switched for each other in the text without altering the file's text flow can be called "metrically identical or compatible."Different typefaces have been formed to be metrically matched with broadly used proprietary typefaces for allowing the editing of files set in these typefaces in virtual typesetting environments, whereby these typefaces aren't accessible. For example, both free and open-source Croscore fonts/Liberation fonts have mostly been developed as metrically attuned substitutes for extensively used MS fonts (Cranny-Francis, 2005).

4.5. OPTICAL TEXT SIZING

During the metal typing era, different typesets were cut in metal plus could simply be printed on a particular size. This was a natural procedure to amend a design at various sizes, making it denser and clearer for reading at lesser sizes. Most digital typefaces are provided with a variety of fonts (even a variable font angle) for various sizes, particularly designs sold for expert design usage. The art of developing fonts for a particular size is referred to as optical sizing.

Furthermore, others may be provided in only a single style, though optimized for a particular size. Optical dimensions are especially popular for serif fonts, considering the fine detail that serif fonts may require to be padded up for lesser sizes. Typefaces can also be designed separately considering the form of paper where they'll be printed.

Generally, designs meant for printing on permeable newsprint paper would be slimmer since the ink shall naturally disperse out while absorbing into the paper, plus might feature ink traps: parts left blank where the ink shall soak while it dries. The corrections won't be required for printing on top-gloss cardboard or exhibition on-screen. Fonts developed for low-resolution presentations, meanwhile, might prevent pure circles, coherent lines and aspects a screen can't provide (Figliola and Stevens, 2012).

4.6. TYPEFACE STYLES

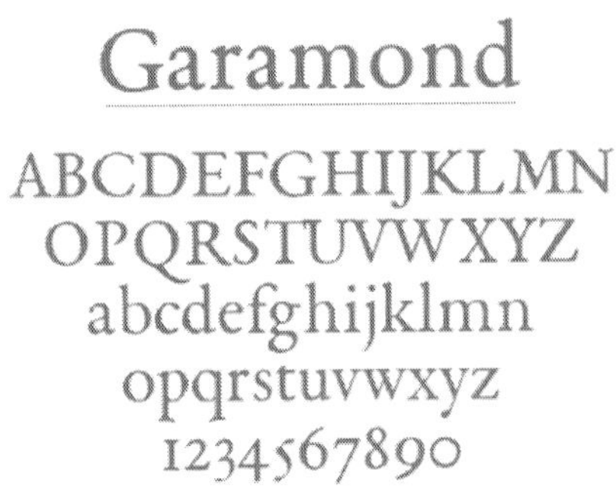

Figure 4.2. There are different classifications of typefaces used in multimedia texts.

Source: *https://visme. co/blog/different-types-of-fonts/.*

Since a variety of typefaces have been developed over the centuries, they're typically categorized depending on their look. At the topmost level (with regards to Latin-script fonts), a person can easily differentiate between Gaelic, Blackletter, and Roman types. The Roman styles have been the most extensively used up to date, besides they are sub-categorized into groups such as sans serif, ornamental, serif, and script styles. Originally, the first Europe style fonts were blackletters, then later Roman serif arose, followed by sans serif and different other styles. While the application of Gaelic faces may be have been limited to the Irish dialect, still these form a special but minority class.

Additionally, typefaces can be monospaced irrespective of whether they're Blackletter, Roman or even Gaelic. Plus, symbol typefaces are mostly non-alphabetic. Equally, the Cyrillic script is available in two forms, the Roman style and conventional Slavonic type. The 3 traditional types of serif typefaces applied for body text are transitional, old-style, and Didone, which are symbolized by Baskerville, Didot, and Garamond. As for Roman and Serif, typefaces are identified for the characteristics at the finish of their strokes.

Both Garamond and Times New Roman are good models of serif typefaces. The serif fonts are perhaps the most common class in digital to print materials. Moreover, serif fonts are typically classified into 3 subcategories which include Transitional, Did one, and Old Style. While Old Style typefaces have been influenced by the earliest Italian lettering designs (Pearson Education, 2004).

Contemporary fonts often showcase a bracketed serif as well as a considerable variance in weight for the strokes. Whereas some argument persists as to if Transitional fonts occur as a distinct group among serif fonts, still transitional fonts exist some place between the Modern and Old Style typefaces.

The transitional fonts display a marked rise in the disparity of stroke weight, including a largely horizontal serif when compared to the Old Style. Furthermore, Slab Serif models have considerably large serifs, plus date back to 19th century, therefore making them among the oldest fonts still in use today.

The first slab serif font however, is Antique, which was later retitled Egyptian and has been in existence since 1815, having been invented by the British type-founder Vincent Figgins.

Equally, Oblique, Roman, and Italic are terms used for differentiating between vertical and dual possible slanted types of typefaces. Oblique and Italic fonts look similar (certainly, oblique fonts are usually just called italics) though there's indeed a difference: Italics applies to fonts in which the letter types are redesigned, instead of just being slanted. Nearly all serif faces contain some italic forms; besides there are sans-serif faces with oblique designs.

(Majority of faces don't provide both since this is mostly an artistic choice from the font designer, concerning how the slanted type should look.) The Sans serif fonts oftentimes but not completely are utilized for display typography like signage, headings, as well as other circumstances requiring legibility over high readability (Pearson Education, 2004).

The electronic media text provides a good exception to print: majority of web pages and digital media are established in sans-serif typefaces since serifs typically detract from readability within the low display resolutions. Most have minimal variation with regards to stroke width, forming the expression of a nominal, simplified design.

The well-known and widely used sans-serif font is Helvetica which was developed by Max Miedinger, and later popularized for computer publishing by addition with Apple PC's LaserWriter laser printer plus having been among the first easily available virtual typefaces. Arial, which has been made famous by MS, is among the most popular Helvetica substitutes. Still, other fonts like Frutiger, Gill Sans, Univers, and Futura have remained relevant over the years.

4.7. CAMEL CASE TEXT

Camel case refers to the activity of writing texts such that every word or its short form at the center of the phrase starts with capital letter, having no overriding spaces or punctuation. Some common examples are "eBay" and iPhone." It's also occasionally used in digital usernames like "John Smith," or to make the multi-word domain titles more legible, such as in advertisements.

Moreover, camel case is regularly used for variable titles in computer programming. A number of programming techniques prefer camel case whereby the first letter is capitalized, but not the rest. To provide more clarity, these two alternatives can be called upper camel case/Pascal case for the initial uppercase letter, while the lower camel case/Dromedary case is called the initial lowercase letter (Pearson Education, 2004).

There are individuals and companies, such as MS, which use the phrase camel case just for the lesser camel case. Here, Pascal case refers to just the uppermost camel case. The camel case is quite different from Title Case, that capitalizes words though still preserves the spaces existing amidst them, plus from Tall Man texting, which appplies capitals to highlight the differences present between same-looking words like "predniSOLONE" and "predniSONE" plus Camel case is also different from snake case that utilizes underscores interspersed using lowercase letters (occasionally with the initial letter capitalized) (Pearson Education, 2004). The mixture of camel case and snake is suggested in Ada 95 styling guide.

4.7.1. Word Groupings

The usage of medial capitals traditionally in the common spelling of everyday digital writings is rare, however, is used in various languages as an answer to certain problems that emerge when two texts or segments are merged. For Italian, pronouns may be suffixed onto verbs, and since the honorific type of 2nd person pronouns have been capitalized, it means this may create a word like Le meaning "to you."

For the English language, usually medial capitals are just found in the Irish or Scottish "Mc-" or "Mac-" names, whereby for instance McDonald, Macdonald, and MacDonald are typical spelling variants pointing to the same name, while in Anglo-Norman names such as "Fitz-" are applied for referring to Fitzgerald or FitzGerald.

Furthermore, medial capitals are typically applied in abbreviations to represent the capitalization which the letters would have if written out in complete digital text. Such as, in academic titles BSc and PhD. For other languages like German, statutes may be abbreviated through embedded capitals, such as, standing for Patentgesetz (Patent Act). Within this context, there may even be more than two camel case capitals (Pearson Education, 2004).

4.7.2. Uses of Camel Case in Multimedia

The usage of medial caps in compound identifiers has been highly recommended by coding style procedures of many companies or software projects. Moreover, for other languages like Java, Pascal, Modula, and NET from MS, the activity is recommended a lot by language developers, as well as authoritative manuals where it has become a component of the language's "ethos."

Style guidelines typically distinguish between the upper and bottom camel case, usually specifying the variety that must be applied for certain types of entities: such as record fields, methods, types, variables, and procedures.

The rules are occasionally sustained by static analysis equipment that review source code for conformity. The first Hungarian notation used for programming, case in point, stipulates that a lowercase acronym for the "usage form" (rather than data type) must prefix the variable names, and with the rest of the name having upper camel case; therefore, it's a type of lesser camel case.

Additionally, programming identifiers typically must contain initialisms and acronyms which are presently in uppercase, like "old HTML file." Through analogy with the heading case rules, a natural camel case interpretation would have the acronym all in uppercase, such as "oldHTMLFile." Nevertheless, this technique is problematic whenever a pair of acronyms happen together (for instance, "parse DBM XML" shall become "parseDBMXML") or whenever the standard requires lower camel case though the name starts with an abbreviation (e.g., "SQL server" will become "sQLServer"). Due to this reason, there are programmers who prefer treating abbreviations like they were lowercased words and mention "sqlServer," "oldHtmlFile," or "parseDbmXml." Nevertheless, this may make it difficult to remember that a particular word is mentioned as an abbreviation (Pearson Education, 2004).

4.7.3. Wikilink Identifier

Camel case text is sometimes applied in wiki markup dialects for terms which should be mechanically linked to each other's wiki pages. The convention was initially applied in Ward Cunningham's first wiki software, commonly known as WikiWikiWeb, plus it's easily activated in different other wikis also. Furthermore, some wiki engines like PmWiki, TiddlyWiki, and Trac widely use the markup language in default settings,

However, it usually also offers a configuration system or plug-in for disabling it wherever necessary. Wikipedia initially made use of camel case links also, but swapped to clear link markup through square brackets plus many other wiki sites also have performed the same thing. There are wikis that no longer apply camel case links, but still use camel case for naming conventions, like About Us.

4.7.4. Further Uses

The NIEM data registry needs that XML information elements apply XML and upper camel-case attributes apply the lower camel case also. Many common command-line platforms and scripting languages can't effortlessly handle file names which contain embedded spaces (typically requiring that the name should be placed in quotes). As such, the users of these systems typically go back to camel case (such as underscores, hyphens or other "safe" characters) when handling compound file names such as "MyJobResume. pdf."

Moreover, social networking and microblogging websites which restrict the amount of characters found in a message may be probable channels for medial capitals.

By using camel case texts between words, this can help minimize the amount of spaces, therefore the total amount of characters, for a given message, permitting more content to be added into the little space available. Hashtags, particularly long ones, typically use camel case for maintaining high readability levels. For instance, #UniversityStudentIssues is easier to read than #universitystudentissues).

For website links, spaces may also be percent-encoded like "%40," which makes the address much longer and not very human readable. But by removing spaces, camel case really doesn't have this issue (Pearson Education, 2004).

4.7.5. Text Data Files

There are two common data programming schemes for text which are Plain text (ASCII) and Rich text. The first one is an electronic text format which can be easily be read and understood by people. As for rich text, it's similar however, it also contains special control elements within the text that provide extra features. As a proprietary document, rich text was originally invented by MS for use in cross-platform file exchange with MS items. This system supports text formatting like underlining, bold, and italics including different types of fonts, sizes, and colored texts. On the contrary, plain text isn't computationally tagged, uniquely formatted or captured in code (Pearson Education, 2004).

4.8. RICH TEXT

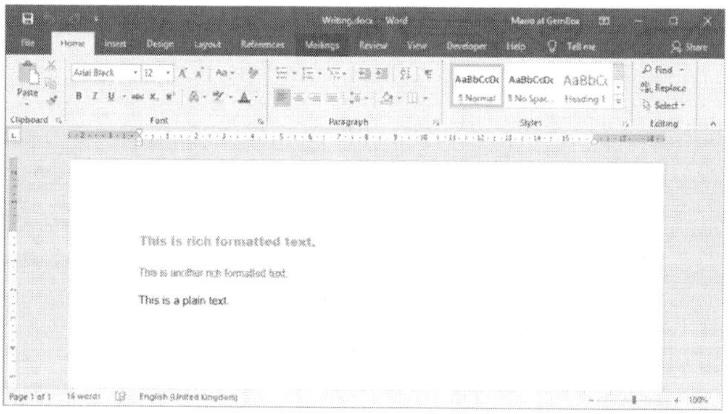

Figure 4.3. Rich Text words can be edited and improved to meet the user's specifications.

Source: *https://www.gemboxsoftware.com/document/examples/c-sharp-vb-net-create-write-word-file/302.*

Generally, RTF is the most readable of all word processors. Rich text documents are compatible with text style formatting, including images found in the text. The RTF files may also be changed into a unique format by modifying the formatting choice when saving the file document.

The majority of word processors can read or write some forms of RTF. Besides, there are many different amendments of RTF specification as well as file portability, depending on the edition of RTF that's being used. However, it must not be mistaken for enriched text, nor IBM's RFT-DCA which are totally different text specifications. Nowadays, most releases of

MS Word for Macintosh devices, including all editions for Windows can easily be read and written in RTF text format. MS, however, still holds legal rights to the format. RTF's final edition was 1.9.1 which was released in 2008, applying features of the Office 07 Suite and other enhancements.

4.8.1. Character Programming

A typical RTF file may comprise of just 7-bit ASCII features, however, it can encode fonts beyond ASCII through escape sequences. Character escapes come in two main types: which are code page escapes as well as, beginning with RTF 1.5, the Unicode escapes.

For a typical code page escape, there are two hexadecimal digits that follow a backslash and the typewriter apostrophe, which are applied for signifying a character derived from a Windows coding page.

To benefit programs that don't have Unicode support, the text should be followed with a close representation of the character within a unique code page. Case in point, \u1576? Can be given the Arabic lettering bā ب, stipulating that older programs lacking Unicode support must consider it to be a question-mark instead.

The control text \uc0 can be applied to show that successive Unicode escape structures within the existing group don't stipulate the substitution character. Up to when RTF specification edition 1.5 was released in 1997, the RTF has just handled 7-bit fonts directly with 8-bit characters programmed as hexadecimal through the \'xx command. Generally, RTF control words also accept signed 16-bit integers as arguments.

Unicode digits higher than 32767 should be conveyed as negative numbers for easier understanding. When a Unicode character falls outside BMP, it means that it's programmed using a surrogate pair. The support for Unicode systems was done because of text handling alterations in MS Word –for instance, MS Word 97 functions as a partly Unicode-allowed application plus it handles text through the 16-bit Unicode text encoding scheme (Figliola and Stevens, 2012).

Moreover, MS Word 2000 and subsequent editions are Unicode-allowed applications which handle text through the 16-bit Unicode text encoding scheme. The RTF files mostly are 7-bit ASCII simple text. RTF comprises of control words, symbols, as well as groups. Additionally, RTF files can effortlessly be transferred between computer-based OSs, since they're encoded in form of text files with 7-bit pictorial ASCII characters.

Additionally, converters that interact with Microsoft for MS Windows and Macintosh must anticipate data transfer as mostly 8-bit characters, besides binary data may consist of any 8-bit integers. In terms of human readability, RTF is mainly a data format used for saving as well as sharing documents, rather than a markup language. It's not meant for intuitive and simple typing by an individual.

Nevertheless, unlike most word processing styles, the RTF code may be human-readable: whenever an RTF file having mostly Latin characters but without diacritics is seen in form of plain text file, it means that the fundamental ASCII text is comprehensible, given that the originator has kept formatting brief – else, the formatting code may hinder readability.

During the time when RTF was launched, majority of word processors made use of binary file formats (MS Word utilized the. doc file layout); RTF was special in its basic formatting control that permits for a non-RTF recognition program (such as, Notepad) to expose and deliver a readable file. Nowadays, most of these systems have been converted to the XML-based text format (for instance, Word has swapped to the. docx text format). Notwithstanding, these files comprise of large quantities of formatting code.

Therefore, they are 10 or more times bigger than the equivalent plain text. For the program to become standard-compliant RTF, it means that non-ASCII fonts must be escaped. Consequently, even with precise formatting, text that applies some dashes and quotation characters is less legible (Patricia MoloneyFigliola and Gina Marie Stevens, 2012).

The Latin languages which make great use of characters featuring diacritics, like\'e9 for é and \'f1 for ñ are especially hard to understand in RTF. As for Non-Latin scripts, comprising of characters like \u21563 are also unreadable in RTF. Furthermore, from its very start, RTF has backed MS OLE embedded items and Macintosh Version Manager Subscription items, which aren't human-readable.

4.8.2. Typical Uses and Interoperability

Many word processing applications support RTF format for importation and exporting of texts (following some edition of RTF specification), plus direct editing, typically making it a "regular" format amid otherwise mismatched word processing apps and OSs. These features contribute towards its interoperability; besides it also depends on the specific RTF version being used. There are various consciously developed or unintentionally spun RTF dialects. Many applications who read RTF texts silently ignore unfamiliar RTF control words.

The RTF is an internal markup dialects used by MS Word. Generally, since 1987, RTF folders can be transferred interchangeably between a number of old and modern computer systems (plus now over the Web) despite dissimilarities between OSs as well as their versions. This makes the text a valuable format for simple formatted text documents like instruction manuals, letters, résumés and moderate information documents. The files at minimum support italic, bold as well as underline formatting (Figliola and Stevens, 2012).

Plus, also commonly supported are the left-, central-, and right-aligned texts, font design and document margins. Both font and margin arrangements, including style presets and different other systems vary depending on the program defaults. Equally, there might be subtle variances perhaps between diverse forms of the RTF description applied in differing programs as well as program versions. However, the RTF file setup is still consistent enough from one PC to another, so as to be regarded highly portable and suitable for cross-platform usage. The structure supports metadata like title, author, and so on, however, not all applications support this.

4.8.3. Texts for Objects and Pictures

The use of MS Object Linkage and Embedding objects, or Macintosh Version Manager Subscription objects restricts the interoperability, since these objects aren't broadly supported in applications for checking or editing RTF texts (for instance, embedding of other documents inside the RTF, like charts or tables from worksheet application (Figliola and Stevens, 2012).

In case a software which understands the OLE object isn't available, then the item is typically replaced with a photo (bitmap depiction of the item) or not shown at all. For photos, RTF supports addition of JPEG, Enhanced Metafile (EMF), Windows Metafile (WMF) and Portable Network Graphics (PNG), but not every one of these photo types are recognized in RTF readers.

Moreover, whenever the RTF text is launched in software which doesn't support the photo style of an inserted image, such an image isn't shown at all. The RTF writers typically convert inserted photos from an unconfirmed picture type (such as, GIF, BMP, and TIFF) onto one of supported photo types (WMF, PNG) or even they don't add photos at all.

For improved compatibility with MS products, there are RTF writers who add the same photo in two unique picture types, which are in a single file for RTF. Moreover, the Windows Metafile copy can be included into the program without factoring any compression. The technique helps to increase the RTF folder size considerably. The RTF specification doesn't need this method, besides there are multiple implementations that comprise of images without the WMF copies (example, Ted or Abiword)

As for MS Word, it's also plausible to set a particular registry value such as ("ExportPictureWithMetafile=0"), for purposes of preventing Word texts from automatically saving the WMF transcript. In terms of Fonts, RTF backs embedding of fonts applied in the document, though this feature isn't extensively supported in software applications. RTF is further compatible with generic font group names applied for font substitution: swiss (sans-serif), roman (serif), script, modern (monospace), decorative, and technical. The feature isn't broadly supported for font switches, for example, in Abiword or OpenOffice. org (Figliola and Stevens, 2012).

RTF specification also supports annotations or comments in texts, since edition 1.0 was launched. The RTF 1.7 specification also defined certain new aspects for annotations: like date stamp (previously there was just "time stamp") including parents of annotations. Whenever an RTF text with annotations get launched in an application which doesn't support RTF annotations, it means that they aren't shown at all.

Likewise, whenever a file having annotations is saved in form of RTF within an application which doesn't support RTF annotations, it means the annotations won't be preserved within the RTF folder. A few implementations might hide annotations on default or need some operator action to showcase them. MS products nevertheless don't allow comments inside footers, headers or footnotes.

Putting a comment inside headers, footnotes or footers can lead to a corrupted RTF file. The RTF system also covers footnotes (but shouldn't be mistaken for annotations), which are usually supported in RTF applications (for example, in Abiword, KWord, OpenOffice. org and Ted, though not in Wordpad).

Also, endnotes are applied as a variant on footnotes so that applications which support footnotes rather than endnotes may render endnotes in form of RTF texts as footnotes. Same as annotations, since MS products don't support footnotes when used in headers, footers, and comments, plus footnotes within those frameworks in an RTF text may cause a corrupted file (Figliola and Stevens, 2012).

4.9. PLAIN TEXT

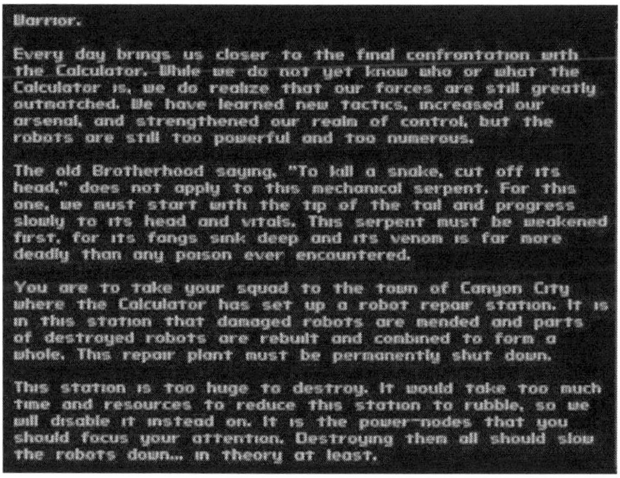

Figure 4.4. Plain Text files are only meant for reading and cannot be modified.

Source: *https://www.dafont.com/forum/read/48056/computer-screen-font.*

By definition, Plain text refers to any text, file or document which has only text. Different from rich-text files, the plain text version can't have features such as fonts, changeable font sizes, bold text, or some other unique text formatting. Many people relate plain text documents with the document extension. txt on MS Windows computers, though, it can still be any non-formatted document. In order to check a plaintext document, a text editor like MS Notepad is used. But, all text editors comprising MS WordPad and Word may also be applied to watch plaintext files since they don't have any special formatting (Pearson Education, 2004).

For computing, plain text can be described as a loose word for data (example, file contents) which showcase only letters of readable content though not the graphical representation, or other separate objects (images, floating-point integers, and so on.). Furthermore, it may consist of a limited amount of characters which control basic text arrangement, like line breaks, spaces, and tabulation characters (even though tab characters may "mean" various different things, hence are barely "plain").

Similarly, plain text is unique from formatted text, in which style data is covered; from structured text, whereby structural aspects of the document like sections, paragraphs, and so on are identified; plus from binary files where some aspects should be inferred as binary objects (real numbers, images, and encoded integers, etc.).

The phrase is sometimes also loosely used to mean documents that feature just "readable" text (or only texts with nothing which the speaker doesn't select). For instance, that could omit any indication of layout or fonts (like markdown, markup, or even tabs); including characters like curly quotes, soft hyphens, non-breaking spaces, as well as dashes, and ligatures.

Primarily, plain text may be in any text programming, however, occasionally the phrase is taken to simply mean ASCII. With Unicode-based encodings like UTF-8 and UTF-16 growing more popular, it means the usage of plain text may lessen.

The plain text file is also occasionally used simply to differentiate from "binary" files, where at least some aspects of the file can't be correctly understood through the character programming in effect. For instance, a string or file comprising of the word "hello" (in whichever encoding), followed by four bytes which express a binary integer that's not simply a character, can be classified as a binary text, and not plain text (Pearson Education, 2004).

Said another way, interpreting the plain-text file to some character encoding which uses totally different integers to represent characters, won't alter the meaning (as long as you understand what encoding is being used), though for binary files the conversion may alter the implication of a few aspects of the file. Texts that feature markup or some other meta-data are normally considered plain-text, as long as their markup is equally in openly human-readable form (like in XML, HTML, and others).

Equally, punctuation is by itself markup; besides nobody considers punctuation for disqualifying a file from getting labeled as plain text). Usage of plain text instead of binary files, allows files to endure much better "through the wild," partly by making them generally immune to workstation architecture incompatibilities.

Case in point, all the glitches of Endianness may be prevented (with encodings like UCS-2 instead of UTF-8, endianness materials, but consistently for every character, instead of potentially-unknown subgroups of it. Based on the Unicode Principle: Plain text is just a plain series of character codes; the plain Un-encoded script is thus a structure of Unicode letter codes. Styled text, is also another word that can be used to refer to rich text (Pearson Education, 2004).

4.9.1. APPLICATION

The main purpose of using plain-text nowadays is basically independence from programs which need their own unique encoding or structuring or file format. The plain text documents can easily be opened, seen, and edited using ubiquitous text editors as well as utilities. Furthermore, a command-line interface permits people to provide directives in plain text then get a response, which usually is in plain text. Most other computer applications are equally able to process or formulate plain text, like multiple programs in Windows, DOS, Unix, and Classic Mac OS; including web browsers (some browsers like Line Mode Browser and Lynx also produce just plain text for show) including other e-text readers.

Furthermore, plain text files are practically all-inclusive in encoding; the source code file having instructions in the programming language is nearly often a plain text folder. Plain text is additionally used for configuration documents that are read for protected settings at the beginning of the program.

Plain texts are equally used for most e mail texts, TXT Records and ." txt" file extensions. These files don't require any formatting and are easy to comprehend by humans. The most ideal format for keeping knowledge consistently is plain text, instead of some binary layout. Before the 60s, workstations were mostly used for figure-crunching instead of text, besides digital memory was quite expensive. Workstations often assigned just 6 bits for every character, allowing just 64 characters—conveying codes for letters A-Z, a-z, as well as 0–9 can leave just 2 codes: which is nowhere near sufficient.

Many computers chose not to include lower-case letters. Therefore, early text programs such as Index Thomisticus and Brown Corpus, among others needed to resort back to conventions like keying an asterisk that precede letters essentially meant to be upper-case. IBM argued solidly for advancing to the next level of 8-bit bytes, since someday people may wish to process text; for which they won the case.

Even though IBM applied EBCDIC, majority of texts henceforth came to be programmed in ASCII, applying values ranging from 0 up to 31 for the (non-printing) control elements, plus values 32 up to 127 for object characters like letters, punctuation, and digits. Many machines stored characters using 8 bits instead of 7, thus ignoring the remainder bit or applying it in form of a checksum. The almost-ubiquity of ASCII came as a decent help, though failed to handle global and linguistic concerns. Furthermore, the dollar-sign ("$") initially wasn't quite useful in England, besides the accented characters applied in Spanish, German, and French languages among others were totally unattainable in ASCII

Many people, firms, and nations described extra characters as required—often reallocating control characters, or applying value in the scale from 128 up to 255. Applying values above 128 differs with applying the 8th bit in form of a checksum, though the checksum application gradually faded. These extra characters were programmed differently in varying countries, thus making texts difficult to decode without determining the originator's guidelines. For example, a browser may show ¬A instead of ` if it attempted to interpret a particular character set in place of another. The International Organization for Standards (ISO) ultimately developed multiple code pages through ISO 8859, for purposes of accommodating different languages. The earliest of these (ISO 8859–1) has been named "Latin-1," covering the needs of many European languages which use Latin-based letterings (there wasn't quite adequate room to capture them all).

Later, ISO 2022 provided methods for "switching" between diverse character sets through mid-file. A number of other organizations established variations on these, besides for several years both Windows and Macintosh processors used mismatched variations. Equally the text-encoding state became quite complex, prompting efforts by ISO as well as the Unicode Consortium towards developing one, unified character programming which could cover various known languages. Following some conflict, these efforts eventually got unified. Presently unicode permits for 1,114,112 coding values, besides assigns codes that cover almost all modern text lettering systems, plus many historical elements and multiple non-linguistic characters like mathematical symbols and printer's dingbats.

Most text is regarded as plain-text despite its encoding. To fully understand or even process it then the recipient should know (or alternatively determine) what kind of encoding was used; nevertheless, they need not understand anything concerning the computer architecture which was used, or even the binary systems defined by whichever program (if any) developed the data. Probably, the most renowned way of openly stating the particular programming of plain text documents is with the MIME form. For http and email, the automatic MIME form is "text/plain"—the plain text lacking markup.

Yet another MIME form commonly used in email as well as http is the "text/html; or charset=UTF-8"—a plain text symbolized using the UTF-8-

character programming with HTML markup. Still another regular MIME form is "application/json" – a plain text symbolized using the UTF-8-character programming with JSON markup. Once a file is obtained without any explicit sign of the character programming, some applications apply char set detection to seek to guess what programming was used.

ASCII reserves the initial 32 codes (numerals 0–31 decimal) for management characters called the "C0 set": these codes initially were meant not to signify printable information, instead to manage devices (like printers) which use ASCII, or providing meta-information concerning data streams like those kept on magnetic tape. These include common characters such as the newline plus the tab character. For 8-bit character sets like Latin-1 including other different ISO 8859 groups, the initial 32 characters that constitute the "upper half" from numbers (128 to 159) are likewise control codes, referred to as the "C1 group."

They're rarely applied directly; once they show up in texts which are seemingly in the ISO 8859 programming, their code positions normally refer instead to various letterings at that point in a proprietary, system-focus encoding, like Mac OS Roman or Windows-1252, which apply the codes to rather provide extra graphic characters.

Furthermore, unicode defines extra control features, such as dual-directional text direction that override characters (applied to explicitly indicate right-to-left writing within left-to-right writing plus the opposite way around) plus variation selectors to choose alternate types of emoji, CJK ideographs and different other characters.

4.9.2. Designing Using Text

When message forms part of a collaborative project or website, whereby users seek information then a great amount of text may be displayed onto the screen. Negligible text on the computer screen needs annoying page turns plus unnecessary mouse clicks as well as waits. Contrarily, too much text may make the screen look overcrowded and unpleasant. Typography is described as the model and exercise of letter as well as typeface design. Meaning, it's an art that's concerned with design features which can be used on letters and texts (Cranny-Francis, 2005).

In its wider sense, typography has ancient roots that trace back to ancient alphabets, hieroglyphic pictures and ideograms. Up to today, a few of its terminology as well as its styles trace back to methods of lapidary inscription which were prevalent in antiquity Rome and Athens. Though strictly speaking, the practice itself remains in printing's history since it was simply with the arrival of print media—including the formation of the standardized, duplicative sets of typeface formats, called fonts—where a proper craft or applied discipline of typography started to emerge.

Formerly a concern mostly of publishers and newspaper editors, the art of typography has nowadays become, with the exponential growth of multipurpose digital-publishing and word-processing implements, a text feature which no hopeful communicator can consider lightly or ignore. Especially with the vast range of font choices available in the current times, the opportunity of facilitating, magnifying, impeding, lessening, intensify, and subduing the effect of a message through modifying typographic variables is even greater than before.

Typography mostly focuses on the style and dimension of typefaces. For printing, a full set of type (comprising of letters, numerals, punctuation marks, or other unique symbols) having the same style or size is known as font. For computerized word processors, the font is a specific kind of typeface of whichever size (Cranny-Francis, 2005).

Most fonts are distinguished in two ways which are; serif versus. non-serif as well as variable width versus. fixed width. The Serifs are unique finishing stokes (running horizontal and vertical) which can be used on letters to create a chiseled, lapidary appearance. Variable width fonts apply proportional spacing between the letters, grouping them together in some instances (note, for instance, the compacted "tt" in the term "letter") whereas widening them out for others. Contrarily, fixed width fonts apply the same spacing amongst letters despite of their dimension or shape.

4.9.3. Points

The overall scope of a typeface can be measured in terms of points: A single point is equal to 1/72 of the inch. Therefore, the 72- point form is 1-inch in height—when measured from the highest stage of the ascender (example., the climbing stroke in "l") up to the lowermost descender (example., the dipping stroke in "p"). Therefore, for example, the term 'lip' in 36-point size shall print out to precisely half inch from the highest of the "l" up to the base of the "p."

Generally talking, most readers prefer going through documents in the 12-point format. Anything less than 10 points seems small and forbidding—same as the tiny print on a lawful contract or insurance sheet. Besides, the fact that only a few individuals ever get to read fine print is exactly the reason behind its existence: the entire purpose is to efficiently conceal data while supposedly publishing it; certainly it's print particularly developed not for reading but artwork) (Cranny-Francis, 2005).

4.9.4. Style Features

Another typographic variable which has a significant impact on the look, texture, and influence of a word, text, or text section is the supposed style attribute (for instance, bold, underlining, and italic, etcetera.) Great communication is mainly an aspect of putting more emphasis and attention, meaning, you need to capture your reader's attention while directing it principally to the key aspects of your message.

Most style attributes, particularly in combination with other types of typographic structures and layout aspects (spacing, for instance), can be of assistance. Certainly it's crucial to remember that whichever discrepancy in the look of a text—particularly a variation highlighting a particular portion of text or differentiating it from the immediate context—may serve to provide emphasis as well as direct the reader's attention.

A lot of font improvements and typographic twists entered onto one page—or continued over a whole document—may really distract or numb a reader's concentration and dilute emphasis. In case there's one recurrent vice that's characteristic of contemporary publishing—particularly electronic publishing—it's the too much application of colorful highlights, colorful flourishes and vibrant fonts. Ultimately, the main goal isn't effective communication instead just mere sensationalism. A brightly colored text often has an especially strong impact. The blinking text, on the contrary, is a great way of pulling attention, though a rather poor way of transmitting complex messages. Also of importance is the layout, which refers to the general design and look of the printed page-especially with regards to positioning and organization of page elements (Cranny-Francis, 2005).

CHAPTER

5

Multimedia Networks

CONTENTS

5.1. INTRODUCTION

In all multimedia applications, multimedia data is pressed then passed on through the network to reach its destination and when received its opened and organized for usage at the received location. Multimedia information systems have allowed the user to regain back, store, and organize different types of data which include images, video, and audio. Multimedia computing has evolved over the years as a field of constant research with close observation in this field we get to see that multimedia can be said it's a combination of three industries, e.g., computer, communication, and also broadcasting industries. With development and research as the two main fields in multimedia networks, in the first area of research, a lot of effort has been put in on the stand-alone network workrooms and the associated software systems and tools such as the composition of music, computer-aided education and training, and video interactive video. With the merging of multimedia computing with distributed systems has created great yields. In turn, new applications that really on distributed multimedia systems include multimedia information systems, collaborative, and also video conferencing systems are on-demand for multimedia services and distance learning. Multimedia communications have developed a protocol for the proper exchange of media and it called the Multimedia Exchange Network over satellite

There are various network requirements needed for the smooth transmission of multimedia data but first traditional networks such as Ethernet, token ring, fiber distributed data interface (FDDI) and Integrated services digital network (ISDN) have evolved over the years and with the new adverse networks have dominated the multimedia market. Tradition media has generally been used in the marketing or the advertising world for several years now and in advertising traditional networks include television ads, newspapers, radio, and magazines. Over the years they are the most commonly used types of communication that are used by businesses to reach the clients and other businesses. Traditional media has several characteristics like its more about the institution as compared with the new modern media which is about the client; traditional media is pre-made and programmed to a particular time frame while the modern media happens in real-time; traditional methods in multimedia might be the oldest method in communication but they cannot be eliminated from the field anytime soon. Despite their capability, over the years, new media has taken over the market. The new modern media is very easy to access through many forms of digital media and in the field of advertising some examples include online, e.g., retargeting, banner ads and many more, or the streaming of online, e.g., radio and television and last the social media advertising. Whereby all of them have the potential to reach consumers and various businesses with a lot of ease (Barz and Bassett, 2016).

Hence, with traditional multimedia methods tending to be more expensive than the modern media but reaching a big audience, modern multimedia methods have allowed businesses to target ads more specifically within the client based age, gender, and marital status. With each day more clients use the internet too quickly and easily to find information giving the new media more advantages as opposed to the old media but also radios and televisions and magazines are still being used hence this creates a harmony between the two methods.

5.2. ADVANTAGES AND DISADVANTAGES TRADITIONAL MULTIMEDIA

Below is a closer look at the advantages and disadvantages of each form of traditional multimedia;

- In radio advertising it has several advantages which are instant delivery of messages which can be repeated several times, low cost used to reach the audience and reaches a specifically selected audience. Its disadvantages are, has very limited audio messages, messages expire immediately with a very high channel switching.
- In newspaper advertising, it has high local coverage and a daily supply for new information to the locals, covers a large population of people, it's an interactive medium, has special sections for shopping guides and other products. Its disadvantages are it has a low life span; it's hard to target a specific audience.
- In television advertising, messages can be repeated severally and reach the audience immediately, has a very high impact on the audience, reaches the highest number of audience but it has a very big cost for production and airtime usage, it reaches a limited audience only those who can afford a television set.

The traditional multimedia systems are hindered by cost and travel expenses but with the new modern media video conferencing has reduced the cost and travel expenses. It has enabled clients and groups to meet face to face without even moving from their comfort places of work, video conferencing has made work become more effective and improves communication within the organization. With this form of communication, it has become the most convenient way to accomplish traditional duties. Because these conferences are much convenient to do than regular meetings, whereby conference is done with more people but at a very low cost. Videoconferencing is also useful for the delivery of broadcast (one-way) audio-video streams. The cost and network challenges are significant but in cases where important delivery of news is highly important such as financial service companies, the network supporting multimedia broadcasts is rapidly installed (Barz and Bassett, 2016).

Traditional media has no accuracy because it has no specific target of the audience at once while modern media has precise accuracy because it targets a specific audience. Traditional media forces an opinion on the buyer and hopes the clients pick them but with modern media, the client can learn about the products online first then buy them. Modern media has a feedback option where one can hear from the customers directly as opposed to traditional media which is one way.

Traditional media is fully based on advertising while digital media is not about advertising it's a tool to create awareness and develop attitudes about the product rather than promote purchase. Digital media is not only data-driven but one can predict the returns and one can improve the marketing efforts.

Traditional media targets a wider audience while social media offers a more targeted audience. Social media is done on the stop as opposed to traditional which is sometimes delayed due to press of timeframe. Social media is dynamic and it can be owned so one can alter any information and adjust it to suit the desired information but in traditional, once information is passed on its final it cannot be changed especially on radios or televisions. Social media gives more control over the information from the publication from time to time when to post it (Barz and Bassett, 2016).

Multimedia networks have also greatly benefitted students as it has brought experts online to help and guide appropriately, also it has allowed students to select courses online that suits them and helps students to schedule their timetable with a lot of ease. Multimedia has several advantages which include increased learning potential, it attracts and maintains attention, significantly reduces training cost, very easy to use, provides high-quality work, it very multi-sensory it uses the senses of many clients such as hearing, sight, and speech. It's very flexible because it can be changed anytime to fit the audience who are present at the time or in different situations. It can also be used for a variety of audiences ranging from one to a group and from the young generation to older generations. It covers a very big part from mobile phones to blockbuster movies also coding of websites, software, and apps and also the film industry.

5.3. MULTIMEDIA NETWORK APPLICATIONS

Multimedia network has many applications in many different fields and below are some;

- In the academic field, learning has become easier, more effective and exciting in schools, colleges, and universities through the use of informational videos, animation, and documentary. Besides, introducing it to children at a young age they become computer-friendly and in later years the knowledge they have gained from multimedia helps them to select various fields in which they can major in.
- By putting up advertisements on billboards, televisions, newspapers, and cinema halls have greatly helped in the growth of businesses.
- By the use of music, movies, shows, and news are all means of multimedia and they help to transmit information.
- PowerPoint presentations are used in offices, events, and institutions is the most common method of multimedia usage, and it shows brief organized content to the students, colleagues or business proposals.
- Multimedia usage can be used in video games, research works, and products. Also, it is used in journalism fields or even magazines and also multimedia plays a big role in many aspects like Facebook; Twitter, Google plus; Pinterest and also in the news channels or even in the science and technology fields.

In multimedia networks especially the entertainment industry, job opportunities have been developed and in turn revenue has increased but has brought life to animation for computer drawings and characters on seen; digital pens have evolved whereby the drawing sketches are done on computers, not like older days when it was done on paper by use of hands; for graphic designers, architectural sets for applying specific forms and this include web designing and graphic designing; a planner in animation is the person who plans the background in games to get 3D image setup. Editors' main job is to watch content, summarize it, make the necessary changes and removes what is not wanted all through the help of multimedia networks. Music composers and movie builders have developed their different fields significantly through the help of the media. Writers who plotting, putting, and outlining the contents of a story use this media too. Preproduction which comes before the animation of a film starts and postproduction which involves the final steps of a film editing, adding voice characters and dubbing are all ways in which multimedia networks have made an impact (Al-Khatib and Alam, 2007).

Multimedia has played a very big role in the education sector, e.g., it has made education very easy for children with special needs; it greatly encourages the students to learn more; for small children, it is easier for them to learn using images rather than text; students with pronunciation problems audios can come in handy; graphics add an interesting turn in learning; in this day and age small children have started learning at a very early age because of multimedia. On the other hand, multimedia has also its disadvantage if students are left to complete studies on their own as they move in different stages of learning the classroom management will be very difficult, because the students are different others are fast learners on the internet others are slow even to understand the basic concept. The expenses of buying quality projectors or computers might be very high for every student to have one and also the amount of time used to download images and videos in a classroom can significantly slow down the pace of the classroom

Multimedia journalism involves the use of texts, images, sound, video clips, graphics to tell stories in a more interesting and capturing nature. A multimedia journalist works for newspapers, televisions, radios or uses computers in social media areas. Multiplatform journalism is a big scope of the field that deals with economical and technology coverage have greatly affected the production, distribution, and consumption of news. Texts, still photographs, video clips, audio graphics when they are brought together they form a multimedia story. Media coverage is the combining of multiple media forms into one place to create a vast experience. Media can be divided into four classes which include printed media, e.g., newspapers and magazines, broadcast media, e.g., television and radio, outdoor or out of home media (OOH) and the internet. New media involves the following examples websites, mobile apps, virtual worlds, multimedia, computer games, human-computer interface, computer animation, and interactive computer installations. New media has been used widely by social media to educate, organize, and share cultural products, movements, and communication. The function of mass media is to let the audience know what's happening around and the truth. New media serves as an important tool for organizations and the nation at large to upgrade their desires and values (Al-Khatib and Alam, 2007).

In today's world, media has become an important tool just like our basic needs, playing that important role in shaping and creating the public and also strengthening of society. When media is used in a democracy it becomes a very lethal tool because it can be either used for peaceful politics or even to start a war if used in an abusive manner. It has also helped to create awareness in the society by gathering views, information, and the attitude of the people towards particular pressing issues. With the intervention of things like satellite, microphone, machinery, and cameras has made life very comfortable to the man from day today. Before ruling out information it's good to find news from multiple sources to be certain about it. In a democratic society, the journalists and the management are expected to use their judgment wisely to create a perfect balance and to check the powers of government and also the businesses in society.

The media is expected to create transparency and trustworthy information to the public without being biased. Free media is the backbone of true democracy and without it, democracy cannot even run smoothly, media is the fourth pillar of governance, the public can use the media to give their ideas in favor of the government or even criticize it for not delivering on its promises or even poor performance.

About 5 years back the media fraternity was divided into two classes which are the electronic media and the print media. However, today a third force has evolved, which is very effective and strong and it's the social media taking over.

Politicians, health care providers, and the public need clear information about the benefits and dangerous effects of the drugs in the market to help them decide what is good for them and what is not. With good communication, the selection of messages and media must go hand in hand with the culture and beliefs of the public so as they can understand the concept and use it comfortably (Al-Khatib and Alam, 2007).

Electronic media uses electromechanical devices to gain permission for the content. By getting people from different places together through the media facilities electronic media has made communication very easy and with it has come many advantages in mass communication;

- People are educated more through media about the current politics and the environment surrounding them;
- Electronic media creates awareness for the public about the world and what's happening;
- Electronic media has helped educate farmers on proper ways to farm and increase their outputs;
- Besides, people can learn about different cultural events around the world; and
- The public gains more knowledge through the media especially today's children have a very sharp mind and learn very fast.

In short, multimedia networks have very many advantages and have a very big impact on the world but it depends on the human race to learn how to use it properly and not to abuse it and create a positive effect.

In multimedia networks, media is divided into 3 general classes and this includes coaxial cable, twisted pair, and the fiber optic cable. The unshielded twisted pair (UTP) is the one commonly used for network cabling used nowadays. The path through which electrical signals move from one point to another is called the network media.

The twisted-pair cabling is a form of cable that is used for telephone communication and Ethernet networks. This is many wires paired together forming a circuit that can pass on data. The wires are coiled together to protect against crosstalk, to reduce the noise created by adjacent wires. Under this class of twisted pair cable it's subdivided into two;

- The unshielded twisted pair (UTP) cable is made up of wires that are used in different networks. The UTP cable is covered by insulating materials; the wires of each pair are connected. This cable depends on the cancellation effect produced by the paired wires to reduce the signal degradation caused by electromagnetic interference (EMI) and radio frequency interference (RFI). To eliminate crosstalk between the pairs in UTP cable the number of twists in the wire varies. It is more exposed to electrical noise and interference than other types of networking media, hence reducing the distance between signal boosts is shorter for UTP than is coaxial fiber optic cables. UTP is slower at transmitting data but with time it's considered fastest due to it being a copper-based medium.
- Shielded twisted pair cable is very expensive and difficult to install as compared to UTP. If the metallic shielding has a good

foundation to enable good antenna signals if the foundation is not properly installed it will pick up unwanted signals. STP is rarely used in Ethernet networks because it's costly and very difficult stopping.

Coaxial cable is made up of a hollow external rounded conductor that circles a single inner wire made up of two conducting essentials. One of these essentials is located in the center of the cable and it's called the copper conductor. Surrounding the copper conductor is a layer of bendable insulators. Around this shielded material is a woven copper braid or metallic foil that works as the second wire in the path and as a protection for the inner conductor. This second protection greatly reduces the amount of external interference. Protecting this shield is the cable jacket. Coaxial cable is less costly than fiber optic cable and it's very common because it has been used for very many years for all types of data communication. It runs with less support from repeaters for longer distances between network nodes than either STP or UTP cable. Repeaters regenerate the signals in the network so that they can cover a greater distance. When working with the cable the thickness and size matter because as it increases in size it becomes difficult to work with. There are two types of coaxial cable;

- Thin or thinnet: This is a cable that is very flexible and easy to work with and it's normally used in any kind of installation. Networks that are on thinnet have the cable attached directly to the computer network adapter card.
- Thicknet or thick: This is at times known as the Standard Ethernet because it was the first cable to be used with the famous network architecture Ethernet. The copper interior is thicker than a thinnet interior.

In bounded medium signals are restricted to the channel and do not leave it, a good example is twisted pair, coaxial, and fiber optic cable. Unbounded medium signals emitted by the source flow into the channel and spread throughout it, e.g., microwave, radio, and infrared.

Ethernet is an old technology used for connecting wired local area networks (LANs) that help the devices to communicate with each other via a particular system. It is connected to the router and serves as a connector to the internet. The router is joined to the modem carrying the signal, transmitting, and retrieving data requests and connecting them to the right computers on the network. An Ethernet cable is the physical outer surrounding wiring through which the data is transmitted. The internet is a wide area network (WAN) that joins together a big number of devices around the globe while

Ethernet is the local area network (LAN) that covers a small geographical part. Ethernet cables are created from 8 wires that are coiled together into four pairs. The pairs are color-coded with a solid color and it stands for dashed or striped white. The cables are in two formats the solid and the stranded, the solid conductor is normally used in wiring buildings (Barz and Bassett, 2016).

5.4. MULTIMEDIA NETWORKS IN MARKETING

This is a method used to join together different forms of media to reach a specific target of audience and build brand recognition. These approaches use traditional media such as televisions, newspaper ads, and radio and direct a mail and also digital systems such as email, mobile, and social media.

Multimedia can spread the information quickly about a new company and help it build brand awareness, it's very powerful and also unique. Other marketing strategies that when used can mark a big difference in marketing are mobile marketing, live casting and podcasting, photo, video, and file sharing are some of them.

Multimedia plays a very big part in advertising, by use of many forms of multimedia to advertise the higher the chances of the product increasing in sales, creating a very big control over the market and gaining more fame.

The most common are television, radio, and print ads which are the most common medium used and still they play a big part in supporting each other (Barz and Gregory A. Bassett, 2016).

The benefits of multimedia learning are that it takes its benefit of brain power ability to make links between spoken and image representations of the substance, leading to a more thoughtful understanding, which then supports the transfer of learning to other situations.

Multimedia product refers to a product where the software allows the communication between the user and various media technologies like the reproduction of sound and image.

Multimedia has been used a lot in the entertainment world, particularly in developing special effects in movies and animation, e.g., VFX, 3D animation. Games which are played on the multimedia are very popular and they are software programs which are accessible either as CD- ROMs or online

5.5. IMPACT OF MULTIMEDIA NETWORKS IN AGRICULTURE

A multimedia network in the agriculture industry has evolved and information and computer technology in agriculture (ICT) also known as e-agriculture is specific on the reinforcement of agricultural and rural development by improving information and communication procedures. This involves creating, building, assessing, and applying new ways of information and communication technologies in the countryside. This field involves the devices, networks, mobiles, services, and the applications this includes innovative internet-era technologies and sensors to other olds school devices such a telephone, televisions, radios, and satellites. By providing up to standard tools, development, methods for the individuals or organization capacities are all main components of e-agriculture. Information and communication technologies in agriculture fields or e-agriculture involvement have been created and vetted around the globe to help farmers advance in their daily activities through bigger production and income or by reducing the risks.

Geographical information systems (GIS) are methods used generally in agriculture, especially inaccurate farming. Here the land is mapped and important geographical data like topography and contours are joined together with other important data for quick and easy testing of the soil. This method is used to determine what to plant and where it's suitable by using previous data and sampling.

In automatic milking systems also known as the voluntary milking systems, these are computer-controlled systems used for milking dairy cattle without human labor involved. This process is controlled by agriculture robots, complex herd software and with the help of expert computers. This process helps the farmer save time from the tedious milking process to creating more time for the farmer to supervise others' works around the farm. It greatly helps the farmers to analyze the effect on milk yields and they can adjust to achieve higher yields and also the effect of animal feeds. With the information being stored well in data, the farmers can track down each cow's information and be able to examine it and enabling the farmer to be well informed when there are unusual changes that would indicate the onset of diseases or injuries. With the intervention of Smartphone apps in the agriculture sector, animal husbandry, and farm machinery the farmers can keep up to date with the changing world and be able to adjust themselves accordingly. Multimedia networks in technology have helped to reduce time, the technology is used to supply water to big farms, e.g., drip systems, machines which have standard techniques are used in sowing of seeds in accurate rows and distance between and also in harvesting and plowing of big acres of land, also in the application of synthetic fertilizers and even spraying of chemical pest.

Multimedia networks have made technology possible because even farmers who are in desert places can be able to plant a variety of crops, that are resistant to the harsh climates and still be able to produce high yields to sustain them. With all the advantages multimedia has brought to the agricultural field there is also very important points that can make the system to fail, e.g., if the farmers lack practical knowledge to handle the machines properly or even to operate them, cost of maintenance of the machinery can be costly to the farmer to maintain if they breakdown, overuse of this machines may lead to environmental changes, with the society becoming more advanced in technology, people are becoming more and more dependent on computers and other forms of technology for their everyday livelihood; hence this is a very big disadvantage because when the machines break down or computers crash they become helpless until the problem is attended to.

This type of full dependency on technology has greatly made people become less self- reliant. This modern machinery such as tractors still has an added disadvantage like soil compaction because most of them are very big and heavy (Barz and Bassett, 2016).

To achieve the best out of agriculture by tthe use of technology it is good for farmers to seek expert help from agricultural experts or farmers who have a broader knowledge with the new technology and have already applied it and its successful.

The use of agricultural drone technology is also among the most important things in smart farming today. Given the job of surveying the crop and livestock conditions from above, their use of time lapsing inside the onboard cameras has helped farmers identify problems that would have gone undetected by the farmer such as irrigation and pest invasion.

Nanotechnology is a technique mostly applied in agricultural products. Used in protecting crops in the field by keeping a closer eye on the growth of the plants and detect the diseases present. Electroscope techniques are used in the absorption of fertilizers and pesticides in the field. Nanotechnology is also used in the study of plant hormones and its regulations while the carbon nanotubes are very useful in detecting and killing the pathogens and viruses seen in the crops (Hwang, 2009).

Through this adverse multimedia network, weather forecasters have been able to foretell the climate changes every single time and with this information, farmers can take up measures which can enable them to plant the right crops according to the weather patterns and still they can create in advance proper water catchments. By proper implementation of information communication technology to the field of agriculture it will become a very powerful tool in empowering both the economy and social status of the society.

5.6. SECURITY MECHANISMS IN MULTIMEDIA NETWORKS

With the big increase in the use of multimedia in day to day communications, it is important to develop good security systems for the transmission of information. Transmission of data by the use of streaming algorithms depends on the availability of the network bandwidth and the characteristics of the movie being streamed. By relying on these characteristics they will reveal the movie information even if it's encrypted, the experiment has shown results that movies can be known using their network traces. Below is a list of different network security devices and tools;

- By the use of access control users, can be able to restrict network access to only known users and devices or even give permission to limited access to noncompliant devices or guest users especially to the sensitive or private sections of the network.
- Malware or malicious software is the most common type of cyber-attack coming in different forms, some work quickly to erase files or even corrupt them while others are hidden for a long time and they allow hackers a back door into other people's systems. By installing the best antivirus and anti-malware software they will be able to keep an eye on the network traffic on the spot, scan activities with suspicious behaviors and even give solutions to eradicate these threats.
- Application of security is the joining together of hardware, software, and the best practices to use to monitor problems and close the gaps in security coverage. It is very important for the user to always keep the programs updated to prevent cyber attackers to access sensitive data.

- To spot abnormal behavior, security support personnel should establish a proper baseline of what makes up normal and abnormal behavior. Behavioral analytics software is created to help identify common indicators of abnormal behavior and can be a good sign that security invasion has occurred.
- Data loss prevention technologies (DLP) are those that prevent an institution's employees from giving out valuable company information or sensitive data either unsuspecting or for ill-nature outside the networking environment such as uploading downloading files or even forwarding messages or even printing them.
- By overloading the network with one-sided connection requests that eventually cause the network to crash is called the distributed denial of service prevention (DDoS). A distributed denial of services is a prevention tool that scrubs incoming traffic to eradicate nonlegitimate traffic that can cause harm to the network, and it's made up of hardware appliances which their main work is to filter out bad traffic before it reaches the firewalls.
- Email security is very important to consider when applying networking security tools because many threat vectors such as scams, phishing, malware, and suspicious links are always attached and incorporated into emails. Many of these threats use details of personal information to appear real. It is very important for the institution's employees are educated more about security awareness training to help them detect suspicious emails. This security software's main work is to filter out coming threats and also can be set to prevent outgoing messages from sharing certain forms of important data.
- Firewalls are also important to network security models which function like gatekeepers between a network and the bigger internet. Firewall filters all incoming and outgoing traffic by comparing data packets against predefined rules and policies hence reducing threats that can access the network.
- Majority of the population have mobile devices that carry some form of personal or sensitive information that is kept safe. This fact, hackers know very well and they tend to take advantage of it but the installation of mobile device security measures can greatly reduce access to a network and is a very important step in making sure network traffic stays private and not leaked through vulnerable mobile connections.

- Network segmentation makes work very easy to allocate or restrict authorization credentials for the employees, making sure one will not access the information they should not have.
- Security information, and event management are security systems also known as SIEMs that join the host-based and network-based detection systems that join together real-time network traffic monitoring with old data log files scanning to provide management with a detailed picture of all the activities taking place. SIEMs are like intrusion prevention systems (IPS), which can scan network traffic for suspicious activity, policy violations, unauthorized access, and other signs of potentially malicious behavior to actively block the attempted intrusions. An IPS can also log in to security events and send notifications to the necessary players in the interest of keeping network administrators informed.
- With the web security software, it can limit access for employees with the sole point of preventing them from gaining access to sites that contain malware. Its other work is to block web-based threats and works to protect a customer's web access point.

Three important pillars make up the concept of network security and this is; confidentiality, integrity, and availability, which when combined are sometimes known as the CIA triad. A network can only be approved secure when it has all three elements in play simultaneously.

Confidentiality works well to keep sensitive data protected and hidden away from where it can be accessed by the average user. This goes hand-in-hand with the principle of availability, which seeks to ensure that data and resources are kept only accessible for those who are authorized to access them. Challenges to availability can include DDoS attacks or equipment failure. The principle of integrity seeks to protect information from intentional or accidental changes to keep the data reliable, accurate, and trustworthy (Rao, Bojkovic, and Milovanovic, 2006).

Each decision made regarding network security should be in favor of at least one of these principles. This means that MSPs need to ask if each decision will ensure that data is kept confidential, that its integrity will be protected, and that it will be made more easily available to those with authorization to access it.

As the world around us becomes increasingly digitized, we depend more and more on the internet and networks to function. This, in turn, requires that the internet and networks provide us with resourceful and secure service.

However, as more of our personal and sensitive data is stored in electronic repositories and archives, hackers are turning their attention to networked systems. For this reason, MSPs, and security support personnel must offer customers robust security systems that protect data from various threat vectors.

5.7. MULTIMEDIA TRANSPORT PROTOCOLS

The main role of multimedia transport protocols is to send multimedia signals from one point to another. These specific points are joined together by communication networks that are using a particular set of protocols. Normally the signals are programmed in codes to reduce the bit rate.

The transportation layers' main job to set up a temporary communication session between two applications and to transport data between them. The transportation layer is the link between the application layer and the lower layers which their main role is network transmission. The request created data that is sent from a request on a source host to an application on a receiving host type. The primary job of transport layer protocols is;

- Keeping track of one communication between the request on the source and the receiving host.
- Dividing data for easy manageability and rearranging sub-divided data into lines of application data at the receiving end.
- By knowing the best application for each communication stream.

5.7.1. Multimedia in the Home

This is a platform (MHP) which is a digital video broadcaster (DVB) standard that is supposed to join together digital television (DTV) with the internet and the global wide web. In turn, the results will create a high-definition television in a collaborating multi-purpose communication set up available to both the consumer and the businesses. Multimedia plays a very important place in society because it runs everything, and is the easiest way to communicate and understand what is going around it involves music, video, and animations. Some examples of multimedia include text, audio, still images, animation, video, and interactivity. Multimedia also comprises of slides which include text and images and also videos. There are five types of multimedia, they greatly act as a pillar in the education process, and they include narrative media, interactive media, communicative media, adaptive media and the production media.

A multimedia device is a tool or piece of equipment that grants permission to the user to be exposed to several different types of digital media at the same time.

The most common types of multimedia players are MP3 players, smartphones, and handheld game devices but computers are the most common type of multimedia devices.

Multimedia is constituted of different elements such as text, video, sound, graphics, and animation. They are very user-friendly and below are the advantages of them;

- Effective learning is increased;
- It greatly holds and gains attention;
- It's very appealing;
- It greatly reduces the training cost as learning can be done online;
- Very easy to use to anybody;
- Information is given a cost;
- Presentations are given high-quality work; and
- It's multi-sensorial.

Also, they are several disadvantages that come with multimedia networks in homes and this include;

- Multimedia production tends to be more expensive because it consists of more than one medium;
- For multimedia to function it requires an electronic device that can be costly to install;
- Electricity becomes expensive to maintain at times yet multimedia solely depends on it for it to run smoothly;
- Multimedia can take away attention from the classroom because it is an attention grabber;
- It is very much time-consuming in creating one;
- It wastes a lot of time and energy for the consumer when they are learning to master it; and
- Multimedia is very fragile any exposure to moisture or other elements would cause damage to it and very expensive to repair it or purchase a new one.

5.7.2. Multimedia in Education

With the quick development and the widespread use of the latest technologies in communication, multimedia has evolved to become the most important technique that is being used in teaching and the learning processes in schools. They include things like the usage of text, images, animation, video, and audio to make ready the courses for the learners in different grades of education, e.g., universities, colleges, secondary, and primary levels. Multimedia has played an important role in improving and enhancing education for the learners and the teachers in a great way. With the significant development with computers, it has created a big change in different fields such as accounting, scientific researches, social communications, medicines, sports, weather forecasting, fashion, engineering, can manufacturing and education as a whole. With computers spreading all over it has come with numerous advantages such as jobs becoming easier, accuracy is improved, very effective and fast. Effectiveness in computer technology has led to high standards in other technologies such as DTV, mobile phone, networks, internet, audio devices, and video devices.

For all ages, technology is user-friendly. In this day and age, old teaching ways are outdated and computer technology has taken place in the learning sectors. The educational technology also known as the learning technology is mainly the use of this technology in the teaching and learning processes while technology in the field of technology refers to the use of different types of tools and techniques such as the laptops, YouTube, Wi-Fi, smartphones, and whiteboards, it also comprises of well-organized and improved management systems, schematic of information distribution and improved teaching methods. With the rapid increase in information and communication technology (ICT) in the society is mirrored in the policies to give more hope in the use of information communication technology in fields of education and also in the building of educational multimedia networks. With its increased capability it offers to the teaching and learning institutions it very good to have an idea of the main role of educational multimedia. Learners, who are well equipped with these methods and tools in their homes like the computers, have a bigger chance in quick absorption and capability to these technologies when used in the learning systems. Many research papers use teaching methods as a teaching aid to examine better methods to increase the learner's capability to be active and be more involved in the classroom and this is very necessary for the current internet wireless connections.

By having students with abilities to use these tools in their education systems, they can also be used for entrainment or even social activities creating a sure strong effect on education, whereby a big impact is created in the learning institutions. By having active class participation, collaboration, and self-explanatory methods the learners are potentially well in tackling problems by themselves. Tools like videos, audios, animated graphics, simulations, and models combined in a well-organized manner. The use of interactive techniques in teaching has played a big part in the learning institutions today. It can be said that computers improve and play a big part in helping learners be smart in their fields. Modern-day multimedia technology is very efficient than traditional methods of teaching. Below are a few results that have come with multimedia technology in education;

- Learner's attention in the classroom is grabbed;
- Learners are more focused and more concentrated;
- It creates more interest in classrooms;
- Students become more relaxed and energized;
- The student has a bigger imagination;
- A better approach towards the content and learning;
- Builds stronger links between the student and the instructors;
- Memory capacity is increased;
- Knowledge levels are increased;
- It nurtures creativity;
- Encourages the smooth flow of ideas;
- It encourages detailed and deeper learning;
- It creates confidence for freedom of expression;
- It creates a smooth flow of working together;
- Learning becomes fun not as boring as before; and
- Learners create memories that are very helpful when learning and in turn, they start liking topics that to them were either boring or even scary to tackle.

Below are the characteristics that multimedia networks have brought to the field of education;

- It helps learners understand better and proper practices to enable them to solve problems;
- Helps in classroom management and administration;

- With multimedia, students can major more in their fields of study by use of drills and a lot of practice; and
- It can create a mirror-like for real-life problems and in turn, the learners can tackle them.

Online multimedia education: Online multimedia education has become a very important pillar in education because learners in the most remote parts of the world can be able to enroll for it as a form of higher education. This has created, surfacing of worldwide information and computer communications technologies. Online electronic education has become present everywhere as an important tool in teaching and learning in schools, colleges, universities, and also organizations. Nowadays, it's not like traditional days because those traditional universities who used to offer classroom only courses now they can offer one or two courses online and turn out successful and also emerging of online universities that offer completely online degree programs (Rao, Bojkovic, and Milovanovic, 2006).

Below are the advantages that come with online learning;

- Learners who are in remote places now have a chance to access higher education or even the disabled, shy students who couldn't attend a classroom set up now can attend online chat-rooms with courage;
- Materials for learning are readily available at any time the learner needs them;
- Creates on time methods that are used to measure and examine student progress; and
- Helps create good communication between student to student and the student and the administration.

Online education has its disadvantages too e.g.

- As opposed to traditional classroom setups which were face to face interactions between the teachers and students, online education has limited social interactions because the teachers interact with students through the e-mail they don't get meet; and
- Online education has made students lack discipline because there is no structure of the self-discipline.

The learners should have enough knowledge when using multimedia tools to enable the successful application of multimedia in education. In institutions like universities and colleges multimedia education is passed on to the learners in two ways:

- By providing hands-on skills of software packages used for building and authoring of multimedia capability as teaching methodologies; and
- Employing multimedia content and technology for proper teaching methods which include interactive information delivery which is personalized and improved access points to materials anytime and anywhere.

Multimedia has played an important role in the teaching and learning sectors as compared to the traditional earlier ways. Multimedia online education doesn't replace the teachers they are still very important to enable the smooth flow of the system because the information has to be prepared then uploaded to a suitable multimedia presentation and later upload it online for the students.

5.8. ROLE OF MULTIMEDIA TODAY IN SOCIETY

Multimedia is anything that we watch or listen to in any form be it text, photograph, audio, and video. They are usually recorded, played back, displayed or accessed by information contents processing devices such as computerized and electronic devices. Multimedia can be used in businesses, schools, homes, and also in public places.

5.8.1. Importance of Multimedia

Used for the transmission of information data like numbers, text, sound, and graphics. Multimedia can be stored, transmitted, presented, and also perceived proving to be the best form of communication. Multimedia has animation, music, and video and it's the best way to get people listening to what is important. Multimedia makes it easier for business people to deliver what they want to the public and also for quick advertisements. The use of the internet can be included to build more multimedia website user interest; it can also help to attract more links to the site to help increase in-line status. To create a multimedia project or a website it requires better writing skills and more high-tech technologies, a good organization structure and excellent business talent.

Places where multimedia can be used;

- Businesses application involves the use of multimedia in presentation, training, marketing, advertising, product demos, catalogs, networked communication, and voicemails.

Presentations are the most common and very important in business to sales, training, teaching, lecturing, and entertainment of the public. They help give a speech in front of an audience to present a project or product, they can also be used for educational or training sessions, multimedia, and PowerPoint presentations. Multimedia in business is very effective in encouraging clients to purchase the products.

- With the cooperation of multimedia in schools, learning has become much easier for learners to learn and also the teaching staff. Helping learners concentrate more in the classroom and eradicating boredom within them and also it has created good learning and engaging conditions for the disabled as they can learn and get what they require online. By engaging students more to doing their projects and hence doing them better.
- Multimedia has played a big part in homes from cooking, design, remodeling, and repairs. DTV sets and radios play an important part in homes giving information to families about multimedia projects. Besides, the use of the home computer to watch movies such as CD-ROM or DVD drives reducing boredom in homes.
- In public places, multimedia is very effective in train stations, bus stations, hotels, and restaurants, etc. playing a very big part in the economic growth rate.

The tourism and hospitality industries have adopted information technology (IT) to low things costs, to improve operational efficiency and to provide high-quality service and customer experience. E-tourism is a reflection of all the processes and value services in tourism, travel, hospitality, and the catering industries being digitalized. The tourism sector is undergoing a very big change like the web was normally used for information gathering but now it is also used for the ordering of services. To be able to improve the tourism industry there is need of in cooperating multimedia elements such as videos, animation, pictures, text messages and virtual reality to enable good communication with the tourists who are using the website to gain more information about the hospitality of the region they want to visit.

The internet has created an extraordinary effect by creating the ability for the customers to communicate effectively and at a very low cost. Creating more revenue returns to the countries' needs The use of growing internet connections has greatly uplifted the industry and still it has altered the industry. The rapid development of information and communication technologies (ICT) for the tourism industry has made hotels and other key players in this industry to increasingly adopt these new technologies. The information communication technology-based products and systems help the hotels to improve on the operational efficiency, improving the service experience as well provide an opening in the global window While ICTs were being used in the tourism industry from the late 80s in the form of Computerized Reservation systems and Global distribution systems, it until the 90s that the ICTs began to make a difference in the hospitality sector. Today the internet has turned into an informative channel providing both individuals and organizations with different types of information making them aware of new tourism and travel opportunities and offers to enable them to compare the offers, online, and be able to purchase and provide feedback on what they want. It has also become a good source for travel agencies and organizations to advertise their services and products to their willing customers. E-Tourism is a new research section that has been developed to in-cooperate Information and Communication Technologies (ICT) in the Hospitality Industry. Web technology is very quickly adopted and used for travel information delivery and travel planning. By use of the web, travelers can get important information such as timetables, routes, plane seat availability, accommodation, where to rent cars, and the available restaurants in the area enabling them to plan the visit without any difficulties. There are also research prototypes of intelligent travel support systems based on the software the agent is using. Most intelligent travel systems have this software's that the agents use to change travel alternatives and even pick the best with less interference (Savage and Vogel, 2009).

CHAPTER

6

Applications of Multimedia

CONTENTS

6.1. INTRODUCTION

Application in multimedia involves an application that utilizes a number of media sources. For example, images, audio, videos, text, etc. Multimedia combines the media sources mentioned above to create content to the end user. Multimedia can be presented in form of a recording; it can be displayed on a screen or interacted with by the use of electronic devices though multimedia can also be part of a live performance. Some of the applications of multimedia have been mentioned and described below.

6.2. ELECTRONIC MESSAGING

Electronic messaging is the transmission of a message through a communications network commonly in form of text that but there's an option of attaching documents. The use of electronic messages is among the oldest and most commonly used forms of communication. In the year 1960s people used to send emails between each other when the users had the same mainframe computer. The use of this technology became common between the year 1960 to the year 1970 where employees in companies used this technique to send each other messages from different branches and subsidiaries. Email technology has developed ever since and in the year 1971 Ray Tomlinson was the first person to include the '@' symbol in order to separate the user's name and the host computers name. Interactions with electronic Mail continued to be rich in features and its usage became easily applicable. Then there was the emergence of popular web services, for example, Gmail, Yahoo mail and Hotmail. In our modern world, the usage of electronic Mail has become so common and this is because emails possess important technical components which make it extremely powerful in the usage of our modern world.

Electronic messaging is extremely flexible: Email services gives you the option to richly format your content from a simple plain text to a survey or a newsletter. Electronic messaging also gives you an option to attach documents and due to this any form of digital content can be sent from one user to another in any part of the world provided that the attachment is not too large. The flexibility of emails also provides for email overload whereby a user can access a lot of information from one channel. Some of the information that can be accessed can be conversation, transactions, and files (Steinmetz and Nahrstedt, 2013).

Asynchronous: In telecommunications, the asynchronous nature of electronic messages has enabled the users of email to either send or receive messages at their own free time without the interruption of other email users. Although there can be a lack of immediate feedback, the asynchronous nature of electronic messages has enabled end users to be more meticulous and has heightened contribution. The display of electronic messages has enabled for users to know the different categories of messages in that it has separated new messages from old messages. It has also provided other categories such as drafts, sent messages, drafts, spam, and outbox messages. This has enabled and users to easily manage their messages.

Broadcast: Electronic messages have the ability to send a single message to numerous email users in a simultaneous nature provided that their email addresses have been inserted. There have been programs, for example, listserv that has enabled thousands of end users to communicate and listen in on the conversation of others.

Push technology: A sender can decide that his or her messages will be push in that he or she decides what shows up on the recipients display though the recipient has limited options to edit what has been displayed. This can be advantages or disadvantages at the same time. It can be advantageous when the sender of the message is trying to capture the attention of the recipient but it can be disadvantages in the event that the messages becomes a spam (sending messages that are misleading and unwanted).

Threaded conversation: The use of threaded conversation in emails leads to organization in that a pattern consisting of messages replies to messages replies to replies and so forth can be created and this can enable the users of the email to follow through in the conversation from one thread without the need to look for other messages from other places. This creates a chain of replies sourced from a top-level message.

With such powerful components in electronic messages there has been the emergence of numerous advantages in the multimedia sector.

- Mobility – multimedia devices such as cell phones and portable laptops have enabled people to be in touch with each other in different locations of the world. This has made people's life to be easier, for example, co-workers don't have to travel long distances in order for them to go for a meeting or submit a job, but work can be sent to their emails and they can do it at the comfort of their home or while traveling maybe on plane. This has enabled professional workers to meet their deadlines without having to struggle much.

- Speed – use of electronic messages has increased speed in transmission of data and information. Workers can now be able to send jobs thousands of miles away with just the click of a button.
- Security – electronic messaging has enabled for data to be stored in the Cloud after it has been sent or it has been generated. This enables for information to be safely backed up online or on a portable electronic device to protect against loss or theft.
- Reduction in costs – electronic messaging has enabled for end users and other parties too heavily save on costs of shipping and mailing. This is because email is free as it enables one to send messages audios videos documents and presentation without having the need to spend money in order to transport the content required.

6.3.IMAGE ENHANCEMENT

This technique enables certain features in an image to be viewed in a different way in terms of appearance when compared to the original image as it enhances graphic display during analysis. The process of enhancement does not necessarily improve the original content of the image but it enhances the dynamic horizon of the image which enables easy detection of features. Research has been conducted and psychological experiments have been done and it has proved that minor alterations in luminance can be noticed by the human visual system in areas of continuous grey tones and cannot be noticed in sectors of discontinuities (Sencar et al, 2010).

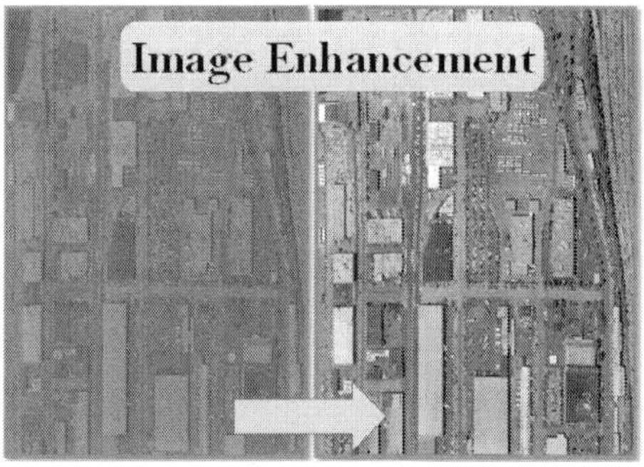

Figure 6.1. Image enhancement involves the use of mathematical formulas which is aimed at improving the standard and quality of a given image.

Source: https://remote-sensing-portal.com/courses/enhancement/.

Due to this image enhancement technique is aimed at smoothening images in more uniform regions but at the same time preserving edges. Another goal in image enhancement is the sharpening of images and this can be done by degrading images by enhancing certain features which leads to simplification of image interpretation for both human and machine observers. Edge sharpening technique is one of the techniques that is normally used in image enhancement and this technique is similar to and unsharp masking type enhancement. Image enhancement improves the human perception of images. Image enhancement also improves the perception of images depending with the application in which the image is being utilized and this makes it more appropriate and suitable for a specific job. The procedure of image enhancement involves altering and changing a particular feature of an image by using a computer to preprocess steps in applications so as to enhance the view of a task. For instance, a robotic gripper is guided more by the enhancement of edges on an image (Sencar et al, 2010).

6.3.1. Techniques Used in Image Enhancement

The main objective of enhancing an image is to enable the data found in images to be easily perceived and interpreted using the human eye and provision of quality input for other image processing techniques. There are two major categories of image enhancement techniques. (I) Spatial domain techniques. This category of image enhancement techniques deals directly with pixels; and (II) Frequency domain techniques. This image enhancement technique makes use of mathematical formulas such as the Fourier transform.

Spatial Domain Techniques. This form of techniques utilizes pixels of images. The numbers of the pixels are altered in order to obtain a desirable image enhancement. In order to directly manipulate the grey level of particular pixels, spatial techniques play an important role and this alters the total contrast of the whole job. During image enhancement, uniformity is practiced and this normally leads to results that are not desirable. This is due to the fact that edges and other data in the image cannot be enhanced in an effective way. For this problem to be rectified other techniques such as histogram equalization can be used.

Spatial domain techniques that are used in grey level transformations include point, linear, logarithmic, power-low, and piece-wise transformation.

- Logarithmic transformation Technique: When it comes to enhancement of dark images in terms of contrast, the logarithmic transformation technique is used and this technique is one of the elementary image enhancement techniques. The logarithmic transformation is basically a grey level transformation. This implies that there is an alteration of the grey level in the image pixels. It involves slender low grade level values in the input to image being mapped to a wider range of output levels. There is a mathematical formula that shows the general equation for the logarithmic transformation and the equation is expressed as S=c log (1+r), where, S is the output grey level, r is the input grey level and c is a constant under the assumption that $r \geq 0$.

- Power – low Transformation Technique: This is a commonly used grey level transformation technique in the spatial domain. The concept behind this technique has similarities to the alpha rooting in the frequency domain. In the power low transformation technique, the input grey level is raised to some power. The logarithmic transformation technique uses the same concept as the power law transformation technique. This is because there is the mapping of narrow range of dark input values into a wider range of output values by the fractional values of γ. S= brγ is the fundamental equation for power law transformation. S represents the output grey level, r represents the input grey level, b is the scaling constant and is the power to which the input Grade level is raised S is the output grey level, r is the input grey level, b is a scaling constant and γ is the power to which the input grey level is raised. Due to the varying nature of the parameter γ, the transformation function is able to be controlled and this makes it advantageous. In equation form, S=T (r) where 0<=r<=1. 2. When using Frequency domain techniques, the orthogonal transform of the image is manipulated instead of the image itself. Phase and magnitude are the two main elements when it comes to the orthogonal transformation of the image. The magnitude comprises of the frequency content of the image. During the restoration of the image back to the spatial domain phase is used. In frequency domain technique the mathematical formula that is the Fourier transform is used in the transfer of image into the frequency domain. The transfer of the image first takes place then the procedure of enhancement is undertaken on the Fourier transform of the image and finally in order to get the resulting image an inverse of the Fourier transform is then performed. The features of the image such as brightness and the distribution of the grey levels are modified with such an enhancement.

6.4. ADVERTISING AND BUSINESS

Advertising has evolved over the last few decades. In the recent years, people only had access to television and newspapers but with a lot of technical technological advancement nowadays most people are on their cell phones. It is estimated people spend about 60% of their time browsing through social media and with this most companies around the world have seized the opportunity to advertise using multimedia platforms in order to reach a bigger target audience. It is now a challenge for companies and marketers to come up with content in order for them to enhance their marketability. Some of the uses of multimedia in advertisement include graphics for print and media advertisement, animation, and Engineering sounds for visual advertisement, editing of all kinds of content and 3D animations.

Figure 6.2. Multimedia advertising pertains the utilization of animation and graphic design to advertise and market a product or a service.

Source: *https://seventhfoundation.com/digital-marketing/.*

Use of multimedia, for example, podcasts, videos, file sharing, photos, live casting and mobile marketing can help create awareness in terms of brand in a very special and Powerful way as it makes the content being advertised go viral in a short period of time over a large number of people.

In as much as the possibility of your institution getting marketed properly relies heavily on fate rather than skill it is still important to consider the impact that multimedia has had on your business.

A principal analyst stated that the ability of multimedia to enhance communication among your business partners and employees and your customers and potential customers is significant.

He stated that " when you think about multimedia platforms and what it is all about it is about being able to communicate mass marketing messages to the device of choice on-demand." "I think what's more interesting is how these tools can be used in conjunction with other multimedia tools to support the business-the marketing, the sales and promotion of their products and services. To me that for small business is probably more important than internal communication."

Below are some of the ways in which businesses can leverage multimedia in enhancing their promotion and advertisement techniques.

6.4.1. Posting of Photos Online

On the internet there are societies whose main function is to post pictures and other contents online. This can be through social media, for example, Instagram, Twitter or Facebook. Due to this many small businesses have spotted a gap and have taken advantage of these services to market their products. Some of the most common marketing strategies are;

- Offering real-time incentives: Social media platforms have an option of enabling the user to post or share a photo over the internet. This helps in marketing in that instead of typing numerous words trying to describe a product one can instead just post a picture that describes a product or a business.
- Interaction with similar minded societies: Some social media platforms such as Pinterest is not only just a photo storage place but also an independent online marketing platform and posting and sharing of photos is free. There is normally a very active community which is Central towards a specific product, for example, pets. One can post a pet he or she is selling online and people who have interest in buying pets will be able to see the photo online and can make a request for the pet. This is a very good way of marketing your products as it is free and it will travel and reach many people at the same time.
- Steering traffic to a company website: One can use social media

to create traffic to their website. Normally most businesses post photos of products or services they are offering and providing and through the photos posted, people can go ahead and click on the link in order to visit your website so as to make a purchase if so. Take for instance, in the event one posts images of products and services they offering on Instagram. The followers of the marketer who are on Instagram will be able to view the products being advertised and at the same time they can be able to repost the same photos or share it to other social media platforms. Interested people will go ahead and click on the link provided below which will direct them to the website where the products are being sold. At the end of the day this will create a traffic of potential buyers of the products which eventually leads to the maximization of profits as more people will be able to access your website and make more orders on purchases.

6.4.2. Hosting Videos and Web Casting

Figure 6.3. Sharing of videos on social media has proven to be a very important tool when it comes to marketing.

Source: https://marketingland.com/create-compelling-content-social-media-221333.

Study conducted in November of 2009 by a digital marketing research firm found out that Google's many video sites accounted for 12.2 billion video views that month including YouTube which accounted for nearly 99% of the total. Webcasting is the main strategy that is mostly being used in advertisement and it involves broadcasting a video or Media in the Internet by the use of streaming media technology and such a video can be seen by a million users at the same time in their own devices at once. Check for instance in the event that a company is advertising their products they will go ahead and use an individual's YouTube channel where content has already been posted and in between the video the advertisement of the product by the company pops up and every time one views the video either on YouTube or Google the video gets advertised every time. This enables for the product to be seen numerous times and eventually the potential buyer can gain interest as there is numerous advertisement on the same product every time. Webcast are also called video blogs or podcasts. There are four basic steps that need to be taken in order to have an effective webcast that is the tool, theme, online home and marketing.

- • The tool/equipment – these are the tools that will be used in the creation of content. Such equipment includes a camera or a wireless microphone and video editing programs. Small businesses can invest in high end camcorders which will lead in the creation of videos that are of high quality.
- • Employ someone – depending on the company's budget, the media team can decide to hire a professional who will help the company in creating a video with all the required content being touched on. In order for one to be a professional in the business they are undertaking it is important for the company to have a media team that advertises and professionals should be hired in order for them to utilize multimedia in marketing as it will go a long way in helping your business to thrive.
- • The show – a company might produce the best video but it will not lead to a significant impact if the video does not intrigue the viewers. The video should be creative in order to create and attract the attention of the viewers online. In addition, the release of the video should be consistent in order to create a regular broadcast schedule which should be airing the videos at a specific time in order to create more traffic. The videos being created should be full of personality since that is the only way that we are going to attract more viewership.
- • Hosting and marketing – once the video has already been made and edited it is now ready for it to be uploaded. Search videos can be uploaded online for free, for example, on YouTube

where it can be viewed by anyone. There are sites where webcast can be uploaded for free. A tagline can be put in order to promote the show. The function of the tagline is to direct prospective viewers to the website or on YouTube where the video has been posted. There are services that are free which can put word-for-word transcript relating to the video and from the transcript the video can be searched by any search engine online, for example, Google Chrome. This will also increase the traffic to which the content is being viewed and searched.

There are many reasons as to why a good video should be created:

- Elaborate on how to use the product – you might have gone on YouTube and saw videos with headings such as "how to use a product" this is known as broadcasting yourself and it is a very important tool when creating a video because in order for someone to purchase your product or gain an interest in purchasing your product, he or she should be able to understand fully on how it operates.
- Extend your client base – in the event that you might be in a business, for example, selling of musical instruments and you find that your market is thin (the only people buying your musical instruments are within your local town). What the owner of the business can do is create a YouTube channel where he or she shows the type of musical instruments being sold and where you can locate the store. This will enable more people to watch his channel and contact him on how they can get the products. Also, this might eventually lead to the owner of the business in creating a website in order for people to go and purchase products online.
- Entertain your customers – in order for your video to be entertaining, one must come up with a video that is relatable, for example, a funny video that discusses about the hardships that people undergo due to slow internet. One should try to create a video that is entertaining as it stands to create many views which in turn will intrigue the viewers and they might be interested in the company and eventually they might purchase the product or service is being advertised. A good example of such a video hosting site is vimeo whose main objective is to bring together a group of people who have passion in the creation of videos in order for them to post online and get praise and worship.

- Provision of unique services – this can be made possible by creating a live video streaming which one can stream a live event and at the same time advertising products in the event, for example, an event that is being sponsored by Red Bull can live stream an event they are sponsoring and at the same time the advertising the product which is Red Bull. This will lead to the creation of a unique service that will intrigue viewers and eventually they might end up being prospective buyers of your product.

Use of multimedia in advertising comes with numerous advantages some of the advantages are there company can create a good customer relationship with the customers, the response time when it comes to prices is enhanced by over 300% due to the inclusion of audio aspect in your website, reviews can be taken down and stored in CDs and DVDs and the reviews are then sold to customers and finally use of multimedia can help a company to build their brands as potential customers can have a stronger emotional connection and a higher engagement with your business. Some of the benefits of using multimedia in building of Brands are;

- The visibility and the influence of the company will develop online;
- With the use of animation, interactive activities, digital stories and games one can be able to fully engage the viewer and make an appealing presentation;
- One leverages the content through the remix in publication, video, and audio information products and marketing materials;
- The portfolio of the advertiser grows as he or she is able to show their unique abilities and expertise which might attract potential employers in the future; and
- Even after the content has been used to advertise a specific product the same content can also be used to advertise other products and this will help in the enhancement of your branding and marketing.

6.5. EDUCATIONAL PURPOSES

For many years the traditional approach of learning has been utilized in many learning institutions and it has proved to work but with the introduction of multimedia in education learning has been made easier. Unlike conventional learning which limits learners to basic presentations like reading a sentence from a textbook, the use multimedia in learning utilizes elements such as video, graphics, audio, and text to enhance the learning process by making it dynamic. You will mostly find that the traditional form of education, knowledge is transferred through context but the use of multimedia in education has provided an opportunity for learners to be exposed to real life scenarios like use of computers. Also, at the same time teachers can utilize multimedia by resourcing a lot of quality information which can help the students in their learning process as it gives them skills that were not available in traditional teaching (Steinmetz and Nahrstedt, 2013). Some of these skills involve critical thinking, discussion problem, solving, and cooperative learning.

6.5.1. Multimedia Elements Used in Education

Multimedia elements have a lot of uses. Computer software such as adobe Photoshop can integrate all the elements in multimedia to come up with a great project that can be used in learning. Below are the elements used in education;

Text: Text is most probably the most fundamental element in multimedia. Though it is basic it carries a lot of weight in that text can impact the standard and quality of multimedia interaction. This is because texts are normally written in fonts and different fonts pass out a different information. Font is a collection of characters of a single size and styling belonging to a particular typeface group. Due to the direct nature of texts, this enables them to be understood quicker than other multimedia elements and for such a reason, it is used in providing vital information. In traditional teaching, texts have been used ever since but when it comes to multimedia texts the words can contain fonts with different designs and this enhances the effectiveness of learning.

Graphic: Graphic is defined as a two-dimensional illustration or an item that can display data on a screen or a piece of paper and by far the use of graphics has been proven to be the most creative way of learning.

Graphic mostly touches on the mental skills of the learners that is once a learner has learnt a content with the help of graphics, he or she will be able to remember quite easily and this enhances the students understanding of the content. At the same time images and pictures uses a lot of different elements, for example, colors, lines, dimensions, and imaginations and all these contribute to the general comprehension of the content.

Figure 6.4. Graphic can be of many forms, for example, a picture, drawing or a photograph.

Source: *https://www.click.in/ahmedabad/learn-graphic-designing-in-chand-kheda-c72-v31353443.*

Audio: The use of audio in education has been commonly utilized. In a class situation a student can be able to record what is being taught by the teacher and in the event that the students have not understood everything clearly, he or she can go home later on and replay the recording in order to get clarity on what was being taught. This is very effective in that it enables the student to interact with the content at any time or location. There are many applications that have been developed that can help in live online discussions through audio and such an application is WhatsApp. This becomes effective as it saves time because instead of meeting the teacher face to face, a lesson can be held online. Long-distance learning has also been made effective. Use of audio is also an intriguing way of transferring information and this opens up a learner's mind to understand more content. Use of audio in learning also provides an advantage to the blind since they can be able to understand through hearing what is being taught and eventually understand. Use of braille can sometimes become tiresome and challenging. Use of audio when done in a proper way can significantly impact the education system positively (Steinmetz and Nahrstedt, 2013).

Video: In terms of performance, use of videos has been ranked to be the best among other multimedia elements. A video can come in different formats such as digital versatile disc, MPEG-2 and mpeg-4 which is especially used for home videos. The main advantage of using videos is that it stimulates the visual part of a student's mind and this leads to a better comprehension of the content being taught. You will find that most of the times using text or other multimedia messages has complexities when conveying information.

An example of such is in the sector of medicine where students found it hard to understand the procedure of surgery by just reading a text but through visual stimulation, that is, use of videos, the student can be able to understand more clearly how a surgery is performed.

Some teachers in different institutions also gives students a task of making a project in video form. This form and technique of teaching helps the student to get in touch with the real element of what is being talked about and at the same time enhance their practical skills.

Animation: Animations are a set of pictures which have been combined and have been made to move in continuous motion and shape changes in order to produce an animation.

Animation heavily influences and stimulates the mind and this has been proved through a biological phenomenon known as persistent of vision and psychological phenomenon called phi. The phenomenon enables us to view animation the way it is. Animation and videos are two different components this is because animations are usually taken from drawings and videos are normally recorded from a real life happening.

There are programs that have been made to create animations by using a computer, for example, Adobe Flash and by using such software, a student can be able to use his imagination and creativity to come up with an animation. This enhances the presentation of the students while at the same time the student is having fun in the learning process.

Animations also provide an easy way of teachers to explain a difficult topic and this in turn enables the students to become first learners.

For instance, in the human body the digestive system can be difficult for students to understand only through text but if a structural framework of the digestive system is represented in form of an animation the student can clearly see how food moves from the mouth to the large intestines and this makes learning easier and faster.

Use of multimedia in the education system has come up with numerous merits. Multimedia application has enabled the representation of data using several different Media and this comes in handy during project writing and presentation as they have the ability to represent their projects in different ways as they apply creativity and imagination. Multimedia application in education has also led to portability in that students are now able to do their assignments anywhere they are depending on their situation because of multimedia tools such as audio and video where students can record and make a connection with other students during discussions. They can be able to submit their projects and assignments in any location they are without having the struggle of needing to be present in the institution. Multimedia elements has also enabled the students to have a higher level of thinking skills and this is because when students are utilizing such elements, they are putting into practice creativity thinking in order for them to combine the elements to come up with quality output. Multimedia approach in education has also enhanced the involvement of students in the learning process. With the use of multimedia elements students are able to provide feedback and ask questions and this keeps the student interested throughout the topic. Use of multimedia enables the student to simulate real-life scenarios and this leads to better comprehension of a particular project and generally, this leads to the improving and enhancement of skills (Leopold and Garcia, 2003).

6.5.2. Multimedia Application in Entertainment and Fine Arts

Multimedia has been used in the entertainment industry to come up with a lot of applications. Multimedia has been used in creation of video games, special effects in movies and animation, etc. For many years it has been known that films and video games have been created with the purpose of presenting an effect to the target audience but in the recent past there has been numerous changes on the nature and level of illusion that films and games provide to the user in their narrative. The application of multimedia has enabled movies and video games to have high levels of Illusions without the risk of having to perform the real stunts by the actors since they are all done in a computer. This has made the entertainment industry to significantly grow because imaginations are being easily portrayed in movies and video games, for example, in Jurassic Park, the dinosaur is able to run and attack humans. With the emergence of special effects using multimedia most impossible things have been made possible. During the making of movies most stunts are done with the help of protective gears like ropes and other things that protect the actors during dangerous stunts, for example, jumping from one building to another. Using VFX, one is able to make impossible and dangerous stunts to look real. You might find that in some movies an actor might jump from a building that is 100 meters high and lands comfortably like a superhero. For such an effect to take place, the VFX can remove the ropes that are holding the actor for safety purposes to show that he was actually jumping freely. In some films like, for example, Avatar, a whole different world is created by the use of visual effects and animation. In the making of cartoons and animated films producers utilize 3D animations and virtual effects and this in this creates the behavior of characters, the effects, movements, and also the background. In our current world, more and more people are getting interested with the use of virtual effects in the creation of movies. This is evidenced by the high sales in movies that involve use of special effects and 3D animations, for example, Avatar, Marvel movies and DC Comics. All age groups enjoy such movies starting from children, teenagers, and the old. Research has been studied and it has been found out that multimedia computer games and Hans is the cognitive processes of Gamers (Leopold and Garcia, 2003).

Researchers suggest that with the continuous playing of multimedia computer games there's a greater overlap on cognitive processes between games and external task and this leads to the transfer of improved cognitive processes to non-game tasks. Most video games that applies multimedia are normally fast in terms of speed and performance and this helps improve the cognitive processes that deals with attention as it helps one to resist destruction. It can be debated that excessive use of video games reduces the amount of time a student has on school work but with the integration and consolidation of both into the curriculum, there is a likelihood for an increase in the probability of transfer from games to curricular goals (Leopold and Garcia, 2003).

6.5.3. Multimedia Application in Software Development

Multimedia software is a program that enables one to combine all multimedia tools that is text, audio, video, graphics, and animations. Multimedia software is used in the enhancement of any type of text document by adding other multimedia components such as interesting photos animations or audio. The program in multimedia software can be used with anyone regardless of their computer skills. Multimedia software enables the user perform numerous tasks from one application. An example of such a task can involve listening to music while adding other sound effects at the same time, it can be recording a speech and the list is endless. Most of this stuff are useful for our day-to-day lives so in as much as the useful, they are also very entertaining. There is numerous multimedia software that one can use in their tasks as they are proven to be very reliable and effective. Some of the applications of multimedia software are in the fields of Engineering, science, and technology, health, and medicine, history, sports, art, and so much more. In order for one to be able to use a multimedia software, he or she must have a computer that meets the specific requirements that is needed by the software in order to have a wholesome experience. Most computers being produced currently have powerful processors which gives it the capabilities to accommodate any type of multimedia software. Multimedia software enhances creativity of the user since the user is able to design and create all kinds of interactive content. Due to the fact that multimedia software gives you the freedom to create, rearrange, mingle, and record different types of music and video, many musicians have found it easy to record tracks, finding the proper pitch, changing the tempo and adding effects on the sounds, for example, Auto-Tune. The software can also connect musical instruments to the computer in order to create something beautiful. Multimedia software also enable the creation of videos that are of very high quality and resolution and at the same time delete some scenes or include visual effects to the video. Editing of videos has been made easy and diverse (Leopold and Garcia, 2003).

6.6. MULTIMEDIA APPLICATIONS IN ENGINEERING

Demonstration in engineering through the use of multimedia has shown that the disadvantages of traditional demonstration can be eliminated. Some of the disadvantages include; rigidity during demonstration, wastage of time, environmental destruction and lack of attraction. Traditional paper-based documents have been replaced by short videos, holographic projection technology and PPT which has significantly restored procedures in engineering and results in engineering which has led to increased intuition.

6.6.1. Current Situation in Engineering Report Presentation

Presentation of engineering reports is a complex system that needs the utilization of huge amounts of labor, capital resources and substantial sources and they are also characteristics of Engineering Construction itself. In our current world, the procedures used in project report presentation, collection of data and materials include recording images, delivery of documents, reporting manually and statistical approximation. Such methods involve tiresome work and lower efficiency and thus it is challenging to make sure that there is timeliness and efficacy.

6.6.2. Multimedia Image Mechanization

Multimedia use of images has been on the rise due to the increasing requirements on reporting of Engineering demonstration systems and multimedia Productions of electronic images. In engineering, presentation of designs is being done through graphic representation, audio, and video Productions.

There has been the emergence of numerous multimedia presentations in engineering which include multimedia bidding demonstration, PPT building demonstration, video bidding, 3D demo bidding, demonstration of indoor and outdoor design scheme, building decoration scheme demonstration, landscape design building demonstration, planning scheme demonstration, project bidding demonstration, interior decoration project demonstration, planning, and design report presentation, post-competition report demonstration, project achievement report presentation, landscape design bidding, scheme optimization report, multimedia demonstration of urban planning scheme and multimedia demonstration to mention but a few (Leopold and Garcia, 2003).

6.6.3. Application of Multimedia Image Technology in Report Demonstration System

Application of three-dimensional scene model in engineering process management: The three-dimensional dynamic visualization digital model of construction scheduled is established basing on the three-dimensional virtual digital model of construction site topography and various kinds of group objects solving the issues concerned by engineering management decision makers and urgent to be solved visualization of Engineering progress. The three-dimensional virtual digital modeling also enables engineers to determine water, temperature, geomorphology, environment, humanity, and traffic around the construction site as it provides detailed information. This is important when it comes to evaluating an area regarding construction conditions. Oblique photography three-dimensional model can help engineers as they will not require the installation of programs since images can directly be uploaded and thus sharing has been made easy. The three-dimensional model also enables the consolidation of light browsing, tagging, measurement, and other characteristics. Real-time measurements of ground objects can be done by the UAV oblique photography modeling and also the three-dimensional spatial analysis can also be done by the UAV oblique photography modeling. The use of the three-dimensional model has enabled engineers to analyze the panoramic view of the situation without them having the need to visit the site and this is effective as it saves on time and Resources.

Improvement of professional standards of reporting: Multimedia imaging technology has improved the transposition and because of this there has been increased efficiency in communication by reporters. Multimedia imaging technology also helps in finding problems, analyzing the problems and solving the problems at different phases of project advancement.

The follow of a logical process by the system design: During reporting engineers have an obligation of clearly explaining the project that is where is the project, the size of the project, what is the project, why the project, are there factors influencing the project and are there barriers being faced during the project. With the use of multimedia image technology such questions can be well elaborated in a report.

Consolidation of holographic technology in presentation system: holographic technique is a form of procedure that records and reproduces real three-dimensional images of objects by means of interference and diffraction. The holographic technique has the ability of producing three-dimensional aerial illusions and at the same time enabling the illusions to interact with the performer. This produces an impressive effect in the performance. The holographic technique enables quantitative analysis by the use of digital images on a computer and with such technology distribution of image can be obtained through calculation and simulation of superposition of multiple holograms. This leads to the restoration of the actual situation of the project and construction process and providing visual impact of authenticity and interest for people who watched the presentation.

6.7. MULTIMEDIA APPLICATIONS IN DOCUMENT IMAGING

Document imaging is defined as the procedure of turning physical paper documents into digital images. The process of document imaging can be done through scanning or by the use of electronic transfer through a COLD application. Document imaging technology has made our current world to move towards a paperless office the process behind document imaging is similar to creating a fax, where by the paper document is digitally transformed through a fax machine and sent across telecommunication lines to its final destination. An equipment called a scanner and document imaging software are used in the process of digital transformation of the paper and once the paper has already been transformed, it is normally stored in a magnetic or an optical Media. A document scanner together with the software installed in the scanner converts a paper document into a digital document in order to consolidate the document into an electronic framework. The document imaging software first formulate a portrait of the digital paper into a preferred format. ITS scans and converts paper documents in different shapes, formats or sizes which include; full color images, grey scale Images, black, and white images, word processing files, spreadsheet files, microfilm, and microfiche, X-rays, aperture cards, handwritten notes, photographs, engineering drawings, graphic files and database files. Examples of formats can be TIFF, JPEG, BMP or PNG. In either of the formats, the computer is not able to read what is in the document but humans are able to read what is contained in the documents. The computer perceives the document to be a picture. An optical character recognition software is then used to recognize the texts in the document in order to make the document machine readable. Once the process of converting the document to be machine-readable is done, the documents are then indexed using Meta data. Metadata involves details regarding the document, for example, the date of creation, the author and a unique identifier. A barcode page which contains tailored meta-data is then attached to the document so as to enable an indexer to immediately index the documents using the meta data provided in the barcode. The machine readable document is then scanned (Leopold and Garcia, 2003).

Document imaging is very essential when it comes to managing documents, for example, in companies that have a heavy and continuous flow of paper documents from numerous locations can be able to transfer these documents to an electronic digital workflow through scanning. The scanned documents are then indexed once they have arrived in order for them to be well-detailed and easily located. This helps in the reduction of paper storage since once the paper documents have been transferred into an electronic workflow, the documents can be shredded and recycled and this eventually leads to the conservation of the environment. Once the transformation of the paper documents has been done, the documents can be backed up and this can help in the management of documents in the event that disasters like fire and flood occur. This is because the documents can be backed up in a different location like the web in the cloud and the lost documents can be recovered. In the event that the documents are needed for the purpose of auditing or the reconciliation of accounts, they can be quickly retrieved due to their indexing which enables them to be easily located. Different people have different needs and therefore before you decide to choose a document imaging system one should consider their needs. For example, if a company has large volumes of paper documents, one must consider a system which has automated functions such as batch scanning, automatic indexing and document classification. Professional and expert help can be sought. A company can entrust a third-party agency in handling all the task involving document management which can be from scanning, sorting of those documents, ensuring high image quality, optimizing the function of optical character recognition and ensuring the safety of the paper and electronic data (Muneesawang, Zhang, and Guan, 2014).

6.8. MULTIMEDIA APPLICATIONS IN MEDICINE

For many years the Department of Health has been searching for technology that will be used in helping to save lives and at the same time improve the standards of treatment and lives of patients. There is the need for technology that has real-time video analysis, storage, indexing, sharing, and retrieval of data in order to help in improving medical activities. A medical multimedia system is defined as a framework that helps in diagnosing, examining, performing surgery, reporting, and teaching in all medical settings by combining all available data sources and putting them in the hands of medical professionals or patients. The use of visual information has often been applied in hospitals to detect diseases and at the same time access them. Over the recent years there has been the urge of developing technology that detect a disease early in the system. Diseases like cancer is rarely detected early but gets detected during the later stages where survival is very minimal. Currently, a multimedia technology known as the gastro-intestinal flexible endoscopy is being used in the detection of diseases. It involves a flexible tube which is inserted inside the body and contains a lens system. Though, this technology still has its limitations and experts have been researching on a new multimedia system which is called the EIR which supports endoscopists in the detection and interpretation of diseases in the gastrointestinal tract. The multimedia system is aimed in assisting the detection of irregularities during colonoscopy and create a fully automated screening of the gastro-intestinal tract using a wireless video capsule endoscope (VCE). This technology will assist doctors in reducing the number of abnormalities that have been overlooked and also assist in the assessment of the abnormalities (Muneesawang, Zhang, and Guan, 2014).

Multimedia technology is used to improve doctor-patient relationships in matters regarding consent of the patient as patient consent for treatment is one of the most important components in the law of medicine. This, is true in that, a patient might visit a hospital and the patient might be required to perform a high-risk surgery or operation and he or she may not have awareness of the procedure. In order to create consent the patient should have the knowledge of the condition and the circumstances that will be required in order for patient to continue with the procedure. The doctor should also be able to tell the patient the available methods of treatment and any complications that might arise with the treatment they decide to go with. This is an informed consent process. Most times the increased growth in technological advancements might cause disparity in communication between the doctor and the patient regarding the scope and methods of treatment prior to the surgery. The informed consent process might be enhanced and improved if the doctor uses multimedia technologies such as videos of the surgical procedures, computer animations and graphics to show the patient what he or she is to undergo in the event that the surgery is to take place. With the use of multimedia technology, patients are able to retain more information regarding the procedure they're about to undergo. You will also find that different patients have different levels of understanding and therefore when the procedure is well elaborated using multimedia technology the patients are able to reduce the difference in the amount of information assimilated. All this improves the standards of preoperative patient education and eventually improve the patient's healing process afterwards (Muneesawang, Zhang, and Guan, 2014).

Multimedia technology is also being used in the medical sector to create a smart medical home. The main objective of medical homes is to develop a consolidated medical framework that is tailored to an individual home. This kind of technology will enable potential patients to be able to detect a disease and at the same time maintain high standards of health at the comfort of their homes. Smart medical home does this by collecting information 24/7 inside the home regarding the patient and this data will accumulate and eventually collected by a doctor. The type of data collected by the program is mostly the standard procedures such as blood sugar, blood pressure, pulse, and weight of the patient. Using this data, multimedia technology will operate to include other forms of measurement of new vital signs like, behavioral patterns, sleep patterns, general exercise and rehabilitation exercises. Smart medical home has the capability of delaying the time in which an elderly is deemed to be dependent on retirement nursing homes and this eventually improves the living standards of the elderly. Patients with chronic diseases and physical disabilities can heavily benefit from smart homes equipments. This is because smart home medical equipment enables patients to detect symptoms early and thus prevent the development of the condition that will lead to spending a lot of hours in hospitals and spending a lot of money to treat the conditions which could have been prevented. Multimedia technologies such as network care systems with integrated sensors that monitor clinical signs can be used in the detection of trends that might cause lead to the development of diseases. Telemedicine is being incorporated in the smart medical home to improve the detection of diseases in clients. Telemedicine involves the utilization of multimedia components such as audio, video, text, and animation to assist in diagnosing medical conditions, treating medical conditions and the general care of the patient. This is made possible through the exchange of information and data regarding the patient with practitioners who cut across different situations. It can be across geographical, time, social, and cultural barriers.

6.9. USE OF MULTIMEDIA FOR RESEARCH

Research projects in institutions can be improved and enhanced by the use of multimedia components such as images, audio, animations, videos, and applications. There are numerous resources and tools that can be found online which can be used in during research. The tools used for research can broadly be categorized into two; Operating with media that is image manipulation, film, and audio editing, building presentation and electronic resources and the second category is finding media that is searching for images, audio, and video which will be used in the research.

When working with media you will find a range of equipments which are available to be used for working. Some of the tools are listed below

When editing images, the tools below can be utilized;

- Microsoft paint – Microsoft paint is a standard Microsoft package that is used in editing images. It is simple to use, uses little disk space and has minimal errors.
- iPiccy – In the event that you don't have advanced softwares, one can find this online as it is a good tool that can be used in image adjusting such as contrast, brightness, and colors and allows one to edit images online.
- Splash up – Splash app has the capability of editing images using advanced functions and it is normally free.
- Photofiltre – This is used in photoshopping images and it is free to be downloaded.
- Web Resizer – Web resizer is a good tool that is used in resizing images.

When one wants to edit films, some of the applications that can be used are;

- Windows Movie Maker – Windows Movie Maker comes with the normal Microsoft packages and it is easy to be used in editing and narrating films though advanced editing cannot be performed.

- iMovie – iMovie perform the same functions as Windows Movie Maker but it has the ability to Perform advanced editing.

During presentation, the following tools can be used;

- Prezi – Prezi enables one to make a nonlinear format kind of presentation and it is available online. Text, images, and videos are placed on a canvas and their features that can allow the items to be zoomed.
- PowerPoint – PowerPoint is the most flexible tools when it comes to giving presentations as it allows for a range of drawing and animation options. It also uses bullet points and corporate styling.

CHAPTER

7

Multimedia Software Tools

CONTENTS

7.1. INTRODUCTION

The world population is growing with each passing day creating more need for the invention of different ways to express our ideas, needs, and desires to each other. Multimedia presents us with different ways, different artistic forms, different ways, which enable us to speak out our minds to our fellow humans and also to animals in a more unified way. It simply combines different forms of information into a unified format which is of high quality, easy to understand and its quantity is worth and appealing to the end user who accesses it.

7.2. ORIGIN OF THE TERM "MULTIMEDIA"

The term "Multimedia" was first used by an American Musician, famously known as Bob Goldstein. He used it to refer to his music work, The Light works, for it combined both audio part and the visual part. It was then used to refer to the work of a political consultant for they would combine information from variety of media such as books, videos, images among others so as to come up with complete information. Multimedia gained its current meaning in the late-90's, which refers to a combination of different ways of presenting information to the end user, and come up with a unified format which is more elaborate and unique (Costello, 2016).

Interactive Multimedia simply refers to a unified format of different ways of sharing information which allows the end user to control the way it displays information, while hypermedia is a type of Multimedia which deals with a structure of linked unified format which the end user has minimal control of how to display the information for it provides them with a navigation system.

The unified format of different ways of sharing information is presented to the user electronically by use of electronic nodes such as a computer. The performances displayed by theatre actors can also be considered as "Multimedia" for they present content to the audience by combining different forms of communication.

7.3. CHARACTERISTICS OF MULTIMEDIA

Multimedia is composed of different components.

Since it is a combination of different forms of sharing information, many formats which have been invented work towards ensuring that information is transmitted faster, in an easier format which enhances the user's experience and motivates its use on daily basis.Multimedia presentations deal with display of unified formats of information to the audience. They can be presented on stage by live actors such as a play based on the advantages and disadvantages of the advancing the technology. It can also be projected on a whiteboard by use of a projector and a presentation software installed on the computer such as the Power Point presentation software. Transmission can also be used to present multimedia data by sending it through electronic mails, WhatsApp messages, messenger on Facebook and the through the normal message phone application. Videos and animations can be presented by playing them through media player application or the famous VideoLAN Client commonly referred to as VLC (Costello, 2016).

In situations where a user is sure he or she will not have access to the internet (where most multimedia information is made available) due to network problems, one may opt to download multimedia information presented electronically for future use. Data can also be streamed in situation where a certain organization need to avail live information in a unified format to its most trusted clients.Games are being made part of the Multimedia group for developers are combining different forms of communicating content to come up with unique gaming soft wares. Special features are being added to games to make the interaction between a player and the software livelier and transcend every day experience. This has gone to the extent of introduction of virtual environments in games to enable the user interact with virtual objects in a game as if they were part of the game.

Figure 7.1. The platform on which Multimedia information is presented must be highly interactive between the user and the platform. Its advantage is that it gives the user.

Source: https://www.wisegeek.com/what-is-a-multimedia-device.htm.

Experience of being able to control what to be viewed and what not to be viewed. For example, in a video, one can forward the streaming to view content at the end or at the middle or go back and view the content at the beginning.

With the advancement of technology and many people opting for the use of the latest technological devices, most Multimedia information should be presented in a digital form. This allows them to be viewed from any device, may it be a desktop computer, a laptop among others (Costello, 2016).

The information shared through multimedia platforms should be integral. Different forms of presenting information ought to be integrated together to come up with a unique and integral format of presenting information all in one format to the end user.

7.4. CATEGORIZATION OF MULTIMEDIA

Multimedia is mainly divided into two categories.

The Linear active category which is mainly about combination of different forms of presenting information which to come up with unique format that does not have any navigational control for the audience. A perfect example is the theatre performances which are only under control of the actors performing on stage for they know what to present next and which way will be more dominant in their presentation.

Non-linear category simply gives the end-user the ability to actively interact with multimedia information. A user is able to control the display of information. Hypermedia which is more of an interlinked system of different ways of presenting information is part of the non-linear multimedia category. This is because it gives the user the ability to control the progress of their viewing.

Information presentations can be either live or recorded.

Live presentation is mostly preferred by organizations which conduct their meetings on a regular basis. It provides different staff members with the advantage of viewing the presentation of their fellow colleagues at the comfort of their homes or personal offices without having to meet at the conference hall. Live multimedia presentation does allow interactivity between the presenter and the one viewing the presentation.

Recorded presentations are used in situation where one is sure he or she will need to use that information for future use. For example, an Olympic competition is recorded to be presented to the organizers later for analysis of the performance. It may allow interactivity through use of a navigation system.

7.5. MULTIMEDIA SOFTWARE

It is basically a set of instruction which enable a developer to combine different forms of presenting information such as texts, videos, audio, and image files to come up with a unique, unified format of all this forms. One can use multimedia software to perform a variety of activities such as the pronunciation of words, viewing of different forms of artwork among others.

The filming industry is making use of the multimedia platform to come up with films of high quality. Effects such as enhancing the view of the production site, adding background music, combining different short videos to come up with a full unique movie, all of this do require the use of a multimedia software (Silva, 2016).

Music industry has also been enhanced and perfected by use of multimedia software. Music producers are able to add special effects to the original recording of a singer. The visual displayed can be enhanced by adding special effects to the environment in which they were recorded. Combination of the audio part and the visual part of the music production to come up with a complete volume of a music set is made possible by use of multimedia software.

The education sector is benefiting a lot from the multimedia worlds. Laboratory experiments which are said to be dangerous can be simulated and availed to students by use of multimedia software through videos streamed live online or by being recorded in safe environments and later downloaded to be viewed by students during laboratory sessions. This has reduced the dangers students face while carrying out such experiments.

Digital cameras are being used to record images in different forms on small digital chips embedded on them for storage purposes instead of having to use a film. Multimedia software enable enhancement of this images by use of different effects which almost completely change the view of an entire image. Such images are mostly used for advertisements posters while promoting a certain business. For example, promotion of most digital cameras use this enhanced images to prove to the buyer that they produce images of high quality (Silva, 2016).

The field of medicine is making use of multimedia softwares to perform different simulations which showcase its possible future. This software can also be modified in such a way that it is able to inform a patient of the possible illness by simply feeding in his or her symptoms to the computer. Medical trainings are being conducted through multimedia presentation providing a learner with a higher change of lively interactions with what is being taught. This reduces the monotony in medicine classes for students do not have to rely only on the lecture to gain knowledge.

Access to information has been made easier through use multimedia software. Most browsers have incorporated in their system the use of speech recognition programs which allow searching of information by speaking out your search term instead of having to type.

The result obtained after a search can also be presented in form speech, such that one has to listen instead of having to read. This integration is of great advantage to the physically impaired people for they are able to access information in an easier way.

Companies are making use of multimedia software to enable teleconferences. It reduces the cost incurred during traveling to the conference hall and it saves on time.

One is able to access the information being shared across during a meeting and even be able to contribute to the agenda of the day at the comfort of their homes or offices (Silva, 2016).

Online trainings are being effected by use of multimedia software. For example, piano trainings can be done online if one does not have the time to attend classes due to a tight schedule. Many students are also doing e-learning instead of having to travel physically to school.

This reduces the cost incurred while traveling from home to school and it offers students with a variety of online study materials from which they can research from.

Telepresence is being used for inspection purposes by many stakeholders in various production companies. Instead of having to pay a visit to the industry, they are able to inspect a certain product by logging in to an online robot avatar incorporated with multimedia software, and controlling its movements for whatever it views is send to the user's computer.

It does save on transport cost and time for one does not have to travel to the industry for inspection purposes.

Figure 7.2. Multimedia software are being used to perfect presentations. Many people are incorporating images, videos, animations, audio recordings among others in their presentations to enhance their view.

Source: *http://news.nidokidos.org/multimedia-software/.*

Reservations such as hotel booking, plane booking, train bookings and bus bookings are being done online via multimedia software. This reduces the congestion in airports, bus, and railway terminals for the purposes of booking and it also saves on the travel cost to be incurred in traveling to and fro different terminals for bookings. It also helps hotels and different transport sectors to offer better services to their customers for at least the number of customers to serve is known.

Travel guides are being used to help in navigations in roads, in big institutions, big hotels, national parks and game reserves among others. With the help of multimedia software, developers are able to come up with maps which guide new people on where to go. Some maps have been advanced to the extent of being incorporated with sound systems and location detectors. This help the user by detecting their current location and then guiding them with the help of sound systems on the direction to follow based on their marked destination as indicated on the map (Silva, 2016).

Many organizational are making use of multimedia software to conduct online trading. E-commerce platforms which are incorporated with multimedia software's are being used to advertise and sell different products and also offer delivery serviced to their clients.

Multimedia soft wares can be used for entertainment purposes. They can be used to stream movies either online or by downloading and watching them later. Some can be used to play music, watch animation clip videos, play videos games or any online games via computer.

The world is being turned into a Global village by use of multimedia soft wares. People are able to connect with each other despite their geographical locations via social media platforms such as "Facebook, Twitter, and Instagram among others."

Online games are also bringing people together for they interact virtually in the game virtual environment to compete for the different rewards offered in the game system.

Certain requirements must be met before the integration of Multimedia Software into any platform. An electronic device able to process data into useful information is required. It must have a good Central Processing Unit which is perfectly function so as to process multimedia data and produce the desired output. Internal or external storage device such as a hard drive or a Compact Disk with enough storage capacity is also a recommendation for multimedia information needs to be recorded for future use.

A Random Access Memory with perfect speed is required to ensure processing activities are conducted within the shortest time possible. A good video adapter cable with high resolution rate is also required to be used during presentation to ensure that the output displayed to the audience is of high quality. Sound cards are needed to enhance the sound system of the computer system to be used while presenting multimedia information. In situations whereby a presenter needs to record the presentation he or she is displaying to their users, a microphone might be of great use for it can be used to record a presenters own voice.

7.6. EXAMPLES OF MULTIMEDIA SOFTWARE

Picasa is an excellent example of multimedia. It mainly deals with images for it allows a user to edit their images by adding some special effects and view the changes. It can also be sued to organize how pictures are to be arranged in a user's storage platform for easier access of different images dealing with different themes or events. A user is offered with the opportunity to come up with a unique album which can be shared through various platforms with their loved ones.

The famous VLC media player developed by the VideoLAN company is used to play media content be it video or audio. It supports all formats of videos and audios reducing the stress of having to use a different platform. It can be installed in laptops, desktop computers and even mobile phones allowing streaming of videos and playing of audio files at the comfort of a client's current location. It is a free software for it is downloaded on the internet and installed in any technological device for free. The main advantage is that it offers a user with different ways of enhancing the experience of interacting with both audio and video files.

Adobe Photoshop is a multimedia software used to edit images. It uses its special effects to ensure that images are edited to the best of format by adding different multiple layers on an image so as to enhance its appearance. Since its invention, it has been advanced to higher levels to an extend of having its own file formats which are created once you edit an image depending on the kind editing features one uses.

Another example is the Media Monkey software. It is used to access and view videos and other media formats. It is a free open source software though if one requires to access its best qualities, they have to pay for the premium gold license.

The only difference between the paid for software and the normal free software is just a few editing features added to it. It organizes the users media files from the hard drive or any other storage device used and differentiates them into video files and music files adding each of them into their playlists respectively. It supports all media formats. Though Media Monkey software, a user is able to subscribe to different podcasts and even be able to keep a copy of the viewed podcast in its storage capacity by grouping them in the right order, either by the topic they deal with or the date of viewing. The only disadvantage of Media Monkey is that it can only be installed into a computer, either a desktop computer or a laptop and not any other technological device.

Inkscape is used to create and also edit images such as illustrations, logos, diagrams, and various types of paintings. It does support images of all formats. The created or edited images in Inkscape software can be animated by adding special movement effects availed in the software such as rotating effects, scaling, and moving effects among other. It only be installed in a computer device with either Macintosh operating system (OS) or the commonly used Windows OS, however, it can also be installed in android for easier accessibility. It is similar to adobe illustrator only that adobe illustrator does have a few more advanced features compared to it.

7.7. MULTIMEDIA SOFTWARE TOOLS

A multimedia software tool is a computer program that multimedia developers use during creation of multimedia, its editing, maintenance, and error checking and testing before its implementation once a software tool has been developed.

They are basically a collection of relatively simple programs, that are used a group to come up with the best multimedia soft wares of high quality.

During development of a multimedia software, some tools may be used more frequently or less depending on the type of software design being used. Tools may be used as small individual programs which are to be used individually in the development of a certain software.

They can also be part of a single larger program which is main aim is to be used in the development of a software system.

The main difference between a software tool and an application program is that a software tool is a combination of simple databases mostly containing a list of important values to be used in the development of a software while an application program is a complete set of database that is thought of as a complete set of software in its own right.

7.7.1. List of Multimedia Software Tools

With the advancement of technology, newer development needs have been discovered, hence the invention of different tools which will aid in the satisfaction of this demand.

The most basic combination of tools used for building multimedia software can be divided into several categories.

Image editing tools are used to edit and add some special features to already existing images.

They can be used to change the format of an image file. Most of the editing is either done by adding some multiple layer to the already existing image or use of special effects to enhance the image's final appearance.

Their use is simply that of reinventing and recreating the image. Examples of image editing software tools include the famous adobe photoshop and paint shop pro.

Sound editing tools are a main component in the editing of multimedia information for the purposes of enhancement of multimedia presentations. They provide the user with the feature of integrating sound into any multimedia file very easily. Sound is required to ensure that multimedia information being passed on to the audience is clear and of good quality.

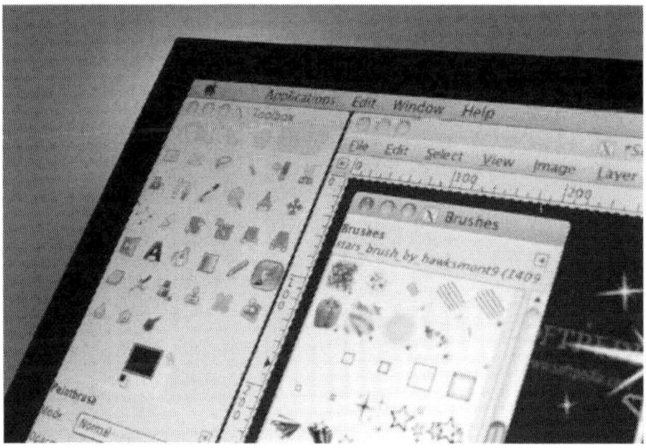

Figure 7.3. Image editing tools.

Source: *https://bluesyemre.com/2013/02/06/5-best-free-image-editing-tools-by-enid-burns/.*

The third category of Multimedia Software Tools is the video editing tools. Most users nowadays are preferring to access information presented in video format. This videos need to be edited by adding some special effects so as to enhance user experience and motivate more use of information presented in video format (Li, Drew, and Liu, 2014).

There are two ways of using both the sound editing tools and the video editing tools. One of them is the linear editing where by a developer makes use of mechanical processes by employing the use of devices such as the camcorder to collect and later edit the information. The other way is the Non-linear editing which is more of a digital for it mainly works on the principle of removing the unwanted parts of a multimedia information and employing some enhancements on the removed parts. The enhanced information is later used to duplicate the removed part.

Digital painting and drawing tools apply the art of the traditional painting methods. They make use of an electronic device such as a computer but mostly a graphical tablet integrated with a software and a stylus. Digital painting tools differ from the other forms of digital art for it does not make use of a computer to come up with a drawing design model. It is more of mimicking the traditional form of painting for it makes use of virtual brushes to draw shape on the screen of a graphical tablet with the help of a stylus.

Figure 7.4. Digital painting and drawing tools.

Source: *https://www.creativebloq.com/news/top-10-tools-for-digital-artists-this-december.*

Animation video tools are used to automatically generate images by use of a computer. They are an advancement of the hand drawn images or painted images on a celluloid sheet which used to be photographed and converted into moving objects and later used to create animation videos. This tools have increased the rate of generation of different animation clips and movies which are of high quality and with different added special effects.

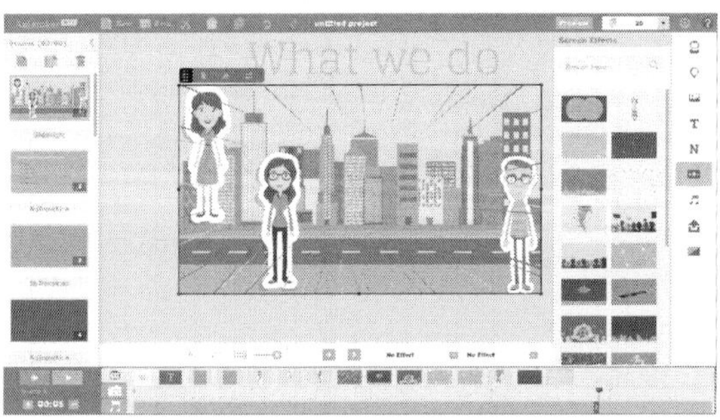

Figure 7.5. Animation video tools.

Source: https://learn.g2.com/free-animation-software.

Another category of multimedia software tools is the Cinema Tools. They are used to combine different film database tools and other editing features so as to enhance different film features and so as to ensure that the final film produced is of high quality and captivating to its audience.

7.8. LIST OF MULTIMEDIA EXPERTS

A Multimedia producer mostly deals with things to do with the internet. The internet involves things such as websites. Their functions involve coming up and producing websites. The website content depends on the client's needs and requirements. For the website producer, he or she has the task of coming up with the pages that make up the websites. Usually the minimum number of pages for a website is six pages so depending on the content they can come up with more than six pages. They are also tasked with the duty of making changes and updates or upgrades to the website and incase of any technical errors, they are responsible of fixing them within the shortest time possible.

The project manager is in charge of the overall projects in multimedia platforms. They make part of the team responsible for making important decisions dealing with the different organizational projects. They are in charge of the development of the project from the start of the project to its final stages. They are also in charge of the implementation of the various decisions by monitoring the day to day operations involved in the project. Project management involves designing the project as well as managing the project. The project managers come together and choose the design that will be more suitable and they actualize it. Most of the times they responsible for choosing the software that will be used during the project. They are therefore required to know the best software available. They make this decision based on the strengths and weaknesses of the software. They choose the individuals that will be involved in actualizing the projects. The individuals are chosen based on the skills that the individuals have. They also relay information from the client to the software team this way they produce the software according to the client's desires. The project managers should therefore have organizational skills (Li, Drew, and Liu, 2014).

A Multimedia Writer has the crucial role of coming up with the content. This is applicable for the websites. They work with the multimedia producer by coming up with the content that will be added to the website. The deal with the scripting of animation plays. They control the voice-overs as well as the actor narrators. This more so for the making of cartoons. They control the synchronization of the actor's narrators and the animations being made. They write proposals within multimedia and carry out test screens for the produced projects ensuring that they are okay before being sold. In the creation of animations, they create the characters in the animation. They coordinate the motion of the characters as well as make them do various actions such as jumping, laughing or even walking.

The video specialists are involved in media platforms mostly dealing with the visual and audio aspect. They know which mode the videos should be delivered in. For instance, those people relayed on video players, videos were delivered in form of Digital Versatile Disk. Newer forms in which the videos are delivered have been developed such as the Compact Disk, or even the internet. They also need to know how to shoot videos with very high quality that will be more appealing for the audience. They are required to have knowledge on how to transfer the video footages from the devices such as the camera to the computer. The mode of transfer that they choose should be efficient in that the whole video is transferred with none of the sections omitted. They should be able to properly use computers as their work involves them editing the video footage. They should be able to use both digital and nonlinear editing systems. The final version of the excited footage should be able to be displayed in digital formats (Li, Drew, and Liu, 2014).

Audio Specialists are more like the video specialists the only difference being that they deal with the audio aspect of multimedia. The fact that the latest digital technology is used in multimedia, the audio specialists are required to store the recorded materials within the computer. They also use the computers to digitalize and edit the recorded materials. They are also required to locate and select individuals with talent. The talent either in music or in narrators. They are then required to make schedules for the recordings. The identified individuals are then given time and date for the recording sessions.

Software engineers have the role of incorporating the various multimedia elements into a project. They do so by using the most appropriate systems. They are required to know the right programming language to be used in incorporating multimedia element into the project. They also control and manage the timings in the progression of videos. They select that the transitions that will be used in the project. Most of the times they are also in charge of keeping records of the projects. Programming deals with the creation of codes. The multimedia programmers write the codes that are later on displayed. The codes are used in displaying the various elements in multimedia. For them to be able to make the codes, they need to have knowledge on controlling the peripheral devices such as the computers. With such knowledge, he or she can be able to manipulate the devices for them to work to his advantage.

Multimedia designing team consist of a variety of individuals. They all have different roles to play when it comes to multimedia design. The team consist of the graphics designers, animators, image processing specialists and the illustrators. For the image processing specialists, their role is to come up with visual content which will be used in making the project more attractive. The animators have the role of coming up with the animation. They make the successive progressions of the animations being made such as the transitions as well as the audio incorporation of the animation (Mitra, 2004).

Graphic designers are the ones who create the graphical content for the project. The instructional designers have the role of ensuring that the content is clearly displayed for the audience. The information designers come up with the content that will enable the team to get feedback. They also choose the most appropriate method of presenting the media.

The interface designers come up with the content map and pathways which may be used in website. They also design and create an interface that will be user friendly for the user. They come up with software devices. These software is created and programmed to facilitate the user enabled modification of content.

Apart from modification, the software allows the user to access the content. The software organizes and presents the content in the mode that the user requires (Mitra, 2004).

7.9. ADVANTAGES AND DISADVANTAGES OF MULTIMEDIA SOFTWARE TOOLS

7.9.1. Advantages

Multimedia software tools enhance the creativity of a user. This is because they challenge us to come up with better soft wares which will make our work easier and help us in production of better and high quality applications.

They cater for all types of learners. People with little knowledge on computational courses are able to able to run and operate different tools provided by multimedia software's for they are user-friendly.

In terms of education, it offers students with better tools which they can use to access different study materials. Some laboratory experiments which are dangerous to students can be conducted in simulations hence preventing any accidents from occurring and educating learners too.

Multimedia software tools provide a user with a more realistic way of solving problems. This provides an easy approach to problem-solving.

With the use of different software tools, one is open to a wide support system which equips them with the right information on how to handle different problems.

7.9.2. Disadvantages

The use of different Multimedia Software tools requires electricity for them to be operated. This source of power might not be available in most rural areas limiting their use in rural areas.

It takes a lot of time to decide which design one should really use because this software tools offer one with different smart and attention-grabbing designs. This software tools are fragile and require lots of caution during their operation.

The cost of installing a full system which uses the best quality of Multimedia Software tools is quite high. This tools require constant testing and maintenance practices which consume large amounts of money.

The use of Multimedia Software tools requires mastery of some skills before use. They also have limited support in the community for not everyone has the slightest idea of how to use them.

CHAPTER

8

Multimedia Learning

CONTENTS

8.1. INTRODUCTION

Multimedia learning is used to refer to a situation in which students are able to learn using pictures and words. It is also possible to use different modes including taste, smell, or haptic devices. These other modes are not used often, however, there is research that is being done to incorporate them efficiently in the learning sector. Most learning institutions use pictures, videos, and texts. In regards to texts, their materials are presented in a verbal form, and are inclusive of spoken words and also words that have been printed. Pictures refer to forms that are pictorial and these are inclusive of pictures that are static including diagrams, graphics, photos, maps, and illustrations, in addition to pictures that are dynamic, such as videos, films, and animations.

Considering the fact that multimedia technology is proliferating at a high rate, it is important for us to explore some of the major questions when it comes to learning. Technology that has to do with interactive multimedia learning can help in creating unity in the learning front, same way doctors are united by medicine.

Due to these times that are run by technology, it is possible for society to consider multimedia literacy as important as knowing how to write. This means that it is important to provide students with the abilities and opportunities for the creation and utilization of multimedia documents.

Figure 8.1. Multimedia learning has proven to be an important tool in learning. It has been able to help in considering the students who prefer to learn using audio and visual aids to better understand the content being taught.

Source: https://www.eschoolnews.com/2020/01/02/multimedia-learning-tools-classrooms/.

One of the main issues that has come up in introducing and providing this opportunity, is the ability to design tools that can be used by the young learners for the creation of multimedia communications. These tools are the ones that will be able to provide students with the opportunity to not only become multimedia consumers, but also multimedia producers. Students need to learn how to control multimedia that is controlled using computers for them to be able to communicate the manner in which they understand information.

Texts, video clips, pictures, and other forms of multimedia are important in the development and conveyance of the understanding that students have, due to certain reasons. Some of these include:

- There is a huge similarity between multimedia communication and face to face communication.
- There are less restrictions with multimedia than there are with texts that are written. There are many people who comprehend texts in an easier manner when it is accompanied by media during its presentation. It has proven to make it easier for one to interpret the information being relayed.
- Multimedia is able to place concepts that are abstract in a context that is specific. For example, when trying to explain to students the manner in which a diffusion in science occurs, using a video can be very helpful in promoting student retention.
- Multimedia provides a better learning environment, as students with different preferences for sensory channels for learning are catered for.
- Multimedia also promotes the coordination of external representations that are very diverse so as to provide perspectives that are different.

It is not that easy to create multimedia composition tools for students. It is actually much more than giving the students the opportunity to make these decisions themselves with a set of options that were previously defined.

8.2. THE TRADITIONAL APPROACH OF LEARNING

The traditional method of teaching, which is also referred to as conventional education, is a custom that has been long-established and deemed appropriate by many different schools in the past and even right now. This method of teaching and learning is more centered on the teachers and it focuses on memorization and rote learning.

In this approach, are expected to passively absorb both authority and Information. This makes students become inactive in the classroom, in addition to having low levels of problem-solving skills. In addition to this, the conventional methods of learning are linear with skill mastery and factual accumulation in comparison to the newer methods that utilize multimedia which are non-linear, having one concept linked to a different one, giving the student the opportunity to choose the path they are interested in learning with.

Figure 8.2. The conventional method of teaching has not been as effective as expected. It expects students to memorize the content instead of fully comprehend and utilize this content for their daily lives.

Source: http://edugrid.pk/are-conventional-teaching-methods-really-effective/.

This approach also has many issues when it comes to resources. This is because all the information the students are taking in can only been absorbed through textbooks and lectures. Having the ability to utilize multimedia helps in having access to many more resources, especially those that can be accessed using the internet. The conventional approach has also proven to also be less creative. Due to the lack in material resources that students require so as to express their levels of creativity, the students become more passive. This can make students loose passion and motivation when learning. This are some of the reasons why multimedia learning is very important in education (Mayer, 2009).

Lectures may be traditional, however, they are the most effective and important tool of teaching. Not only do the teachers think so, but also the students. This is because the lecturers are able to compress the learning material, which may be very vast, and thereafter deliver it to the students in a manner that is well organized, helping to lower the level of stress on the students. Despite the fact that this traditional method is considered important, it has both advantages and disadvantages.

Some of the main advantages include:

- Lectures are very important when it comes to meeting the student's needs. This is because they are able to make the workload easier for the students.
- Lectures help in condensing large quantities of Information and this helps in presenting it to more people.
- There are students who prefer to learn by listening, and this method can appeal greatly to them.

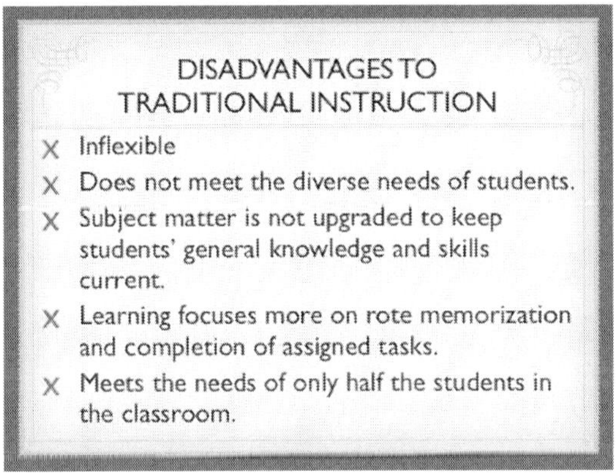

Figure 8.3. Above are some of the disadvantages that have been noted in the conventional method of teaching. One of the major concerns is that it is not able to meet the needs of all the students in the classroom.

Source: https://www.slideshare.net/maverikeducation/a-balanced-approach-combining-traditional-and-differentiated-instruction.

Some of the disadvantages include:

- This method makes students passive during the lessons and therefore avoid giving the teachers feedback.
- It also makes the teachers assume that all the students are normally at a similar level of understanding, and also that they all learn at a pace that is similar, despite the fact that they are not.
- Lectures are only efficient for students who are effective in communication. Having to read the information on slides is ineffective during lectures.

8.3. THE MULTIMEDIA APPROACH OF LEARNING

Multimedia has proven to be very important in the education system. This is because it is inclusive of many different forms of media, including videos, sound, text, animation, and graphics. It is possible to see all these elements in our surroundings. In addition to education, multimedia has also been used in technology, games, science, training, and business. This is a major sign that multimedia is paramount in our daily lives today. Due to the advancements in technology, multimedia has helped in providing new ways in which students can learn in an effective and efficient manner. It has helped in providing other methods other than the use of textbooks, thus making many improvements in the education sector by the addition of many different elements that have made learning much more dynamic.

Figure 8.4. Research has shown that the use of multimedia in the classroom has led to an increase in the number of students who perform highly in the classroom. This is because it is known to improve student understanding of the concepts being taught.

Source*:* https://www.tes.com/lessons/Rw-N_eIwbKfY4g/multimedia-in-classroom-eed21604.

Skills, knowledge, and education courses have often been taught in a certain context. So as to deal with this issue, using multimedia in the education sector has helped in the provision of real world examples by utilizing computers that can provide a lot of high quality content. There are also many different softwares in the market that can help in providing methods of learning that are both friendly and interactive.

Using both multimedia and the internet in learning can give teachers the opportunities to access many different teaching resources that are available. These materials can give the teachers with the ability to provide their students with skills that they should have to succeed in this world, including critical thinking, problem-solving, discussion, and also cooperative learning. This is all proof that using multimedia is much more beneficial than using traditional methods (Mayer, 2009).

8.4. MULTIMEDIA ELEMENTS USED IN EDUCATION

The different elements of multimedia can be used for many different things. There are computer software's that help in the creation and combining of the different elements of multimedia for the creation of projects, such as Adobe Flash, Adobe Illustrator and Adobe Photoshop. So as to apply these elements into learning, it is important to have knowledge on the functions of each element. Below are the descriptions.

Text: This is considered the most basic multimedia element and it is also the easiest to use. It however, should not be underestimated because it helps in providing the highest impact when it comes to the quality of the interactions with the multimedia, in comparison to the other elements. This is because there are many fonts that are contained in texts.

Fonts are considered a group of characters that are of one size and style. They belong to a specific typeface family. Generally, texts help in the provision of information that is important. This is due to the fact that texts help in making the information being relayed much more direct and easy to comprehend in comparison to other elements of multimedia. Texts are the multimedia elements that are mostly used in learning. They may seem boring, but when they are used as a form of multimedia, the words tend to draw much more interest in comparison to using textbooks that have plain texts, therefore leading to an increase in the learning effectiveness.

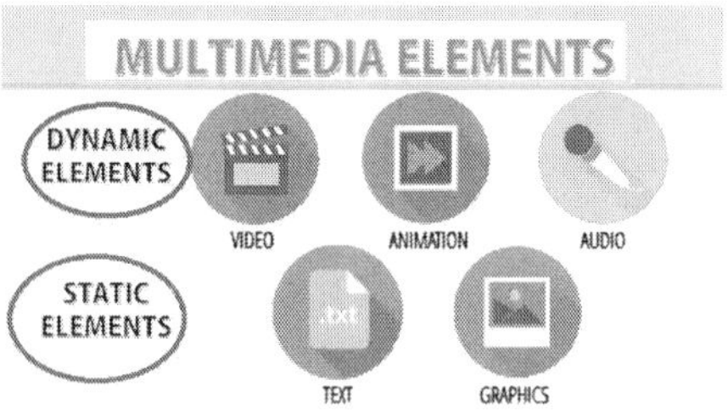

Figure 8.5. There are two types of multimedia elements. The static ones that include graphics and texts and the dynamic ones that are audio, animations, and videos.

Source*:* http://www.netnic.org/concept-of-multimedia/.

Graphics: These are illustrations or figures that are in two dimensions. These are considered the most creative method of learning. One can either use a drawing, a picture or a photograph. Picture formats come in many different types, including PNG, GIF, and JPEG. Utilizing graphics in the education sector can help in increasing the level of student comprehension. It also helps in enhancing their retention skills due to the fact that they are much easier to remember. This is due to the fact that images utilize a large amount of skills that are cortical, including line, color, imaginations, dimensions, and form. They allow for students to gain a clearer picture of the aspects that they are learning.

Audio: This element has been utilized for many years in the education sector. This is because majority of the things we learn are easily recordable, making it a tool that is very effective, because the students can use it for interaction with the content of the course that is being taught by their teachers wherever and whenever they want to.

Audios have also helped in making it much easier for students to conduct live discussions online through audio platforms and tools. There are a couple of software's that can be utilized for this purpose, such as Skype, WhatsApp, WeChat, among others. This not only helps in saving time when one has no time to meet face to face with the teacher, but it can also help in long distance learning.

It is also possible for audio to be used by teachers for the delivery of high amounts of information at once. This allows the teachers to make explanations of the information being relayed in ways that are much more interesting, therefore allowing the students to properly understand the topic being taught. Audio learning can also help in teaching people who are disabled, such as the blind, allowing them to learn through sound because they are not able to see nor read. If used in the correct way, audio can help many different people in the education sector.

Video: Video is a multimedia element that is used widely. Among the five elements, it has the highest level of performance on any device or computer. For educational use, there are a couple of video formats that are standard such as MPEG-2 which is utilized for the DVD, or MPEG-4 which is used for the home video.

Sometimes, the use of texts and also other elements of multimedia to relay information has proved to be complicated. Videos are used because they help in providing the students with visual stimulation, allowing them to fully comprehend what they are learning. They have proven to be very effective, even in training surgeons, where they may nit be able to fully understand a certain procedure just by reading on it; however, using a video that has a surgery taking place can help them to better understand the procedure.

Teachers are also able to ask their students to create projects using video as their element of multimedia. This is due to the fact that it is able to provide them with the ability to get in touch with the actual aspect of the content they are learning. This also helps in peer to peer learning because the students can show each other their projects.

Figure 8.6. Video multimedia is the element that is mostly used in education. It is able to include all the elements of multimedia into one. Videos can help in explaining procedures that the teacher would not be able to explain by talking, thus making the learning process much more effective.

Source: *https://www.shutterstock.com/image-photo/video-screen-multimedia-technology-education-graphic-445113493.*

In addition to all this, video projects can also help in enhancing the practical skills of the student. This is because, they have exposure to the external element when they are asked to do the video project, in comparison to sitting in class all day. All this allows them to improve their skills at the same time gaining much more experience. Videos can be very helpful in the improvement of the educational system.

Animation: These are created through having a motion that is continuous together with changes in shape for the production of an animation. The psychological phenomenon called phi and the persistent of vision are biological phenomenon's that account for the introduction of animations. They allow us to visualize animations as they are. They are dissimilar to videos. This is due to the fact that videos are taken from events in real life while animations are normally made from drawings.

There are a couple of software's that can be used to create animations in the education sector. These include Director, Authoware, and Adobe Flash. Students are able to use these software's to make use of their creativity for the creation and presentation of school projects. Not only do they enhance creativity, but also make learning fun.

Students are also able to learn easier and faster using animations. This is due to the fact that they are efficient in allowing the teacher to teach a topic that may harder for them to understand without the animations. For example, the teacher is able to use animations to show the students the inner parts of the body and how they function, making it easier for the students to understand the inside if the body despite the fact that they are not able to see it. This helps in improving student retention and understanding. Learning and teaching can be made much easier, amusing, and fast with the incorporation of animations.

8.5. ADVANTAGES OF MULTIMEDIA IN LEARNING

Being able to understand the capabilities of multimedia can help us in understanding the reason why we should integrate multimedia into education. Apart from being a very powerful tool when it comes to creating presentations, it also provides great benefits in the educational field. Using textbooks only keeps students from fully experiencing the learning experience. For example, reading a Shakespeare play is much different from listening t it. Even when teaching sciences, it is possible to use multimedia to bring the lesson to life. It helps in providing a manner in which the students are able to fully experiment the topic being taught in a manner that is vicarious (Saddik, 2013).

This can all be achieved by using audio, video, graphics, and text in a simultaneous manner, instead of in a sequential manner. It is possible to see the appeal that multimedia learning has brought in our world today, through the illustration of the level of popularity of video games that are in the market currently. Video games are multimedia programs that have been able to achieve the combination of video, audio, text in addition to animated graphics, all in a fashion that is easy to use.

In addition, in a conditions where the school has low funds, utilizing multimedia can help in providing a learning experience that is augmented or enhanced, at a cost that is lower per unit. There are many things that can be done so as to unleash the full power of multimedia, so as to ensure the provision of long-term benefits to everyone. It is through discovery, experience, and exploration that multimedia is able to provide a learning experience (Saddik, 2013).

It is not true to say that technology drives education because that role is dependent on the need of the students when it comes to learning. Using multimedia helps in making the learning process more flexible when it comes to space and time, more oriented on goals, it also makes it unaffected by long distances, the students participate more, and it is possible to tailor multimedia to learning styles for each individual student, therefore helping in increasing the level of collaboration between the students and the teachers. Multimedia helps in making learning become friendly and much more interesting, at the same time reducing the level of fear in students when it comes to inadequacies and failure.

Figure 8.7. The use of projectors or personal computers provides students the chance to see the content being taught up close. This allows them to use their imagination to experience the learning experience, thus allowing them to retain the content in an easier manner.

Source: https://education.seattlepi.com/advantages-disadvantages-schools-using-multimedia-3099.html.

There are some benefits to the students. This include:

- Gaining a deeper understanding – in accordance with research, students benefit from multimedia learning due to the fact that it takes advantage of the ability the brain has when it comes to making connections between visual and verbal content representation, which leads to an understanding that is deeper. This ends up supporting the transference of learning to different situations. This is very important in classrooms of today, because students are being prepared for future that expects them to have collaborative skills, problem-solving skills, and also the ability to think on a higher level.

- The students get to improve their problem-solving skills – there is a large portion of the brain that is able to dedicate itself to processing visual multimedia. This means that the use of videos, animations, and images alongside texts helps in stimulating the brain. This helps in increasing student retention and attention. These circumstances provide students with the ability to make identifications of and solving of problems in an easier manner in comparison to using just textbooks to teach.
- It helps in increasing the students' positive emotions – psychologists have proven that being able to experience positive emotions allows students to see many more possibilities in their lives. The use of multimedia to provide a set of instructions is important in impacting the mood of a student during the process of learning. They are able to have a better learning experience and also become much more proactive in the classroom.
- The students are able to access large amounts of information – having access to tablets, smartphones, computers, and the internet allows students to be well equipped with the tools that they can use for searching and finding the desired information. Researchers were able to show us that around 96% of the students who use the internet normally utilize it to search for information online. This allows the students to be confident when it comes to sharing information as well as participating in class, due to easy access to information with the help of the internet.
- The students get to explore the world – multimedia has helped children in exploring and learning about locations they have never traveled to. Students are able to explore various parts of the world in a geography class. This includes forests and mountains, among others. It is now possible to explore plants and space in a science class. Multimedia can also allow students to view dissection videos and even different habitats for animals.

This being said, we can now discuss the main advantages of multimedia in education. Multimedia provides a pedagogical strength which is the ability to utilize the natural abilities of processing information, that we as humans already have. The fact that information and communication technology is growing at a higher rate in the society has led to encouraging the use of Information and communication technology in education.

Students who are able to access the modern technology as well as educational tools at their homes through interactive learning and computers, among others, have a higher potential when it comes to absorbing these technologies when they are being utilized for learning in the school. One of the main aspects that are being looked into in research papers when it comes to multimedia teaching methods, is the manner in which they can be able to improve the ability of the students to be involved in a much more interactive manner in the classroom. This has proven to be a big issue considering the fact that due to the availability of Internet, wireless, etc. students have many distractions in the classroom when they have and use these tools (Mayer, 2009).

Figure 8.8. Teachers need to be able to use the multimedia content in a way that enables interaction in the class so as to ensure that the learning is effective. The students need to stay engaged and not distracted by the content.

Source*:* https://www.emergingedtech.com/2014/07/ways-video-conferencing-bringing-collaboration-teaching/amp/.

Being able to provide the opportunity for the learners to utilize these tools for learning purposes instead of only using them for social or entertainment activities, will have a major beneficial impact on multimedia learning. Multimedia helps in providing a learning environment that is very beneficial and based on technology. It allows students to solve many problems all while depending on themselves, and this is referred to as self-exploration method, active participation and collaboration.

Some of the multimedia materials such as animated graphics and still graphics, audio, and video, not forgetting models and simulations, should be integrated in a manner that is well designed. They help the students learn new knowledge in a manner that is much more effective. There are many people who consider utilizing these multimedia and e-learning tools to help in supplementing the normal conventional classes; this however, should not be used to fully replace the conventional classes.

The use of interactive multimedia in the classroom has shown to be a phenomenon that is growing almost every day. It has really helped students in the learning process. It is possible to conclude that the use of multimedia helps in enhancing and enabling students to learn in a manner that is much more effective (Mayer, 2009).

In addition to all this, the use of multimedia in the classroom helps in providing researchers with much more information on how students adapt and react to it, so as to promote the efforts in the creation of newer programs using the elements of multimedia and tools that are used to author multimedia, so as to provide learning software's that are rich in content. There are many researchers who are studying the manner in which the use of multimedia impacts the different field of education during teaching. This includes mathematics, sciences, engineering, languages, etc. There are some potential positive outcomes that all schools need to consider when integrating multimedia in the classroom. Here are some of them:

- Multimedia is able to retain the attention of the students;
- It is also helps in allowing the students to focus and concentrate;
- Multimedia can be used to make the lessons interesting, thus generating student interest;
- It also helps in creating a level of expectation;
- Multimedia can help in energizing or relaxing students for the learning process;
- It also activates the students' level of imagination;
- It also helps in the improvement of the students' attitude to learning and also the learning content;
- Multimedia also helps in building a bond between the teacher and the students;
- Student retention of learning material is also greatly increased;
- The students tend to understand the content better with the use of multimedia;
- It helps in fostering creativity;
- Multimedia helps in stimulating the flow of ideas;
- It also helps in fostering deeper learning;

- Multimedia serves a collaboration vehicle;
- It gives the students an opportunity to exercise freedom of expression;
- Students get inspired and motivated when using multimedia;
- It also helps in making the learning experience more fun;
- Multimedia can be used for setting a tone or mood that is appropriate; and
- It helps in providing visual images that the students find easier to remember.

8.6. DISADVANTAGES OF MULTIMEDIA IN EDUCATION

There are two main aspects that we can consider when we discuss the disadvantages of multimedia in education. The practical disadvantages and educational disadvantages. Firstly, we will discuss the practical disadvantages of using multimedia in the classroom. When you think about it in a practical manner, delivering multimedia lessons or aspects of a lesson using images or videos needs for the teacher or school to have either a computer, tablets, a projector, or a different computing device, all depending on the topic being taught and the size of the material that the teacher was able to create.

Figure 8.9. It is important for the teacher to remember the downsides that come with the use of technology in the classroom. Access to the internet can end up distracting students due to platforms such as social media. Teachers should always make sure to use platforms that are not distracting.

Source: https://theconversation.com/amp/students-distracted-by-tech-leave-professors-longing-for-eye-contact-120933.

Purchasing projectors or computers that are of good quality for each student can be quite expensive and having computers that are not of good quality can reduce and slow down the students' pace of learning, due to the size of the videos and the images, which may not be supported by low quality computers and projectors. Students that are able to access computers at the homes may also run into some troubles. This is because they may have access to information that is not appropriate for them. In addition, when students have their own electronic devices from home, the different qualities can lead to presentations and projects that are not equal (Saddik, 2013).

Secondly, we discuss some of the educational disadvantages of using multimedia in education. When a teacher designs a multimedia presentation for the students, his or her role as a teacher changes from being the instructor to the person facilitating. If the multimedia lesson permits the student to finish the learning material at a pace of their own, the ability of the teacher to manage the classroom becomes much more difficult. This is more prominent especially when the students are working in groups to view the presentation or even when they are sharing computers.

In addition, the ability to use these tools depends on the computer literacy if the person using them. Students who are not that literate in computing technology have to take much more time to learn these skills, so as to be able to use these tools to access the learning material that the teacher provides. It is also important to consider that the teachers who are not familiar with producing and designing multimedia coursework or packages have to be trained, which can be both expensive due to additional costs, and complicated (Saddik, 2013).

8.7. WAYS IN WHICH MULTIMEDIA IS USED FOR LEARNING

There are many ways in which multimedia can be used in the classroom. Here are are some of the ways.

8.7.1. The Use of Audio Books in the Classroom

Audio books can be used to improve the reading skills of students. They have proven to be much more effective than watching videos due to the fact that the students tend to focus more on the background music and the pictures that are playing in the video instead of the texts and the pronunciations. This is also similar with books, because the books do not provide the students with the proper pronunciation to the text that the students are reading.

Lit2Go is a site that teachers are able to use in the classroom to play audio books. It helps in improving the students' reading skills. This site has recordings of many different classics such as Heart of Darkness by Joseph Conrad. This can also be achieved using CDs that have recordings of different books that students would enjoy to listen to. All this can be very beneficial in improving student literature and pronunciation (Konert, 2014).

8.7.2. Using YouTube in the Classroom

This method of teaching is referred to as digital storytelling. It involves the use of tools that are digital to relay a story. There are other forms of digital storytelling, such as electronic memoirs, computer-based narratives, digital documentaries, etc. They are able to tell a story using the different elements of multimedia including video, audio, graphics, and web publishing. It can be used for the presentation of materials that are new to the students, in a different way.

Figure 8.10. YouTube can be used in the classroom to show educational videos to the students. The amount of educational content on YouTube is a lot, and this can help in preventing boredom by changing up the teaching style.

Source: https://u.osu.edu/piemonte.4/2014/03/04/YouTube-in-the-classroom/.

It is a method that has proven to be very useful in capturing the attention of the students and also in increasing their level of interest when it comes to the exploration of new ideas. It also helps in the engagement of students with images that are colorful, elements of videos, and audio.

8.7.3. Using Videos to Create Mini-Lessons

Teachers are able to create lesson plans by utilizing videos as stand-alone overviews for certain topics. Video content that is created by teachers can be hosted by many different websites which are available as previews and reviews of skill. An example is the education version of YouTube called Teacher Tube that helps teachers cover major school subjects.

This platform makes it easy for one to search for a certain topic or also in browsing by categories, which helps one to find specific videos that are relevant. A student can be able to search for "middle school geography" and the search engine will provide a page of results that contain study guides, reviews of exams, and even in specific lessons. This method of integrating technology in the classroom is easy and also includes an element of multimedia to the teaching plan. This can help in effective resonance with learners who prefer to use a visual aid. There is also a study that has shown that using videos that are animated in the classroom can help in impacting the development of a child positively, in areas such as creativity, memory, problem-solving, etc. (Konert, 2014).

8.7.4. Coordination of Live Videos

Teachers do not have to pre-record videos to teach their students, because there is the availability of video conferencing that allows for teachers to deliver lessons using videos, live. This can be done even by teachers that are found in other schools or teachers that too far to teach the class in person. Being able to bring in experts as well through conference calls can help in exposing the students to newer ideas and also make the workload lighter.

This person can be added as a contact either through Skype or Google hangouts, allowing them to give the lesson using the program. Skype also provides a list of guests that speak on topics they are experts in voluntarily. You can make this more interesting for the students by asking them to prepare questions that they can ask during the video conference call. This also promotes student participation.

8.7.5. Playing Podcasts

Being able to play podcasts that are relevant does not only help in the supplementation of lessons, but also in engaging learners who prefer audio learning and thus allowing it to act as a station for learning. There are many podcasts that can be found online. They are made by both media specialists and even just the ordinary person who is passionate on a specific topic. Some of the topics that can be found are:

- Lessons on the techniques and strategies of learning;
- Lectures from popular professors;
- Recorded interview with authors of books that the students might be reading at the time; and
- Exploring of topics that are related to the curriculum.

It is also beneficial to allow students to make and presentation their own podcasts, which can be achieved by designing projects within the school course. Podcasts have been confirmed to be one of the easiest ways to integrate technology into the class. All one needs are effective speakers.

8.7.6. Using Virtual Manipulatives

During the teaching and reinforcement of certain mathematical concepts, students are able to use virtual manipulatives in ways that are not only physical. For example, Geo-boards can be used in 6th grade geometry activities, from the National Library of Virtual Manipulatives, to help in the illustration or areas, perimeters, and concepts that are rational.

Despite the fact that there are not many websites that can provide these manipulatives, the most versatile and engaging website that is used by most teachers is the National Library of Virtual Manipulatives. It includes different tasks that target students from the stages before kindergarten, all the way to the 11th grade. It is an appealing method to most hands-on learners.

8.7.7. Using the Interactive Whiteboard to Present Multimedia

This tool helps to promote interactions with content that is digital, as well as multimedia, in a learning environment that has multiple persons in an effective manner. Some of the ways this tool is used include:

- Being able to display and view certain website together as a class;
- Manipulation of images and notes;
- Being able to save notes so as to allow reviewing of the notes at a later time;
- Writing notes in digital ink;
- Using images and other different forms of multimedia to create lesson activities that are digital;
- Being able to show the class ways in which they can use a certain application software without having to use the small screen in the computer;

- Adding notes over video clips that are educational;
- For the enhancement of materials that are used for learning;
- For the students to be able to display the work that they are presenting to the whole class;
- The board is equipped with presentation tools that the teacher or student can use to make presenting easier and efficient; and
- This is a tool that can help in improving interactivity in the classroom.

Figure 8.11. The interactive whiteboard can be used in the classroom to allow the students to get in touch with the aspects being taught. Is can display any element of multimedia.

Source: https://www.thetechedvocate.org/are-you-maximizing-the-impact-of-your-interactive-whiteboard/.

8.7.8. Using Computer-Supported Problem-Solving E-Games to Learn

Quizzes and computer-based tests have been recommended in improving the problem-solving skills of students in the classroom. Especially when one uses online adventure games and asks the students to solve some problems that are in problem sets. Teachers are able to use multimedia adventure games as sets of information, where potential pathways as well as the questions that may be asked, are previously determined.

Generally, these games have many different potential pathways when it comes to the level of sophistication and difficulty, as well as how complex the answers to the questions or problems that have been predetermined, are.

There are certain aspects that help in supporting the use of these games as an approach for problem-solving. These are:

- The student is able to get help, feedback, and support from the computer due to the interactive nature of these games. It is still possible for the students to require an instructor for some guidance in this learning environment.
- It is possible to determine the level of cognitive demand that is available in these games through the range of responses that is provided. It is possible to solve different problems in very many different ways. These games are very beneficial because the students have to find different ways of dealing with these problems in accordance to their different perspectives, thus confronting many different possibilities. This however, may have a downside due to the fact that, the many solutions to the problems can end up limiting the creativity level of the students.
- These games provide students with the opportunity to save their progress at any point they would want to and also be able to return to that same point later on, thus making them time effective.
- Students are also able to experiment on many different potential solutions for one problem when it comes to solving it. They are also able to experiment with these options in a short period of time. Without these games, it is hard to ensure provision of these form of trial and error learning in a period of time that is deemed appropriate, and also often quite difficult to test this solutions in reality.
- These games help in gaining the students' interests and commitment due to the fact that they enjoy these games, because they are able to put everything in a context that is more meaningful of a world that is fictional and they are able to interpret this context in the real and living world.

Being able to solve problems is a process that is intellectually complicated and deals with having to coordinate a range of skills that are demanding and interrelated, including:

The ability to understand and represent the problem and identify the specific information that is necessary for the solution.

- One also needs to be able to gather and organize interactive information that is relevant.

Figure 8.12. E-games can be used in the classroom during a break. These can keep the students interested in the content being taught. There are a couple of educational e-games that can help students in improving their problem-solving skills.

Source: https://www. facebook. com/EGC. mmu/.

- The ability to construct and manage a plan of action or a strategy that is interactive;
- Students need to reason, test hypothesis, and make decisions in the process; and
- The students should also be able to use the different tools for solving problems, making evaluations of results that are interactive, and monitoring solutions.

8.7.9. Using Editing of Videos, Sound, and Graphics to Learn

Some schools provide their students with the opportunity to perform in ballets, musicals, plays, interviews, and even conferences. These can all be broadcasted on TV channels that are run by the students, or even online. For this to be effective, the students need to be equipped with a computer that has a microphone, an internet connection, a video camera, and an account they can stream on. The teachers can also ask the students to listen to podcasts on the regular by well known lecturers, and have discussions on the topics being talked about. The students are then able to make their own content from this content which helps them to also better understand multimedia.

There are also many different websites that are found in the multimedia collection, and these websites have content that us relevant to the educational subject in general. The Adobe TV is one of these platforms. It is able to provide content on different multimedia software's that can be used.

Students in higher learning are also able to use software's to turn photos into videos. Photo to Movie is a free software that both teachers and students can use. It can be used for displaying photos, music, effects, adding titles, zooming into certain parts of a photo, and even adding backgrounds. They can also use different video editing software's such as Adobe Premiere and Windows Movie Maker to also learn more about the aspects of multimedia. The teacher can ask the students to select certain educational videos and ask them to add music, sound or even texts. In addition to this, the students are also able to use recorders and audio editors to handle certain elements such as music, sounds, and speech. The teacher can ask them to record certain files, such as a lecture and later on edit them by changing the recording speed, etc. All these can help students become more aware on the different ways they can use multimedia to learn (Konert, 2014).

8.8. THE COGNITIVE THEORY OF MULTIMEDIA LEARNING

Multimedia learning refers to using pictures and words to learn. Watching a power presentation, or a lecture that has been pre-recorded are both examples of multimedia learning.

8.8.1. The Multimedia Principle

This is the principle helps in serving as a foundation for The theory of Multimedia Design. It helps in asserting the fact that deeper learning happens with the use of both pictures and words, instead of using just words. However, there is no assurance that the simple act of adding graphics and images will promote a level of deeper learning. Students are more likely to have a learning experience that is much more meaningful with multimedia instructional content that has been developed with certain cognitive science assumptions in mind. Some of these assumptions include:

- An assumption of the active processes – for one to experience active learning, there is a need to carry out a set of cognitive processes that are well coordinated, during the learning process.
- An assumption of Dual channels – it is important to consider that one may need dual channels, one for verbal and auditory processing and another for pictorial and visual processing.
- The assumption of limited capacity – each channel is equipped with a capacity that is limited for processes.

8.9. THE NECESSITY OF USING THE MULTIMEDIA DESIGN THEORY

The Working Memory – The working memory refers to the section of the memory that is able to process information consciously. This part of the memory is very limited. Due to the fact that most of the multimedia instructional content that the students interact with it novel, the teachers are required to remember the fact that the working memory is limited when they are designing multimedia instructional content.

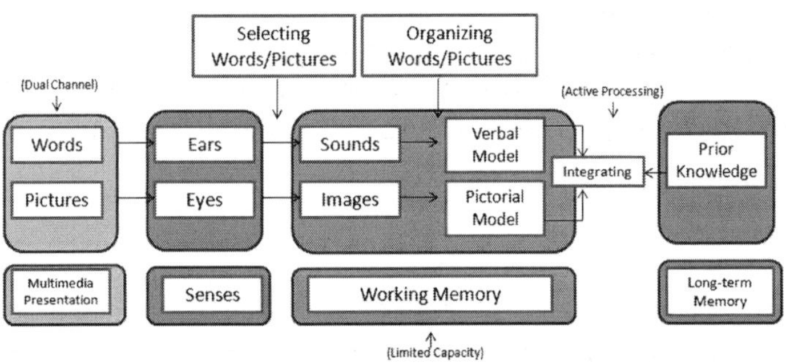

Figure 8.13. Above is an Instructional design that can help in reducing the cognitive load on students. Cognitive load can reduce the level of the learning experience.

Source: https://en.wikiversity.org/wiki/Cognitive_Theory_of_Multimedia_Learning.

When teachers develop lessons while considering the fact that the working memory of the students' is limited, these lessons tend to be much more effective in comparison to lessons that are developed without this consideration. For example, providing the students with instructions that have been written down as an activity for a small group, instead of just stating to the students the instructions one by one, giving the students the opportunity to do their work without having to remember the instructions.

The Cognitive Load – One of the issues that occur when there is a combination of pictures and words in the same situation, is a cognitive overload. In this situation, the demands for processing information that are associated to the task of learning end up exceeding the cognitive processing capacity of the student. Cognitive load can be described in three different ways: intrinsic, extraneous, and germane. When the instructional design is poor, it can lead to an increase in these three factors. These are described below:

- The Extraneous cognitive load – this type normally happens when the learners are required to utilize their working memory for work other than the main objectives that are set out in the learning process. These designs have a problem with pushing the resources of the working memory towards automation and the construction of schema. Using the above example, learners are expected to utilize their working memory to ensure that they are able to remember the instructions that the teacher has given, for performing the small group activity, rather than paying attention to the major concepts that have been taught by the teacher. This shows that they have an extraneous cognitive load.
- Intrinsic cognitive load – this load is due to having complications that are inherent when it comes to processing information. For example, having to understand an equation that is complicated and is inclusive of Greek symbols requires the learner to have the ability to remember and know what each Greek symbol means. It is not possible for the instructional design to get rid of the intrinsic load; however, the teachers need to understand that they have led to the automation of different concepts and skills, that the learners require the working memory to comprehend and process.
- Germane cognitive load – this load is due to learning that is effortful, which causes the production of schema and automation. This is dissimilar to the intrinsic load in that the intrinsic load deals with the inherent work that is part of the task, and the germane cognitive load involves the work that is put in when learning from a certain task. For example, a mathematical equation that involves multiplication has an equal intrinsic load for a sixth

grade student and the teacher as well, however, the student has a higher germane cognitive due to the fact that the student has to learn more from the task.

There are a couple of ways that teachers can work at lowering the cognitive load in multimedia learning. When teachers are presenting multimedia content to the learners, they should be able to follow certain steps so as to ensure the reduction of the cognitive load, and also to make sure that the material is effectively transmitted. There are nine strategies that have been outlined by Mayer and Moreno in 2003 to help in lowering the level of cognitive load when presenting multimedia. These are:

- Offloading – this involves moving some of the important processes from the channel that is visual to the one that is auditory, or vice versa, especially when the verbal explanation that is given is too much. The learning process is much more effective when the concept being taught is relayed in the audio form instead if in the text form on a screen.

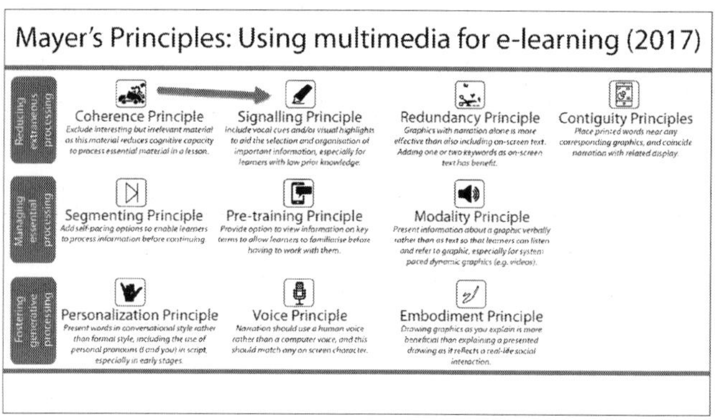

Figure 8.14. Above are the 12 principles of multimedia. They help in reducing the three forms of processing.

Source: *http://michaelseery.com/home/index.php/2017/07/mayers-principles-using-multimedia-for-e-learning-updated-2017/.*

- Segmenting – this involves taking time to take pauses between different teaching segments so as to give the students an opportunity to process the information being relayed. The effectiveness of multimedia learning can be seen when lessons are presented in smaller sections at a time in stead if an entity that is continuous.

Previous training – Learning becomes much more effective when students are well knowledgeable on the behaviors and names of different components of the system. They need to be aware if the relevant characteristics and names of the system components.

Weeding – it is important for teachers to get rid of materials that are extraneous and not interesting. Excluding extraneous information helps in making learners much more effective. There is a study that has been able to show us that additional extraneous material does not generally necessarily harm the performance of the students if it is material that is motivating and interesting.

Signaling – this involves including cues for the students to follow when it comes to having to process materials so as to prevent processing materials that are extraneous. It is important for the teachers to understand that learning is much more effective when there are signals. For example, the teacher can include directions using arrows on the manner in which the students should follow a system diagram that us not equipped with a path that is clear.

Aligning – placing words that have been written near graphics that correspond helps in lowering the need for scanning visually. Learning gets to be much more effective when the texts are put right next to image parts that correspond.

Eliminating redundancy – teachers should avoid using repetitive written or spoken words. It is easier to use audio to teach, instead of using in-screen texts. This being said, teachers should avoid reading PowerPoint slides to the learners.

Synchronizing – teachers should be able to present images and audios in a way that they are able to correspond with each other. It is possible to make learning much easier by using images while narrating a presentation, in a simultaneous manner instead of a successive manner.

Individualizing – teachers should be able to communicate with their students to gain assurance that they are able to hold mental representations.

8.10. ISSUES ARISING FROM MULTIMEDIA TECHNOLOGY IN LEARNING

In spite of the benefits that are evident with the use of multimedia technology in learning, there are still a couple of issues that arise in practical teaching. These include:

8.10.1. Major Means Take the Place of the Assisting One

The use of multimedia technology has proven to be a very assistive teaching instrument that has helped in achieving a teaching effect that is well projected. However, if it totally depends on the devices during the process of teaching, the teachers tend to turn into workers for the multimedia, and therefore they do not play the major role of teaching.

There are many teachers who actively use multimedia technology for their teaching process, however, they are not skilled enough to ensure that they can handle it in a confident manner. They tend to stand next to their personal computers during lessons, and this means that the learners are putting all their attention into the screen. This being said, there is not eye contact or verbal connection with the teacher. Regardless of the essence of the conventional methods of teaching, the trend of multimedia technology teaching appears to the extreme ends (Mayer, 2009).

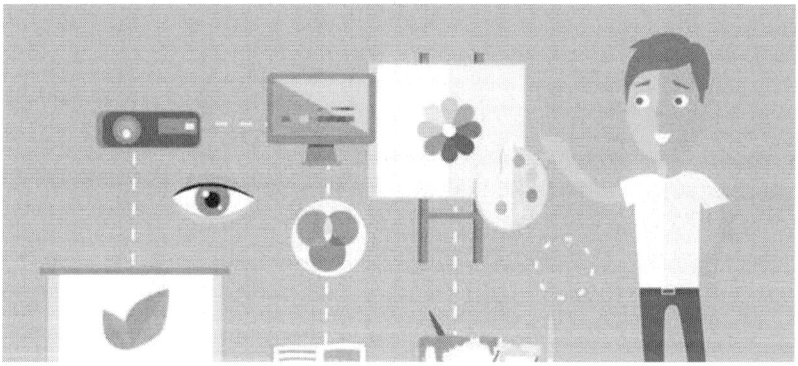

Figure 8.15. Multimedia technology needs to be used as a tool that will help in assisting the learning process. Teachers should still speak and ask questions to ensure that the students are keen and active.

Source*:* https://www.edsurge.com/amp/news/2016–07–18-visual-instructional-tools-are-essential-when-teaching-common-core-standards.

Therefore, it is important for teachers to note that the modern methods of teaching, such as multimedia learning, are tools that need to serve as an instrument of assistance, instead of fully replacing the conventional methods. This means that this technology should not dominate the lesson. They should be considered as substitutes to ensure that learning and teaching is fully effective.

8.10.2. Losing the Speaking Communication

Some of the subjects that use multimedia technology still require proper communication between the students and the teachers. For example, in English, students need to be well equipped with the tools that allow them to improve on their pronunciation and comprehension, as well as improving their oral expressions and thought patterns.

Whereas, when using multimedia technology that features texts, visuals, audio, and video these help in enhancing the interests of the students, however, it also leads to a lower level of communication between the students and the teachers due to the teachers' voice being replaced by the sounds from the computer.

This also means that there are lower chances of the teacher and the students speaking due to visual image and audio.

When this environment of communication that is supposed to me mutual between the students and the teachers fades away, due to image and sound multimedia introduction, this affects the initiative the students have to speak and think, therefore turning the lesson into a more of a show, making the students more of viewers instead of participants in the activities of the class.

8.10.3. The Thinking Potential of the Students Is Restricted

Teachers are supposed to be able to raise questions in real-time and impromptu in addition to getting the students to promote and cultivate their thinking capacity, so as to be able to find and solve problems.

However, multimedia technology has a limitation in that, it over-demonstrates and provides an order of solutions that has been previously arranged, therefore it is difficult to provide the real-time effect and feedback cannot be given. Multimedia technology ends up ignoring the importance and emphasis in teaching.

This leads to the neglecting of instructions in the thinking of students, their strengths in the capacity they have to contemplate and solve problems, and even the inspiration of their thinking paths.

Teachers need to be notified that cultivating the thinking capacity of the students should be considered the main objective in teaching and also in the use of multimedia technology. They should also ensure that this technology does not take up the time the student has to think, analyze, and explore questions (Mayer, 2009).

8.10.4. Imaginable Thinking Replaces Abstract Thinking

THINKING STYLES		
	CONCRETE	ABSTRACT
TYPE	Logical	Creative
INPUT	Detailed, literal and physical facts	Observations Examples
ACTIVITY	Visualising Objective Reasoning	Generalising Hypothesising
OUTPUT	Solutions to physical problems	Analogies, formulas patterns, relationships
USERS	Engineers Programmers	Scientists Mathematicians

Figure 8.16. Above are the main differences between concrete and abstract thinking. Both are important and they should not supersede each other.

Source: https://www facebook.com/Learnsystemsthinking/.

There is a rational stage and a conceptual stage that the process of cognition goes through. This also applies to the process of studying. The education system aims at making sure that students are using the perceptual recognition to adopt the outlook cognition and thereafter move from thinking in a perceptual manner to a rational manner, making it a major teaching objective. So as to ensure that the abstract thinking of the students is enhanced, multimedia technology helps by making the content being presented to the students much easier, and due to its unique benefits, it is able to ensure clarification of the teaching emphasis. The problem comes in with the fact that multimedia is able to show the images and imagination of the students' mind on the screen thus leading to a restriction in the abstract thinking, as well as the logical thinking. As of now, there has been a decrease in the reading competence of students, and this has become a huge problem due to the fact that sound and image in multimedia technology replaces textual words. This means that students are not able to utilize the logical thinking as well as the abstract thinking. In general, it is important for teachers to make sure that multimedia is not completely replacing the main role of the teacher, and it is instead being used as an instrument of assistance in completing the process of teaching (Saddik, 2013).

CHAPTER

9

Multimedia Management

CONTENTS

9.1. INTRODUCTION

Multimedia management is a branch in business administration that tries to identify and strategize operational functions of media. Some of the elements that pertain multimedia management is strategic management, procurement management, production management, organizational management, marketing management and problems encountered in the leadership of multimedia firms.

Multimedia management is also defined as the ability to integrate the operations of resources and facilities in a manner that is cost-effective. Media professionals need to have the proper skills in order to become successful in management.

This is because media management is very dynamic as it changes over time due to the rapid advancement of technology in our current world therefore, professionals need to be flexible. It is vital to have a multimedia management team in an organization in order to increase the general productivity of a company, improve the efficiency and control of multimedia components and reduce the general costs of operation.

In our current world, multimedia has become a very important tool in conveying ideas, messages, and projects in presentations. Businesses and academic institutions have popularized their presentation using multimedia. Some of the presentations that are being conveyed include marketing strategies, yearly growth in sales, advertising, teaching to mention but a few. Multimedia has become effective because it integrates all the components and this enhances visualization. Visualization normally adds interest and excitement to presentations and this enable viewer to remember the message being conveyed more easily.

Richard Meyer studied multimedia principles and found out that words and graphics are more suitable in utilization compared to just using text or graphics alone.

He found that when words and graphics are combined together, viewers will be able to mentally organize the materials in a well-represented cognitive coherence as they blend the materials with their existing knowledge.

9.2. CHARACTERISTICS OF MULTIMEDIA MANAGEMENT

9.2.1. Media Strategy

When creating content, it is important to understand the exact demographic you want to attract. Media strategy is defined as a plot of action that is employed so as to capture the attention of an audience and to improve the general conversion rate of customers. When viewers come across your content, the desirable action they engage in afterwards, is what is defined as the conversion rate. Take for instance, if a business is trying to improve their direct sales of a certain product, the number of viewers who will be able to directly purchase the product you are promoting after viewing the website, will determine your conversion rate. This is done by dividing the number of viewers by the number of viewers who have purchased the product. Media strategy has different objectives depending on what is being hoped to be achieved. Although media strategy has different objectives, they all have the same approach during its creation. They must all have a particular objective and a demographic in the creation process (England and Finney, 2002).

9.2.2. Components Used in Media Strategy

During strategy formation, there are certain steps that are taken:

Researching and identifying your target audience – research is important during strategizing this is because the more you know about your target market they more effective your strategy will be come.

Through research, one is able to identify the market and their behavior for example, where they spend their time, how they spend their time, the type of media they use and the most effective messaging technique that will be employed in order to reach them. Different target markets use different types of media for example, the youth mostly use social media and therefore application of printing and other traditional forms of media will not be effective in conveying the message intended.

Setting reasonable objectives – during the creation process it is important to always keep in mind the goals and objectives that need to be realized. The objectives need to be realized should be quantifiable and particular. The SMART procedure has often been employed when setting measurable objectives and goals. SMART stands for specific, measurable, achievable, realistic, and time-based. To illustrate this, take an example of a company, if a company's goal is to generate more revenue, the objective is measurable but if the company's objective is made to be more specific like to increase the revenue from 30% to 50% by the end of the fourth quarter, the goal gets to be more realistic as it offers a way to create a timeline that keeps you within the scope of your objective.

Marketing budget determination – without a properly laid out strategy in the usage of finances, an organization will spend lots of money on a strategy that will not be optimal results. Creating a budget will enable a manager to be more creative and tactical when trying to solve a problem and it protects the organization from overspending money that they don't have or they could have spent it on other important issues.

Crafting the message that you want to convey – before formulating how to craft your message, it is important to identify the customer problem that is being experienced by the end user. This is done through intense research on the desired target audience. Through the research, different problems will be identified and for each problem, a specified message will be designed in order to stress on that issue. After the message has been crafted, an appropriate call of action will be followed.

Learn from your outcome – once a media strategy has been created and employed, the organization will be able to measure and gauge the performance afterwards. From that, the company will be able to improve on what was bringing about barriers in media strategy optimization. This is important because most effective media strategies evolve over time due to the rapid advancement in mechanization.

9.2.3. Marketing Communication

Different marketing communications provide different results and therefore it is important to know the type of marketing communication that will be best employed in a given strategy. Marketing communication utilizes various channels of marketing and tools. Communication channels can be of various types ranging from physical transmission such as wire or logical connection medium such as radio channels and computer networks. Different channels have different capacities in transmission of information and it is normally measured using bandwidth or data rates (bits per second). In order for data to be communicated from one area to another, it requires a pathway or medium. These pathways are called communication in channel. There are two types of communication channels that is cable which include fiber optic cables, twisted pair cables or just ordinary cable and the second one is broadcast, for example, microwave, satellite, radio, and infrared. Promotions sales branding and advertising are examples of marketing communications. This communication has an objective and objective is to enable the viewers to understand a brand. In order for a marketing communication to be successful, an organization needs to target an audience who will appreciate the organization's specific marketing program. Institutions have recently use professionals in trying to determine the best communication medium. This is because professionals are able to identify different channels that will provide optimal results in different situations. The other reason that organizations are employing the use of professional engine seize is for the purpose of control. This is because when an influencer or a promoter has been paid to promote a certain product, the organization has control over what is being promoted that is, they can tailor their messages to suit their purposes and they're able to give instructions and dictate the kind of information the influencer should convey and the keywords that are important to reach the target audience (Herrick, 2012).

Traditional broadcasting methods have proven to be very effective over time. The use of radio and television to broadcast a message is able to reach very large numbers of people. This is true because most people in our current world either own a television or a radio. Though this is advantageous, the charges of promoting products using these traditional forms can be very expensive compared to other types of marketing media. Research finding show that radio is the best form of media to communicate and convey information. Other forms of traditional methods of marketing medium include advertisements in newspapers, journals, and magazines but their popularity has been reducing overtime due to the advancement of technology. Another form of traditional marketing is in-person marketing. This involves hiring a representative to go from door-to-door of households and organizations trying to promote a brand and raising its awareness. Another form of in-person marketing is hosting community charities and letting prospective customers know about your brand. During the charity the representative discuss about the brand while giving reason as to why the brand is beneficial to the end user and why they should buy the brand from you. Finally, networking has also been an effective form of communicating and promoting a brand. Examples of networking include joining professional associations, attending forums and seminars and going to trade shows. This increases awareness of your brand to different target audiences as they will be able to view your brand first from other competitors. Also, while attending the seminars, one can present their products and brands and this will improve to customer relation and we all know that for a business transaction to take place, a certain level of respect needs to be gained in order for someone to purchase your product or brand in the first place (Herrick, 2012).

There has also been an introduction of modern types of marketing channels. A good example of such is social media and other online platforms. This includes working with online influencers. Using influencers to promote your brand and product is a very cost-effective method of marketing but there are other ways of increasing brand awareness online such as using networks like Facebook, LinkedIn, Twitter, and Instagram but this has proven to be very expensive and most businesses will be unable to afford such a strategy. Another way that can be used to generate a great deal of brand awareness is using word of mouth. Your mate you normally you find that entrepreneurs and other organizations invites uses to like their page and others tag friends so as to enter a contest and from this contest a brand can be popularized online. This is where influences play a huge role because they are able to use such tools to create traffic on your website and online users will be able to see your products and brand and therefore generate interest. Another way that you can market your products online is by paying search ads for us to get your brand name on top of search results in your category. Content marketing has also been employed especially by organizations and individuals who are not willing to pay for marketing. This is done by creating content that is unique, has value and is entertaining and at the same time showcasing your brand. This form of marketing enables online users to gain attention from your posts. There have been numerous successful stories where companies and individuals have created entertaining content online and they use such strategies to build their customer base and reach their target audience. The question that most organizations and institutions ask is what kind of channel is best suitable to be used in promoting their brand. This question can be answered by conducting meticulous research on your target audience and examining the kind of strategies other competitors have employed. With this, one is able to assemble a strategy that will work best in optimizing their promotion. Some of the procedures of research that people are employing are interviews, surveys, user tests and focus groups (Herrick, 2012).

There are four types of marketing strategies that is being used by people in our current world.

Research: Before a communication medium is employed, thorough investigation on your target audience is critical. During research 3 basic elements needed to be considered they include needs, interest, and motivations. When researching about needs, it is important to know what your client considers as a need, a want and a luxury and from that you will be able to know what your customer purchases because they have to and what is important enough to the consumer. With investigation, one is able to get a detailed information of what interests the end user and from the information one is able to tailor an appropriate strategy to employ. Last but not least, we check what motivates the client. This data is very important because different demographic share different ideologies and using an ideology of a particular demographic in decision-making, one is able to customize the strategy. In all methods of research confirmation bias is to be avoided at all costs. This can be done by ensuring that you have impartial data.

Online media: In a study conducted in 2018, 79% of smartphone users purchased commodities mostly via their phones. This is enough evidence to show that in modern times most companies use online communication and digital marketing mediums as their primary marketing device. Business-related institution is using the sponsored results on Google search where ad space is purchased online for varying price points. The purchase of online Google search will depend on the budget the company has. Although online media is being used on a wide scale, there are situations where different demographics do not necessarily respond to website advertisements and because of these other strategies will be employed. Another unique way of marketing your products online is using social media outreach where you utilize your resources to identify and locate areas where your potential customers spend time online the most.

Promotions: This strategy is used when a business wants to stretch hands and reach customers who are outside of normal customer base. This is done by advertising products and raising brand awareness and at the same time it helps in improving the reputation of the company. The purpose of promotion is putting advertisements where people will be able to see them and eventually gaining new customers. For this to be made possible, good deals must be put for example, giving offers on products by reducing prices for a specified period of time.

Advertising: This strategy is slightly different compared to the three other strategies explained above. A large portion of the budget will typically go in physical advertisement. Through thorough marketing strategy, the appropriate form of advertisement will be identified. This is because in-store promotion and other traditional promotional methods are still being used because they create more customer attention compared to paid advertising.

The most common form of paid advertising that is being used include paid broadcast, podcasts, print, television, radio, and aerial messages.

The reason why advertising is the most effective means of communication between consumers and providers is, it provides the business communication benefits particularly related in developing long-time brand imaging. Because advertisements involve paying the influencer time and space, this gives the business power to control the messages that are being conveyed. This gives the company time to create a multimedia that will properly convey the message that is intended to reach the potential customers.

For an effective media promotion, the communication vehicle that should be used to needs to be relatable for example, if you repair computers and you want your business to be promoted, you can place advertisements in magazines that talk about computers and technology. Also, if you are trying to reach an audience that uses a specific language, you can promote your brand by placing advertisements on local stations that speak that specific language. This is mostly done by politicians when they want to promote their popularity in a particular region (Herrick, 2012).

Advertising gives a business opportunity to build a long-term brand image. This is because of the control factor that is obtained once you've paid for advertising because the business is able to provide a concise and consistent message about its products.

The messages can include the quality of products, the services provided by the company, durability or prices. Finally, the reach and frequency of promotional communication is very important. Reach refers to the overall number of clients who will be able to view your adverts. Frequency refers to how many times consumers will be able to view your advertisement.

This is critical because it enhances the attraction of the products being advertised and this increases the size or viewers as it builds loyalty and develops a high level of brand awareness which generates proceeds.

There are 10 kinds of advertisement namely; display advertisements, social media advertisements, newspaper, and magazines, outdoor advertising, radio, and podcasts, mail, and personal self-video advertisement, product placement, event marketing and email marketing.

9.2.4. Public Relations

When managing multimedia, public relation is a very important component to be considered. This involves working with media for the purpose of giving information to the public regarding the policies, practices, and missions of an organization while maintaining a credible, consistent, and positive reputation. Because of this, there is need to directly co-ordinate with parties that are involved in using multimedia to produce content and features in mass media. The main objective of Media relation is to ensure that the optimization of positive coverage in mass media without the need of paying directly through advertising. Public relation is aimed at creating coverage for clients for free instead of marketing or advertising. Institutions use public relation techniques to give information to potential customers, partners, investors, employees, and the public and using this information to hopefully portray an image showing a positive and favorable view regarding the organization in terms of leadership, product or political decision. You will find that every institution in our modern world has a public relations department that hires professionals. Examples of such professionals include media relations managers, account supervisors, account executives and account coordinators. The job of public relations professionals is to create a rapport with the intended target of audience of the organization, the media, the relevant trade media and other opinion leaders. Their obligations is to establish communication campaigns, write new releases and other content for reports, writing speeches for the directors of organizations, becoming a spokesperson of the organization, preparation of press conferences for clients, hosting interviews, designing websites, creating social media content and generally managing crisis. Publicity is the core objective for that professionals need to cohere to.

You will find that media is such a powerful tool in that, any form of negative reportage regarding a business or a person, can adversely affect their reputation. On the other hand, any positive reportage has a positive impact to the reputation and image of an individual and an organization. The perception of customers is heavily altered by the type of information they are being fed concerning the organization, brand, service or products. When an organization is looking for foreign financing, it is important to have a credible public relations department that puts out a good word regarding your company and this can be clearly portrayed by a nice multimedia team. A good relation with the media is vital and critical in order to create opportunities for the organization to send certain messages about their organization to the public and other stakeholders. Due to the fact that there's the assumption that media has no direct interest on an organization, organizations take advantage of this assumption to gain third party endorsement. When developing communication strategies, the department of public relations normally adhere to the endorsement effect. This was proven by Howes and Sallot. The public relation practice normally holds such view in a higher acode. This is because information published or broadcasted in the media includes on an added value because it is assumed to be an independent third-party body and because it approves of the content being conveyed by an organization, the review is considered to be unbiased. This notion arose because of the assumption that organizations are biased and driven by self-interest which it wishes to advance. When an independent media covers a certain information regarding a business or organization, there is greater credibility because it is assumed that the information being conveyed by the media team is factual, vetted, and screened and it has not been paid for and this brings about stability when it comes to other voices giving out opinions. There is the bother by public relations practitioners when it comes to reporting about content being dished out by the organizations. This concern is caused by reporters who never let the facts get in the way of the story through selectively including or excluding information or failing to check the facts (Herrick, 2012).

There are situations where you find that media bodies are being politicized and due to this, information being given out by the media gets corrupted. A country like Zimbabwe has led to growing mistrust between corporates and reporters. Such situations arise due to poor working conditions of journalists. The credibility of media houses in Zimbabwe has significantly dropped due to inaccurate reporting and lack of fact-checking by professionals. There is a huge coexistence between public relation officers and the media. Multimedia is a very vital tool in steering and promoting the reputation of an organization. Basically, the function of public relation is to facilitate the promotion and maintenance of a conducive image of an organization among its target audience and the media is a useful tool in doing this.

The public relation department has become a very important component in reputation management over the recent years by steering the communication strategy among the corporate world and its stakeholders. New York Times has stated seven components that public relations professionals and their management need to consider when handling the media. The first component is honesty. This is vital because the main objective is winning the trust of customers and stakeholders. Although an organization is not obligated to disclose all its information, the information that an organization is willing to give out concerning its practice and product should be truthful. In order for honesty to be enhanced, an organization must look for media reporters who are well-versed and knowledgeable on issues regarding their operations in order for them to investigate and look into factors that is relevant and needed by the stakeholders and the general public.

An organization should not expect for a reporter to give details word for word concerning their operations and products because reporters are biased and they're providing information from their point of view but reporters are also expected to give facts and report messages that are accurate, intelligent, and fair. In the event that a reporter has given out information that has errors and is inaccurate, the organization concerned is obligated to reach out to the concerned media house and request them to rectify the error they have made. A credible and professional media organization is obligated to correct any errors brought to their attention provided that the error is factual.

There are situations where media houses fail to revert or rectify the error they made and when it reaches to this point, the organization is obligated to go forth and use other means such as legislation by going to the court and making a case out of the situation. In the case of Zimbabwe, the organization can report the misconduct to the voluntary media commission of Zimbabwe whereby the organization will arbitrate the complaint and reasonable action will be taken. It is advised that when such an error occurs, the affected organization should handle the situation in a professional manner.

The rule of thumb states that one should not shoot the messenger for being the bearer of bad news and in the event that a disaster occurs, one should be prepared to handle the problem directly.

Media coverage has become more intense and aggressive due to the advancement of mechanization where there has been the introduction of online and social media into the mix. Due to this there, has been fast dissemination of information whereby information is being released quicker and it is getting more and more inaccurate.

There has been the emergence of bodies where mismanagement and shady business deals are being exposed and revealed. In order to avoid being charged for gross misconduct, organizations are being encouraged to cultivate a good relationship with media houses where inaccurate information and corrupt deals are being discouraged and honesty is being emphasized in reporting (Herrick, 2012).

9.2.5. Talent Management

With the advancement of technology, there has been the introduction of the digital age. The digital age has forced organizations to change ways in which is a hire, selects, and nurture skills for a new generation of employees. Organizations are now emphasizing on improving the organizational performance by engaging factors that involve the use of multimedia. Talent management is being structured upon the following criteria; Relationship between the employer brand, talent management program and engagement and the second is digital skills for managers and employees. In relationship between employer brand, organizations are creating a framework that incorporates the retention and engagement, commodities, and promotion communication, innovation, value of customers and financial performance. In digital skills for managers and employees, organizations are creating a model whereby employees will be trained to develop skills that will optimize performance in leadership, analytics, solving of problems, making decisions and decision thinking. With the incorporation of the above processes, professionals in an institution will enhance the production skills in creative content and storytelling, distribution of content through social media platforms, receiving, and creating, engagement through selective replies, analyzing dynamics of social media industry, enable, and support everything involved in the use of social media platforms and leverage social media for key business functions. The objective of the framework is to create a culture in an organization that will incorporate leadership and career development with multimedia technology (England and Finney, 2002).

In employer brand and talent management in our current world, the search for talent is a never-ending task. This is because there is increased economic competitiveness and digitization due to rapid technological advancements. Therefore, to attract and retain top talent has become a major challenge in our current world. Organizations are aiming to incorporate talent management in their long-term business framework in order to optimize performance that is, by reducing operational costs in performance, enhancing marketing communication and innovation and heightening the value of services and products to potential customers. When it comes to employer branding, brand associations usually alter the image and reputation of an employer which in turn affects the attractiveness of the organization to potential customers and brand loyalty is used to improve the culture of an organization and the identity of a brand. The strategy employed behind employer branding is to motivate workers and managers in an organization to 'live the brand' which represents factors that make an organization appealing to its present and future employees. Employer branding also creates a culture that aligns the employees brand experience win the client's brand experience during marketing. Edwards defined brand experience as identifying the unique employment experience by considering the totality of tangible and intangible reward features that a particular organization offers to its employees and this is commonly known as employee value proposition. Employee value proposition involve career development, salary, and remuneration policy, working conditions and psychological benefits like job satisfaction. This comprises of functional and economic benefits. Therefore, the human resource department in organizations is employing such strategies in solving the difficulties that come with talent acquisition and retention thus helping employees to internalize company values and organizational culture. Employee engagement is important because the brand promoters in organizations are the employees in the context of multimedia information about organizational culture, leadership, remuneration policy and career opportunities as they directly affect the desired image and reputation of the company. An engaged employee is passionate about their role in an organization and they are incorporated in the strategic component of the company. There are factors that create a powerful employee brand that is, asset, and shape an authentic, consistent message of what your organization considers to be of value, communicate, and message by leveraging the right channels and developing employer branding metrics and measure their effectiveness against talent goals (England and Finney, 2002).

In 2008, William Rothwell conducted as a study that found out that in order to attract millennials who have high potential, talent management programs should consist of the following components;

- Get commitment on behalf of senior managers and employees – employees in an organization should possess technical expertise career, proper transmission of information and knowledge and a clear management succession planning.
- Analyze the jobs being administered at the moment and the people working on the jobs in order to determine the definition of talent – an organization needs to analyze the current work that is being administered in an organization in order to create clear job descriptions that realistic Ali summarizes work requirements. A competence model is designed in order to analyze people in the respective departments and creating a profile that shows how individuals are performing at every level of the organization. Organizational leaders need to determine the talent that the organization requires by analyzing the kind of job employees are doing, who are doing the job and where they are. With this, high

performers that is, individuals who are most productive when assigned a certain job are determined and high professionals that is, individuals who are most expertise about a specific area of the organization is also determined.

- Recruit and select talent – when recruiting talent, the most important factors that an organization needs to look for is digital and employment branding. This can be done through proper training and developing talent inside the organization.
- Evaluate performance – when evaluating performance, the organization needs to check on the current productivity of an employee, the competence and the behavior they demonstrate during working.
- Analyze the work and people needed in the future – In order to align the organizational strategic goals, project managers need to foresee the requirements of assignments and competent needs that will be required by the organization in the future. The organization's strategic objective clearly indicates the key performance indicators required by the organization, the personal characteristics of an employee that is essential to success and the kind of job assignments needed to be performed.
- Evaluate potential – in order to evaluate potential, there are things that managers need to check when employing someone. Some of the things being checked involve psychological tests, rotation experiences, assessment based on the competencies required and supervisory nominations.
- Develop people – the main function of developing people is to identify development gaps and close them by finding strategies that can be employed to create competency that is, organizations establish leadership development programs, action learning programs, training programs, rotation experiences, mentoring programs and other planned efforts to close the gap.
- Retain the best performers – after jobs have been given, the human resource manager is advised to interview potential employees in order to know high potentials, high performers and high professionals. This is important because it helps the manager to determine and know different people in order to incorporate them into the future recruitment.
- Evaluate program results – the following question enables

managers to measure the rate of successful talent; how well is the program achieving the measurable goals established for it? how many people are available in the event that vacancy occurs? how quick can these qualified people be identified, selected, and oriented? what kind of people are available and ready to perform when the vacancy occurs?

9.2.6. Licensing and Copyright

Due to the increased technical advancements and evolving of market practices, intellectual property rights in the multimedia environment is facing huge challenges. Organizations are setting up strategies that will help in solving the issues as they have put millions of dollars in trying to establish standards when it comes to corporate management in multimedia. Currently across acquiring intellectual asset is very expensive and difficult. Developers in the multimedia industry wants licensing to give them the opportunity to purchase and utilize existing intellectual property rather than creating them themselves. This is because you find that multimedia developers realize that the owner of content they are using do not necessarily own the rights to the content they are licensing and this makes parties to be in a state of confusion by which rights they should sell. Currently, multimedia developers basically utilize devices that publish stand-alone storage base. Universities are using emerging models and frameworks such as wideband transmission which is easily available publishing through wide area networks (WANs). Although per use licensing has worked fairly for online database industry, it is proving to be difficult to be incorporated well for storage based publishing. Pricing of usage-based requires a network system which has an advanced mechanical and marketing overhead and due to these new users are disadvantaged. There are Solutions that are being the design to solve such a problem, for example, transclusion. Transclusion is where once a developer has purchased the access to some contents in a system, then the developer has purchased a permanent access to it. This is closely related to buying a product. Another solution being used is concurrent use licensing where a standard fee is charged based on the number of users who can access the service at the same time. Once these strategies have been put in place, multimedia creators will have easy access to libraries of program content and multimedia will become a preferable communication vehicle for education (Herrick, 2012).

Currently the laws governing copyright does not give clear and detailed instructions on the distribution of protected work over the internet. This has prompted the United States Department of Commerce to release recommendations for creation of copyright laws that protect content creators, for example, movies, books, recordings, and other forms of information in the internet. Without the creation of such copyright laws, software developers have the ability to convert content online into a computer language and this enables them to easily use other people's content to create their own content and distribute to other users. Although it will be extremely challenging to counter stealing of content online, the main aim of rewriting copyright laws is to create a strong and solid legal framework in order to enable violators to be sued and be charged with civil lawsuits.

Digital rights management has been a concept that has been recently introduced due to heightened creation of digital content without the proper licensing and regulation. It covers a very large scope of intellectual property management and enforcement by providing secure and trusted services to control the use and distribution of content. Digital rights management was also established in order to enable the proper management of multimedia as it has proved to be a great enabler for future services both mobile and fixed and the vital responsibility it plays in commerce and the community. As I had earlier explained, one of the most challenging Factors in multimedia management is controlling all aspects of intellectual property that is, the content creators and their rights. Digital rights management clearly describes the technical processes involved in managing the life cycle of content with the objective on exploiting the intellectual property rights of that content. Digital rights management is closely related to security and the encryption of online content. It pertains factors such as content conception, creation of content, use of content, reuse of content and final archive of content. Right management is a strong tool to be use when dealing with multimedia content. This is because you will find that content can be created by numerous people online and there's normally an issue that arises when it comes to the commercialization of such content as its aparks up debates on who owns the content in the first place. This is because those who claim to own the content try to exploit the benefits that come with the subsequent commercial sales of the multimedia content. Due to this, rights management is critical at the beginning of the life cycle of the multimedia content creation just as it is important as the content evolves and becomes commercially significant. Right management gets complex because there are other factors that influence the management of the content that is business, legal, and social components. The business element is directly related to the rights management because it involves the commercial sales of the content. The component of legal rights also utilizes rights management as it requires the adherence to copyright laws in the local jurisdiction and finally, when it comes to the social component it encompasses the requirement and regulation that the content being displayed online should contain and should have in order to maintain the ethical and disciplinary thinking of the society (Herrick, 2012).

9.2.7. Multimedia Production

Multimedia production is the process of creating an interactive medium using multimedia components that is audio texts video and graphics. Multimedia projects are normally complicated as it involves experts and professionals who have the skills create such a content. There are six stages involved in the creation of multimedia and each stage is designed to refine the projects with attention to the client's needs, technical requirements and audience preferences. Below are the steps involved in multimedia creation;

Planning meeting to initiate the procedure: The planning meeting is a crucial stage in the multimedia process of development this is because it brings together the desired multimedia team. Once the desired multimedia team has been brought together, a common idea regarding the development of the multimedia is shared and visions are aligned. The project manager gives out clear goals and objectives and lays out the milestones that is need to be achieved during the creation of multimedia. Also, during this stage, the manager can discuss particular target audiences and assigning task to different professionals in the group so as to cater for the target audience.

Creation of brief and scriptwriting: Once the meeting has been cleared and the group has been formed, a story behind the multimedia project is formulated. The team assigned to create the background story come together, write a script, create briefs and outline the main points of the project and during this process professional language that is appealing to the target audience is emphasized. From the Script is there complete content creation will be created as it will be used as a checking point.

Storyboarding to tie the elements together: During multimedia creation the multimedia components that is texts audio video and animations are used and due to this there is need of a team to find all these components together in order to come up with content. This stage helps the media team to stay within the scope of the process, keep everyone in track and give structure to the project.

Designing the visual aspects: Once the multimedia elements have been put together, the design team takes over the visual aspects of the project to determine how it looks and feels. with the help of the notes discussed during storyboarding the design team comes up with graphics and design the navigation and give direction to videographers and photographers regarding the correct shorts. During designing, the main focus and aim is the target audience and because of this, the design team will decide on the type of design they will employee it can be graphic design, web design, information design or photography collection.

Review and editing: This is the most demanding stage in the process of multimedia creation. The group that is responsible for reviewing and editing the project are obligated to integrate all the different aspects of design together taking into consideration the time constraints, storyline, and creative specifications. Depending on the type of multimedia creation the designs of the projects can be edited either separately or can be edited together. When editing a project that involves videos, it can take hours and hours because there are a lot of components that need to be integrated together during editing, internal review is critical as they will act as the targeted audience so as give their view.

Production and user testing: Using the storyboard as a guide the production staff come together and gather all the edited and reviewed projects. They gathered edited projects and then put together as one in a logical sequence show us to put the multimedia content together. The gathered content is then reviewed through multiple rounds as they keep on doing minor editing and fine-tuning until a desirable final project has been realized. The client end internal viewers are involved in fine-tuning the project. User testing can be employed so as to ensure that the project has the desired effect on the target audience. At this stage, the user testers act as the intended audience and they use the multimedia to judge while the team members observe and take notes of what needs to be corrected or improved. While the testers are analyzing and judging the project, the staff observes the reactions on their faces and they go ahead and ask questions related to the objective of the project in order to see if the project hits the right marks. After testing, further adjustments are undertaken to the project until the team and the clients are fully satisfied. Finally, the project goes out for distribution.

Product management: In the field of economics and marketing a product is normally defined by its properties and attributes. Product management is essential as it plays a very big role in determining the attributes that a product should possess in order to meet the diverse needs and goals of target markets in a desirable, sustainable, and profitable way. The material components, that is news, friction, and persuasive contents together with the material components that is, medium – means by which it reaches the consumer should be integrated in order to solve the unique and complex naturc that is related to multimedia. The key feature of media products is its ability to satisfy the potential customer needs and objectives of an instructive, convincing, and pleasurable nature.

CHAPTER

10

Emerging Trends in Multimedia

CONTENTS

10.1. INTRODUCTION

Multimedia has seen a great improvement in its field in the last few years since many people use the media and many different types of media for communication. This has therefore contributed to the growth of the multimedia sector and research has been performed to find how the trends can be improved further. This has therefore led to the emerging trends in the multimedia and they have affected the multimedia industry either positively or negatively as more people use multimedia and also multimedia has become a widely studied course in the higher learning institutions worldwide.

The following are the various emerging trends in multimedia being explained further;

10.2. MULTIMEDIA SYSTEMS

In the contexts of multimedia, under it is the multimedia systems. The multimedia systems are put in place to ensure that the quality of the media produced is good and also ensures the efficient transmission of the products of the multimedia. The multimedia systems help improve the quality of the multimedia products by availing a variety of tools that will be incorporated into the generation and transmission of the products to the audience. The multimedia systems are also a way of increasing the audience for the multimedia products. Some of the emerging trends in multimedia systems include:

10.3. MULTIMEDIA NETWORKING

Among the latest trends in multimedia is the incorporation of the latest tools of networking into multimedia. So many advances have been made in using networking aspects in multimedia and has led to the birth of new multimedia tools. One of the latest trends in the multimedia networking is the peer-to-peer streaming. The peer-to-peer streaming refers to the use of redistributing video systems to allow the transmission of signals in real-time. Networking involves creating a link between computers allowing the computers to communicate amongst each other. The peer-to-peer follows this principle. It makes a network between users who view the similar content.

For the peer-to-peer streaming to work, there is the use of the peer-to-peer software applications to facilitate the connection between the users. Apart from the peer-to-peer streaming being used in televisions, with advancements with technology it has been incorporated into other system. It has led to the emergence of the streaming applications being used in mobile phones. The streaming mobile applications include the streaming TV that allows users to stream television and internet TV content from the comfort of their mobile phones. It also has generated the peer-to-peer streaming movies.

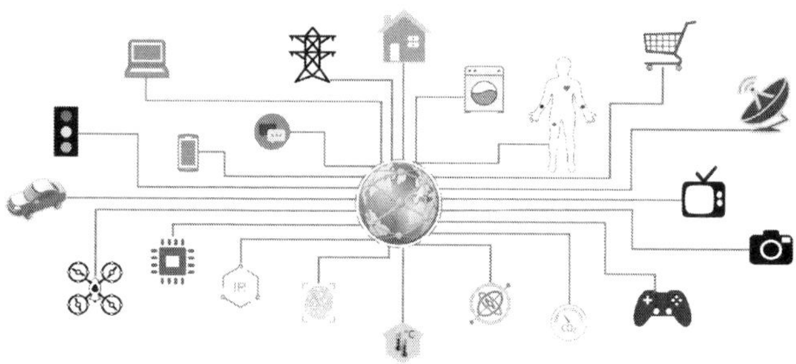

Figure 10.1. An image showing multimedia networking.

Source: https://eecs.ceas.uc.edu/MNCL.

The peer-to peer streaming also uses the principle of segmentation. The content to be viewed is divided into segments so that the user gets to download small chunks of the content instead of downloading a huge single file that may end up being costly. The advantages of using the peer-to-peer streaming is that it is easy to set up. This is because most of the applications made are generated to be user friendly and the user can use basic knowledge to set up the peer-to-peer streaming. For most of these applications, they contain icons where the user can get instruction on how to setup the streaming.

Also among the multimedia networking is the content distribution in multimedia. Content distribution refers to the promoting of content to other viewers through use of other channels. This essential involves third parties assisting in the promotion of such content so that the audience for the content increases. This involves the use of socials media platforms such as twitter and Instagram to create awareness for the content. It also entails the use of the press conferences as well as product reviews. For one to increase the chances of the content being viewed, they have to ensure that they content is of high quality that will appeal to the user (Hwang, 2009).

There are various categories of the content distribution. They include earned, paid, and owned. For the earned content distribution is as described above where third parties are involved in the distribution of content. For the paid content distribution is when the owner of the content has to pay up in order for their content to be distributed to other individuals. The owned content distribution involves the distribution of content in the internet through sites that are owned by the distributor of the content. This includes use of blogs or websites.

There is also the wireless multimedia which is kind of similar to the wireless networking in networking. As in networking, the wireless multimedia is also referred to as WIFI multimedia. It is essential used in the multimedia extensions.

The wireless multimedia is a service that gives priority to multimedia enabling it to run through a wireless network. For such a system, the process is mostly automated to make it more efficient and also to save on time. The wireless multimedia involves the transmission of multimedia products such as videos and pictures through the use of a network. This is done by organizing the content data packets into small sizes to ensure that the transmission is error free.

The content to be sent is usually categorized in to four groups where by the sending will be done on the basis of the type of data that should be given first priority. The categories include voice, video, best effort and back ground. Voice when given the highest priority, gives of a higher quality of the transmitted voice content. This is because the voice packets to be made will be properly packaged and transmitted at a minimal latency. The video is given the second priority in transmission. Most of the wireless multimedia allows the transmission of data in three or four standard definition television.

This ensures that the quality of the transmission is good. It allows the transmission of the video data packets to high definition televisions. The best effort are the data packets generated from devices that do not have QOS standards and therefore assists in the transmission of such types of data. The background is different from other categories. It mainly prioritizes on the downloading if files and the printing of such files. It avoids the scenario where the data is not transmitted due to increased latency (Hwang, 2009).

With the use of the emerging trends in the multimedia networking, it has been advantageous to individuals as it has enabled the generation of various job hence the emerging jobs in multimedia networking. Some of the job opportunities include one working as an employed content distributor. One can also work as a website generator or a website designer for the owned content distributors. One can also get employment as a hardware and software developer and specialize in the field of OSs (Hwang, 2009).

10.4. MULTIMEDIA SYSTEM SUPPORT

The emerging trends in the support system includes the adaptive support, internet protocols (IPs), QOS, middleware, OSs and multimedia servers. For the adaptive support, it is used in scalable media. This is when there are expansions to be made to the multimedia. The IPs allows the proper transmission of the multimedia products. It also creates pathways for the generators of multimedia products to upload their content in the internet for it to be accessed by the users. It also allows them to gain information on multimedia. The OS has also been upgraded so that the OS used has a very fast processing speed.

With such an OS, the applications in computers and phones will be able to run smoothly unlike before where the system used was outdated and experienced a lot of trouble shooting problems and would pose a challenge to the multimedia developers. Wil the use of the latest OS, it creates an environment for the applications to run without any problem. It also allows for the easy identification of problems within the device being used. This will save on time as the easy identification of the problems will allow the specialist to fix the problem easily and within a short period of time.

10.5. MULTIMEDIA ANALYSIS, PROCESSING AND RETRIEVAL

The latest trend in the multimedia systems involves the use of the latest software packages available to make the analysis and processing much easier. It has led to the development of systems such as the multi-modal processing allowing the multimedia developer to access various processing tool that will improve the quality of the multimedia. There have also been upgrades in the multimedia content description and indexing which allows the use of a more modified system in giving multimedia content description. Along with this, a system has been generated to cater for the retrieval of multimedia content. This allows the quick recovery of the lost content or misplaced content.

In case the content got exposed to the wrong person, to avoid the content being stolen, there was a mechanism that was put in place to ensure that the content is not stolen. This involves the use of digital multimedia management rights that allow the protection and the attribution of the content. The use of such systems allow the protection of the content and prevents unruly individuals such as hackers from accessing the content. It also gives licenses so that a generator of content has the full rights to the content and is able to assume all rights on the content. The multimedia analysis, processing, and retrieval as a trend has many advantages one being that it has led to the generation of job opportunities.

The emerging job opportunities in this field include multimedia analysis expert. One can also work in the digital multimedia rights management as a licenser.

Software specialists can get employment as a software developer coming up with the packages that will be used in the analysis and processing of multimedia. The emerging trends have also been useful in making the multimedia production process to be easy (Costello, 2016).

10.6. MULTIPLE PLATFORMS FOR CONTENT DELIVERY

In the current era and with the coming up of many new technologies that were not present before, there is a change in the preference of the ways each consumer prefers to get the content he or she needs from.

Though some people may prefer to get content using traditional ways most people prefer using the technologies as they are more entertaining and easier to use than using traditional methods. With the preference in the way, a consumer prefers to get information in or content in it has led to multiple platforms for content delivery. Platforms that are created for content delivery have assisted and led to emerging trends in multimedia.

Some of these platforms that exist are since many people find having to go to the library and spend a lot of time perusing through books tiring and annoying whereas they can use their mobile phones.

The individuals in the multimedia teamwork to ensure that they provide videos and clips that can enable students to get the information they need in easier and more interesting ways and therefore it is an emerging trend in the field of multimedia. Companies have come to realize that each consumer has a preference for the way they would like their content to be delivered and they have therefore these companies have begun putting their content in ways that it can be accessed by any individual according to their preference of the kind of platform they would prefer. A good example is teenagers may prefer to use their mobile phones to watch a video as compared to using the computer of having to watch it on the television and therefore the companies work to ensure that they provide their content in this platforms.

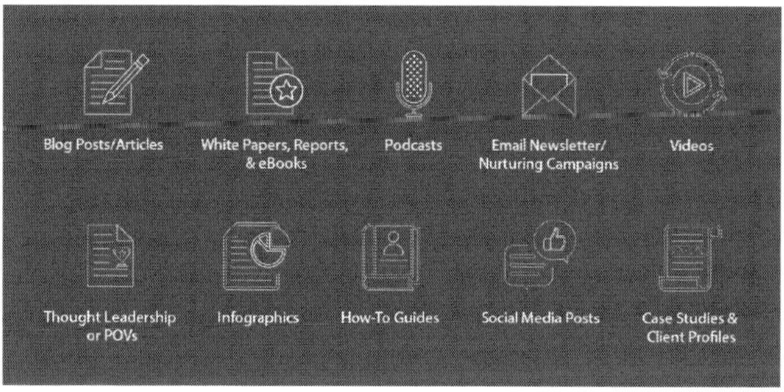

Figure 10.2. A multimedia platform for content delivery.

Source: https://www.e2msolutions.com/blog/content-distribution/.

Multiple platforms for content delivery is, therefore, a tool that can be termed as an emerging trend in multimedia because with the change in time new content is being introduced in any of the platforms such that the consumers can access content in any form of media and they can, therefore, enjoy getting the content in the media that they prefer more. This has led to the increase and growth of the multimedia sector as more individuals get involved in using these technological devices and using various media to acquire the content that they need (Costello, 2016).

10.7. SOCIAL MEDIA

Social media is a platform that connects many people through communication. They are computer-based technologies that enable people to get engaged in conversations no matter the distance between them or how far they are. Social media connects people all over the world and it enables individuals to pass the information they desire to pass in a very fast and convenient way. Unlike in the olden days when communication was enabled when the information was passed through the use of messengers who could travel far and wide to pass the information, the use of social media has eliminated the disadvantages that came about with the use of messengers.

Social media is an emerging trend in the field of multimedia that comes with many benefits which include:

Social media makes the world a global village. By the introduction of social media, it has enabled the interactions of different countries in the world together such that one can easily know what is happening in the other countries and countries in another continent hence it makes individuals feel as if they are one small village. It has enabled countries to pass information to one another unlike in the past when information could not be easily passed to individuals in other countries.

It has enabled other countries to take part in businesses and to take part in businesses. By the introduction of social media platforms, it has enabled people to be able to advertise their goods to potential customers in the social media platforms. This has enabled a growth in the business sector as many businesses can make a lot of profits as they make their goods and products known to many people and therefore they can make very many new customers that come to buy their products hence it is advantageous.

It is also advantageous in the fact that it is a source of entertainment and a platform that enables people to pass time enjoyably. Social media has platforms like the WhatsApp that enables people to communicate with each other, share stories, update WhatsApp status where they share their life and pictures. Instagram is another social platform that has become a major addiction to many people as they use it for communication and sharing their pictures and it connects many people as they can many people all the way can get to know what their friends are doing and the places they visit.

Social media is a very important tool as it enabled many people to get to know each other and it has enabled many people to pass information to one another though it can also be disadvantageous in the sector where an individual might get too addicted to social media that they forget their roles and many individuals cause accidents because they are too addicted to their phones that they cannot put their phones aside even when they are driving. It is also disadvantageous in the sector where it may lead to a rise in crime, for example, when people take part in hacking other peoples accounts (Leopold and Garcia, 2003).

10.8. THE DIGITAL ADVERTISING ECOSYSTEMS

Digital advertising ecosystems is the opportunity that companies have to advertise their goods online through the internet and the various media in the multimedia sector. It is an emerging trend in the field of multimedia because many companies and organizations that produce goods and give out services which use the internet and various media to advertise their goods products and services. The digital advertising ecosystems and using of media to advertise goods is advantageous in the following ways: It enables an increase in the sales of goods and services since there is the increase in sales it has brought about to an increase in output, it has also led to the company attracting new customers and consumers of their goods and it has led to the organizations and business gaining fame and being known by individuals in the world. These advantages have led to many advantages in the company as discussed below.

By enabling an increase in the sales of goods it has prevented many business organizations from closing their companies as their goods get sold. By the use of media to advertise their goods many business organizations have can ensure that all their goods find people to buy them.

The use of media to advertise goods has also enabled businesses and organizations to attract new consumers and customers for their goods. This is in the way in which an individual who may not know a certain company and they need goods,

When they are using their devices they may come across these organizational products and they may gain interest and therefore by these, the organization gets new customers through these and they can also maintain their customers because they remain their customers that the goods still exist.

Digital advertising ecosystems also enable business organizations to gain a lot of fame and this has been advantageous because the products of these companies become more preferred than the goods of the other companies because they believe in what their companies offer rather than what new companies have to offer. The gaining of fame and popularity is advantageous because it has enabled the business organizations to beat the competition in the market and even if they increase their prices they will still be bought from the goods. After all, they are believed to be of better quality than the other goods.

Lastly, it has enabled much business to do work together with such as they can perform certain duties and they can also partner together to come up with a good, for example, Safaricom partnered with M-Pesa which enabled an increase in the services and the output too, therefore, the customers increased too relatively (Leopold and Garcia, 2003).

10.9. VIDEO STREAMING

Video streaming is an emerging trend in the field of multimedia. Video streaming is the use of media and other technologies to show a video live rather than one having to undergo the process of downloading a video.

A lot of people watch movies and videos and they get fascinated by them in a way that they may get addicted to them. In the olden day's videos could only be watched after they were downloaded and they were burned in the compact disks but with the coming of the new era of technology, videos, and movies can be watched online by streaming them live.

The advantages that are associated with video streaming include;

It is cheaper to video stream than to download: By video steaming, individuals can save more than they would when they do when they have to video stream and they have to burn it in a compact disk so that they can view it.

Live streaming is way cheaper than downloading and hence this factor has led to an increase in the population of people who live stream to those who still watch the videos traditionally by having to download it first then watch it later.

It has also enabled the saving of storage space: In case an individual downloads a video it occupies a certain percentage of their internet and therefore it is disadvantageous because it leads to the filling up of storage space way faster.

With the coming up of live streaming it has enabled individuals to save a lot of space since they view the videos live and when the movie is complete it does not save and hence this enables individuals to view a lot of videos without having the fear and trouble of having less space or lacking storage space.

Figure 10.3. An individual streaming a live video

Source: https://50wheel.com/category/live-streaming/page/2/.

Video streaming is very easy to access as one only needs the required technology and data and they can watch the videos any time. The advantage of video streaming is that you can watch the videos at any one time as they are always available and one can get videos that are dated very many years ago. These videos are always ready for consumption from the internet using the technological tools and this has enabled many people to get information that they require from the past easily without having to undergo the pressure of carrying out a lot of research.

Lastly, video streaming is an interesting process that can be used by many people as a source of entertainment as one watches videos that range in any class from funny videos to the educative videos. Many companies have sought to make their videos have the ability to being streamed live as this has enabled many organizations that provide videos to have an increase in their profits greatly. Video streaming is, therefore, a trend that is being incorporated into the multimedia sector greatly on account of the many advantages that it holds and the limitations it avoids and eliminates downloading videos.

10.10. INCREASED AUDIENCE CONTROL

Increased audience control is another factor that has proven as an emerging trend in multimedia. By increased audience control it means that the audience can have control of what they watch, at what time they want to watch it, where they want to watch it and the number of times they want to watch it. Audience control is a key factor because different people have different time limits and people may fail to have the same time of rest as the others and therefore important information may pass these individuals because they are busy. Increased audience control may benefit the audience in the following ways;

It enables the audience to have to use the media at their own free time in a way that they don't have to push themselves too much. For instance, if the favorite television show for a particular person is being aired at a specific time, the individual may feel bad when they fail to watch it in case their schedule was too tight and they could not make it but with the new media, it is much better because individuals can view what was aired before easily and at their convenient time and therefore they do not have to push themselves too much and affect their time. They can, therefore, concentrate on their work first and then they view their show later on when they are done with work (Costello, 2016).

Another advantage that is associated with increasing audience control is, individuals can also review a play, video or movie that they watched before and may want to repeat it once more. Unlike the media that were available in the past that could only show a show once, the new media and technologies enable the individuals to watch as many times as possible and hence no major point can skip their mind easily.

Increasing audience control has also enabled the audience to have control of what they want to hear and when. The use of technologies and media has enabled individuals to have a wide variety of content and hence individuals can choose the desired time that they want to watch a particular thing and in case the content of what they are watching proves offensive, they have the opportunity to switch to something that is more desirable to them and hence this has increased the possibility of people using the mass media.

Increasing audience control has also led to an increase in the sources of information which include the blogs. This is advantageous because with an increase in blogs it has led to an increase in the number of sources of information and therefore with this more sources of entertainment also increase greatly. Lastly, it has led to making the consuming of goods easier as individuals only need to get information by a single click that has enabled more and more people to use the multimedia sources widely and therefore making way as an emerging trend in the field and sector of multimedia (Costello, 2016).

10.11. USER GENERATED CONTENT

User-generated content is an emerging trend in the sector of multimedia because many people come up with new ways that they use multimedia to develop and generate content. User-generated content is a major field that many people are getting involved in as it can employ some individuals as many people lack jobs in the competitive world. The providing and generating of content can bring about a certain percentage of income when the content can acquire a lot of views and likes from the people, for example, through YouTube and other platforms.

The advantages of user-generated content include; It enables individuals to take part in sharing their ideas and talents with the world hence their talents do not go to waste. By user-generated content an individual can sing a song or make a cover of a song or even perform a short play that they can post for the public to see and with this, they will be able to showcase their talent and they may get a lot of fame from this. They post their content to the media platforms that are providing such services and many people can view these content easily (Costello, 2016).

It has also enabled a lot of individuals who may have lacked jobs that is the unemployed individuals to gain source of income since when the user generates content and updates it in the media platforms they can get a certain amount of money from these platforms in case the videos and other content are liked by the people watching them and this content can acquire a lot of likes and views from the public. It is, therefore, a source of income for some people and this can provide money that the individuals require to come up with better forms of businesses.

It has also led to the possibility of the users who generate this content to get fame from the public. When people update their content they may get to be known by many people and this may be advantageous because in case the people viewing the content are pleased with what they see, the individuals can acquire jobs easily as they will have the connections they need. It may also assist others to aquire scholarships that will enable them to follow and pursue their talent and become better in what they are doing and therefore it is advantageous.

User-generated content is a fun process because the process of generating content is fun as one does what they enjoy doing more. User-generated content is easy to create and the process of uploading it is also very easy and it may not require a lot of manpower or training to do it. It is also not as expensive as it may look and therefore many individuals opt to go this direction and have some fun when they are doing what they love doing and as they share their talents with the world at large. It is, therefore, an emerging trend in multimedia (Costello, 2016).

10.12. WEB 2.0 TOOLS AND APPLICATION

Initially, individuals had to wait to create time to meet with other individuals, this reduces the chances of individuals being able to get feedback from other individuals. It also made it hard to share information more so for individuals who live in distant areas. This is because the multimedia system used in those ages were outdated. This has changed with the incorporation of technology in multimedia. This has improved the multimedia tools used in communication. Among the emerging trends in multimedia is the use of web 2.0. This trend involves tthe use of technology in the communication process through the use of the internet.

The use of web 2.0 has availed a variety of tools that enable various groups of individuals such as educators thereby allowing them to share information through the internet; online sharing of information. It has contributed to the establishment of the Web Media Brands Inc. which was founded in 2009. The web 2.0 provides a variety of tools which includes:

10.12.1. Podcasts

A podcast is an internet service that gives users a platform to create audio files which are usually in MP3 formats usually in a podcasting website enabling other listeners to access the recorded podcast on their devices. The podcast is a trend that is on the rage among users and this is attributed to increased numbers of podcast listeners. Studies show that between the year 2016 and 2017 the number of podcast listeners has grown from 13 million to 16 million. Podcasts are usually a combination of the vocal qualities of the host/hostess and the formatting of the podcast. If both the conditions for the combinations were well met, then the podcast will be listened to by a larger audience which will keep on growing.

There are different types of podcasts used in multimedia. They include the nonfiction narrative storytelling which is commonly used by most of the podcast hosts. It is mostly used by the journalist who aims at getting in-depth knowledge on the subject matter. The podcasts involve the stories of the interviewees being retold by replaying the audio clips of the recording session. The challenge of using this type of podcast is that the formatting of the podcast is difficult to master (Costello, 2016).

There is a narration style which involves the host of the podcast plays a variety of roles to make the podcast successful. The host has to play the role of a writer, editor, reporter, and producer. For such a host, he or she needs to have conducted research. The host allows the audios of the other character to be played and later on, he or she gives a summary of what the characters have said. This is to help the audience to have a much better understanding of what the characters have said and they can get a flow of the concept.

The second type is the hybrid podcast. It is different from the nonfiction in that it allows from for other individuals to host the podcasts and they are referred to as guest hosts. It follows a certain procedure. It first starts with a monologue from the host. Here the host gives information on the subject matter. It then moves to either a panel discussion, interview or contribution for the guest host. This type of podcast is preferred as it gives room for new opinions to be shared out. An example of a hybrid podcast is Slate's The Gist.

The third type of podcast is the panel discussion. As the name dictates, this type of podcast has one host and more than two guests or interviewees within the course of the interview. It provides the listeners with a broader source of knowledge and therefore different points of view. This type of podcast is mostly used in political podcasts. The narration style of the podcast is mostly conversational as it involves the host and the guests discussing the subject matter. The last type of podcast is repurposed content. In this podcast, the content is presented in the repurposed style. For the host of these podcasts, the main aim is to improve the user's experience. This enables the audience to connect (Costello, 2016).

10.12.2. Blogs

Blogging is the use of blogging applications to create content for consumption by the readers. The content is usually dependent on the creator of the blog. The bloggers have to juggle a variety of roles. For instance, they need to come up with the subject matter, conduct research on it and later on publishing the content. Blogs are more of multimedia. It incorporates the use of the written word, pictures as well as videos to make the content to be easily understandable to the audience. For most blogs, it makes the use of all the aspects of communication to make the content to be more appealing for the audience. This puts more emphasis on the visual appealing of the content presented to the audience. For some of the bloggers, if their blogs deal more on photography they make use of slide shows this way they can present more pictures and save on space. It is also a good method contributing to the good visual appearance of the blogs. To make the blogging experience much easier, the bloggers tend to know about photography and videography so that they get to do these aspects of blogging on their own therefore they get to save money on photography, videography, and editing (Costello, 2016).

Other components of the web 2.0 are the RSS feeders, Wikis, and social networking. The main aim of the web 2.0 tools is to create broad opportunities for sharing, coming up and creation of content. There are various advantages of web 2.0. For one, it gives room for the engagement and participation among various groups of individuals including the business experts and professionals. This is demonstrated in the use of the repurposing podcasts that facilitates communication between the host and the audience. It is also among the most flexible work as it can be done with no limitations of time or distance. It is also affordable or expensive as the internet can be easily accessed by every individual on earth.

By using the web 2.0 one can get feedback from the audience based on the research or products. In the current system, the modifications have facilitated immediate feedback from the audience. It also provides a variety of tools that can be used in various aspects of multimedia. For instance, it has enabled easy designing of graphics. The tools are used in facilitating the management and updating of the multimedia systems. It also allows the use of the latest advancements in technology more so for businessmen. This is in the sense that it allows actual-time conversations made possible through video conferencing. It also allows instant messaging making the communication process to be much easier and much faster (Costello, 2016).

Microsoft (MS) is a company that develops MS products. Some of the products include the word, excel, PowerPoint, and access. These products are some of the tools used in developing multimedia products. For instance, the word is used by the content developers in writing and the generation of scripts. PowerPoint is mostly used in making the presentations. They include presentations that are used in meetings. This application is useful as it is equipped with tools that can make the presentation to be livelier. It enables individuals to create animations as well as slide shows. Excel is mostly used in tasks that deal more on computing and analysis of data.

The MS surface is a recent platform that is mostly used in multimedia in recent days. It is a computing platform that has been greatly used commercially to facilitate the digital sharing of information. The sharing of information is made possible through the use of touch and three-dimensional objects to make the content to be in digital format. The MS surface shares information in a manner that all the individuals who were to receive the information, all receive the information at the same time. This platform is made up of both software and hardware parts. The two are incorporated together for the working of the platform meaning that if one of the two fails, then the platform will not work. The hardware used is multi-touch hardware meaning that it is based on vision. Software used is mainly composed of a variety of software that was put together embracing diversity hence improving the quality of the platform. It makes use of the windows software that is used to generate a natural user interface which the users will find to be friendly when interacting with the platform. It also makes use of a 360-degree application design that can be used by several users hence it is a multiuser application (Costello, 2016).

10.13. PERSONALIZED ACCESS

This refers to the multimedia concepts being given a human touch. This means that the concepts incorporated embrace the various elements of human life that may be of more preference to the individuals. The personalized access also involves how individuals are able to get access to the various multimedia products. There are various roles of the personalized access in multimedia. For instance, it gives individuals crucial research directions. For one to conduct successful research, they need to know where they can access the information useful in research. Depending on the topic, the personalized access gives the individual important research direction as guidelines for them.

This it also a gives a sense of vision as the research direction assist them in getting a vision of what they are to accomplish after the research. The research in this case is referenced to multimedia. The other duty of personalized access is that it enables some visions to be obtained from it. Take an example in giving research directions, from the directions one can be able to obtain vision for the research from the directions. It is also useful in the representation of multimedia content. The representation is usually for the content description (Gries and Gries, 2005).

The personalized access ensures that the content description gives out a clear summary of the content so that the user after reading the content description, he or she already gets an understanding of what the media content entails. Apart from the content description, it gives a representation of the user preference as well as the context of the multimedia. With this kind of representation, the successive of the multimedia is guaranteed. The current trends involve the automation of content annotation. This is made possible through the personalized access. The automation of content notation makes it easy for the users when accessing content. They find it easy to navigate within the multimedia.

The personal access is also used in presentation authoring which is in an automated format. The presentation authoring refers to coming up with the presentation with a given format. An automated presentation authoring involves the use of automated media devices in coming up with the multimedia content. This involves the use of multimedia tools that have been automated do that the system automatically backs up the multimedia content. It also provides for tools that will give upcoming searches on the content that are to be included in the final multimedia product. The personalized access gives the creator of the content the privilege of using these tools (Gries and Gries, 2005).

10.14. DIGITAL SPOKES PERSON

They are also referred to as live actors. These individuals play a crucial role in multimedia more so in the field of websites. Among their roles includes them making the websites to be lively. Their participation in websites makes the website have life. Their participation may include them making videos that will be attached in the website. It may also include them making live stream videos. The live stream videos mean that the audience get to engage with the individual in the current time. It's more like television broadcast. This is the largest contributed in making the websites to be lively.

They also add a human touch to the website. Through the live streams and videos, they get to incorporate the human presence into the websites. They discuss on subject topics that affect human beings giving illustrations. As they do so, the human presence is represented by them in the videos. They can also contribute to creating a human touch in the website by coming up with topics that talk more on the human beings. The digital spokesperson gets to discuss on topics tailored for a specific group of individuals. Some of the website are meant for parents, adults, and children

The digital spokesperson is a digital trend in multimedia because of the part they play in coming up with the multimedia product. One of their role involves them contributing to the scripting of the website. Basically a website consists of several pages. The first page is usually an introduction on the website. The next page gives a description of the website content. The other pages that follow are made up of content concerning the website. The digital spokesman play part in coming up with what is to be incorporated to the website. This is called scripting.

They choose the content to be added as well as how the information is to be presented. For instance, they may decide that using of images may more effective so they may incorporate the images into the other pages of the website. If they are to use videos, they contribute in coming up with concepts that will be used in the video from the characters who will play different roles in the video. If a theme song is to be used, they work with audio specialist so that the song chosen will be effective and will draw the users to want to listen more to it (Savage and Vogel, 2009). The digital spokesperson is like the face of the media that is to be accessed by the users. If it's a website, then they are the face of the website and this means that they are a physical representation of the website. With this at hand, most of them play the role of marketing the website. If they are influences, they use their social media platforms to market the website to their users. If they do public appearances, then they market the website as they make the appearance. This strategy has been employed by most of the individuals in multimedia.

They are a useful resource when it comes to helping users to navigate in the website. This is more so for the individuals who are using the website for the first time. The digital spokesperson as they market the website, they give an illustration on how the user can navigate the website. Some of them opt to make video tutorials which is more convenient as the users can watch their tutorial at their own time and they can play it in slow motion so that they are capable of using websites and other elements of multimedia.

10.15. VOICE ACTIVATION

Voice activation has been among the emerging trends on multimedia. It is among the ways that most of the developers on multimedia have used to ensure the safety of the product that they have come up with. Each and every person's voice is unique and this principle is being applied in the various multimedia tools. The voice activation has been used along with finger prints to secure content. The voice activation works by the owner of the multimedia product creating a voice input. This input is then compared to other inputs to ensure that no other person with a voice different from the one that has been put gets to access the content.

10.16. VOICE ASSISTANTS

This is an application that has been emerging in multimedia. It a useful resource more so for the project managers. It helps them to manage their time. This application has been placed in mobile phones and computers that has access to the internet as most of the voice assistants are online. But for the most advanced ones, they can work while offline. Some of the voice assistants include that of google which is the Google assistant and Siri which is used in most of the I phones.

The reason why these applications are referred to as voice assistants is due to the fact that they are voice activated. The voice assistants are usually given access to all the applications within the device. This way if the user commands it to carry put a task, it is able to do so using the access granted to it. For instance, if the user was to give a command to the device to open the calendar it will be able to do so. The voice assistants have access to the schedules so they are able to remind the user of the activity that was to be carried out next.

10.17. ARTIFICIAL INTELLIGENCE

The artificial intelligence has been incorporated in multimedia production more so in the multimedia rooms that broadcast news. It is mostly used in the editorial rooms. This is due to the fact that robots have been incorporated into the writing aspect of multimedia. They are referred to as robot writers. The robots are designed with data and algorithms to enable them to come up with a story and write it within a short period of time. In time, the robots will be used as assistants in the editorial rooms. The robots are also fitted with grammar tools such as the thesaurus to enable them to produce published news that is error free in terms of grammar.

Before the robots are used, they are given instructions on what to write. In the instructions, things such as the font to be used as well as the size of the font are indicated. They use their ability to access the internet in the writing process.

10.18. MOBILE MEDIA

Mobile media is the use of mobile phones as media devices as the small screens allow media to become increasingly mobile. Mobile phones and other mobile devices are increasingly becoming a trend in the field of multimedia. Multimedia devices have grown from television to a popular mobile phone. In recent generations, mobile phones are used and every individual owns their mobile phone including teenagers and small kids. Mobile can perform a lot of functions that are associated with the media and therefore it makes them a multimedia trend. The following are some of the functions that mobile phones play in the media field (Cranny-Francis, 2005).

Mobile devices include the tablets, mobile phones and other communication devices. By using mobile devices individuals can watch or stream a live video. Mobile phones have apps like the YouTube and the Netflix apps that individuals who own phones can live to stream a movie and enjoy it at the comfort of their homes. They do not have to download these movies so that they can watch them later but they can stream the movies and enjoy them at any one time. Live streaming a movie proves as entertainment for the individuals owning the mobile devices and them, therefore, find a suitable means to pass time. Using mobile phones individuals can also take part in the social media platforms where individuals use their mobile devices to communicate through platforms like the WhatsApp where they can send a message to people as far away as other continents and get feedback from them immediately. They can also share WhatsApp statuses that help them to know how other people are faring on as they can also share their pictures. Applications like the WhatsApp are very enjoyable and entertaining and many individuals become increasingly highly addicted to them. Another social media platform that the children and adults may become highly addicted to that is found in the mobile devices is Instagram where individuals create accounts where they share their pictures, pictures of food or pictures of places they visit. Many people invest a lot of money on the perfect picture where they can either buy expensive phones with powerful cameras or they can pay a photographer to take their pictures and edit for them. Many people spend a lot of time on the internet such that they forget most of their duties as most people fight to gain popularity from Instagram and get a lot of likes and many followers too. Other social media platforms also exist and are used widely by people as a means of communication and entertainment (Cranny-Francis, 2005).

Mobile devices are also used as a content-generating platform. Many people use their mobile phones to generate content that they use to pass information. Content created can be a video recorded using the mobiles phone camera or making and editing pictures and short videos that the individuals can post in their YouTube accounts and they can gain a lot of fame and popularity from them and they can also get money.

The advantages of a mobile device as a multimedia tool and an emerging trend in the multimedia sector include the following:

Mobile devices can be used as a source of entertainment that is cheap and affordable. When a person is bored, they can use their mobile phones as an enjoyment platform or a source of fun and pass time. This can be achieved by watching videos from the internet, listening to songs, or passing information through communication and watching stories and statuses of other people. It is termed as a cheap multimedia tool and entertainment tool since mobile phones are cheap and affordable and easily accessible.

Mobile devices are also used to pass information in the sense that a lot of communication takes place using mobile phones than other devices like computers. Mobile phones are portable since they are small devices that can fit in an individual's pocket, unlike laptops and computers. They also contain a battery that can keep the charge and therefore this means that they do not have to use them only in places with a source of power and therefore this makes mobile phone communication to being possible anywhere and they can be used at any one time (Cranny-Francis, 2005).

The use of mobile phones as multimedia trends can also be advantageous in the form where one can generate income using mobile phones. The use of mobile phones has enabled many people to acquire employment as they work using their phones, for example, when one creates a content and they post or upload it in a platform like YouTube When the video gains and captures the interest of the people and it can acquire a lot of lives and vies from the population then it can enable the owner of the account to get paid an amount of money from the YouTube and hence many unemployed individuals can get employment.

Apart from the possible advantages that mobile devices have brought it has also come with disadvantages that include, Mobile devices are very addictive and many individuals have become very addicted to their phones such that they fail to perform their duties. Individuals can spend the whole day using their mobile phones and this has made many people lazy to the extent of not performing their duties. Accidents have also occurred as a result of people being addicted to phones such that they cannot put their phones down and concentrate on one thing.

The other disadvantage among many others is that mobile phones can lead to the rise of crime such that malicious people can start hacking accounts and companies where they get access to this accounts of companies and they steal a lot of data that is useful, private, and confidential and through this, they lead to the company being in a lot of risks. These individuals are tracked down and arrested before they can cause any more harm and they are detained while investigations go on and in case they are found guilty they can be detained for a long time (Cranny-Francis, 2005).

10.19. LESS MASS MEDIA AUDIENCE

Mass media is the technology that is desired to reach a specific mass audience. By mass we mean a lot of people and by the audience we mean the targeted group that the information is desired to reach. The less mass media audience is an emerging trend in the field of multimedia because; it has reduced the audience for a single mass media. By less mass audience it has enabled the desired information to reach the desired group and the desired population at large. This field is rising gradually though and change is seen slowly.

By less mass audience, the media have found ways in which the content they create can reach the desired population without being distorted and lost in a case where it reaches a mass audience but does not reach the required population. Many individuals and groups have a specific liking such that they prefer a particular source of enjoyment which a different group may not enjoy. This has therefore created the need to ensure that any content that is created reaches the demanded group, for example, children prefer watching cartoons and animations to watching news and documentaries.

Less media audience has been made possible by diversifying media in was that sources of information and media become so many such that it reduces the probability of there being only one thing to watch and this will hinder the process but when there is a lot of media then the individuals in any group will look for a media that will be more interesting to them and therefore information can be passed to the desired group more effectively than before without making a particular group uncomfortable. An example is how many television stations have cropped up each with an audience they desire to reach like the cartoon network may be set with the desire to reach children and the little teenagers and the news broadcast channels may be set to reach adults and the more mature individuals.

The advantage of less mass media audience is that information reaches the desired group, for example, if it is a warning against accepting sweets from strangers who may be kidnappers, this information can reach children faster if it pops up in a media that many children are using as it may prove useless if it pops up in a media that adults most of those who are not parents use.

Less media audience is, therefore, a major trend in multimedia because it comes with a lot of advantages and very few disadvantages. Many media devices are therefore set such that they do not have to be a trouble when information is reaching the desired audience such that it ensures a certain media is meant for a particular audience and another media is meant for another audience. Therefore, the use of less mass media audience is advantageous and widely being incorporated into the multimedia sector as an emerging trend in the multimedia sector.

References

1. Costello, V., (2016). Multimedia Foundations: Core Concepts for Digital Design (p. 486). Florida: CRC Press.
2. Cranny-Francis, A., (2005). MultiMedia: Texts and Contexts (pp. 1–88). London: SAGE.
3. David, G.,& Paul, G., (2005). Multimedia Introduction to Programming Using Java (pp. 2–51).Berlin: Springer Science & Business Media.
4. DiMarco, J., (2004). Computer Graphics and Multimedia: Applications, Problems and Solutions (pp. 1–87). Pennsylvania: Idea Group Inc (IGI).
5. Elaine, E.,& Andy, F., (2002). Managing Multimedia: Project Management for Web and Convergent Media, Book 2 (pp. 1–80). Buenos Aires, Argentina: Editorial Dunken.
6. Hans, W. B.,& Gregory, A. B., (2016). Multimedia Networks: Protocols, Design and Applications (pp. 1–19).New Jersey: John Wiley & Sons.
7. Helmut, L.,& Narciso, G., (2003). Multimedia Applications, Services and Techniques – ECMAST'99: 4th European Conference, Madrid, Spain, May 26–28, 1999, Proceedings (pp. 1–83). Berlin: Springer.
8. Herrick, D. F., (2012). Media Management in the Age of Giants: Business Dynamics of Journalism. Second Edition (pp. 1–87). New

Mexico: UNM Press.

9. Husrev, T. S., Sergio, V., Nikolaos, N., & Shiguo, L., (2010). Intelligent Multimedia Analysis for Security Applications (pp. 1–79). Berlin: Springer Science & Business Media.
10. Hwang, J. N., (2009). Multimedia Networking: From Theory to Practice (pp. 1–62). New York: Cambridge University Press.
11. Ivan, V., Ignacio, S., Albert, B., Jaime Garcia-Reinoso, Ivan, L., & Gonzalo, C., (2019). Multimedia Networking Technologies, Protocols, and Architectures (pp. 1–69). Massachusetts: Artech House.
12. Kamisetty, R., Zoran, B., & Dragorad, M., (2006). Introduction to Multimedia Communications: Applications, Middleware, Networking (pp. 1–5). New Jersey: John Wiley & Sons.
13. Konert, J., (2014). Interactive Multimedia Learning: Using Social Media for Peer Education in Single-Player Educational Games (pp. 1–83). Berlin: Springer.
14. Mayer, R. E., (2009). Multimedia Learning (pp. 1–89). London: Cambridge University Press.
15. Mazen Al-Khatib & Mohammad, S. A., (2007). IPTV Multimedia Networks: Concepts, Developments, and Design (pp. 11–27). New York: Intl. Engineering Consortiu.
16. Mitra, U., (2004). Introduction to Multimedia Systems (pp. 1–85). Massachusetts: Academic Press.
17. Paisarn, M., Ning, Z., & Ling, G., (2014). Multimedia Database Retrieval: Technology and Applications (pp. 1–100). Berlin: Springer.
18. Patricia, M. F.,& Gina, M. S., (2012). Text in Multimedia (p. 20). New York: DIANE Publishing.
19. Pearson Education, (2004). Multimedia Texts for Whole Class Teaching, Year 4 (p.48). London: Rigby.
20. Ralf, S., & Klara, N., (2013). Multimedia Applications (pp. 1–87). Berlin: Springer Science & Business Media.
21. Saddik, A. E., (2013). Interactive Multimedia Learning: Shared Reusable Visualization-based Modules (pp. 1–92). Berlin: Springer Science & Business Media.
22. Silva, M. M., (2016). Multimedia Communications and Networking (pp. 1–79). Florida: CRC Press.
23. Savage, T. M.,&Vogel, K. E., (2009). An Introduction to Digital

Multimedia (pp. 1–79). Massachusetts: Jones & Bartlett Publishers.

24. Tai-hoon, K., Hojjat, A., William, I. G., Niki, P., Timothy, K. S., Edward, J. R., Byeong-Ho, K., Seung-Jung, S., (2011). Multimedia, Computer Graphics and Broadcasting, Part I (pp. 1–79). Berlin: Springer Science & Business Media.
25. Tan Wee Hin & Leo, (2009). Handbook of Research on New Media Literacy at the K-12 Level: Issues and Challenges: Issues and Challenges (pp. 1–49). Pennsylvania: IGI Global.
26. Ze-Nian, L., Mark, S. D., & Jiangchuan, L., (2014). Fundamentals of Multimedia (pp. 1–81). Berlin: Springer Science & Business Media.

INDEX

C

D

E

F

N

O